Battles of a Gunner Officer

This book is dedicated to the members of the
Honourable Artillery Company
who sacrificed their lives for their country

Battles of a Gunner Officer

Tunisia, Sicily, Normandy and the Long Road to Germany

John Philip Jones

Based on the unpublished diary of
Major Peter Pettit, DSO, TD, HAC

Foreword by

General Sir Richard Barrons, KCB, CBE, ADC Gen
Commander, Joint Forces Command, and Colonel Commandant HAC

PRAETORIAN PRESS

First published in Great Britain by
PRAETORIAN PRESS
an imprint of
Pen and Sword Books Ltd
47 Church Street
Barnsley
South Yorkshire S70 2AS

Copyright © John Philip Jones, 2014

ISBN 978 1 78337 606 3

The right of John Philip Jones to be identified
as the author of this work has been asserted by him
in accordance with the Copyright, Designs and Patents Act 1988.

A CIP record for this book is available from the British Library.

Printed and bound in England by
CPI Group (UK) Ltd, Croydon, CR0 4YY

Typeset in Times by CHIC GRAPHICS

Pen & Sword Books Ltd incorporates the imprints of
Pen & Sword Archaeology, Atlas, Aviation, Battleground, Discovery,
Family History, History, Maritime, Military, Naval, Politics,
Railways, Select, Social History, Transport, True Crime, and
Claymore Press, Frontline Books, Leo Cooper, Praetorian Press,
Remember When, Seaforth Publishing and Wharncliffe.

For a complete list of Pen and Sword titles please contact
Pen and Sword Books Limited
47 Church Street, Barnsley, South Yorkshire, S70 2AS, England
E-mail: enquiries@pen-and-sword.co.uk
Website: www.pen-and-sword.co.uk

Contents

List of Plates

There is a portfolio of sixteen glossy pages in the middle of the book, containing twenty-six images. These are listed below.

1. Armoury House.
2. 25-pounder guarding Armoury House.
3. 11th Regiment Group, 1941.
4. Officers' Mess trench, Tunisia.
5. Longstop Hill, Tunisia.
6. Victory Parade in Tunis.
7. Centuripe, Sicily.
8. Major General Vivian Evelegh.
9. Group, HQ 481 Battery.
10. Group, A Troop in 481 Battery.
11. Group, B Troop in 481 Battery.
12. Instructions for Compo ration.
13. Page from the original diary with transcript.
14. Lieutenant Colonel Ian Freeland.
15. The Falaise Gap.
16. A Sherman tank.
17. A Flail tank.
18. A 25-pounder gun crossing the Orne.
19. The Reichswald.
20. Wesel.
21. The Rhine Crossing.
22. Greeting from Brussels Burgomaster.
23. PP in battledress.
24. PP after the war.
25. PP's medals.
26. Painting of an HAC 25-pounder at gunnery practice after the war.

List of Maps

Foreword

by

General Sir Richard Barrons,
KCB, CBE, ADC Gen.
Commander, Joint Forces Command,
and Colonel Commandant HAC

More books and papers have been written about the Second World War over the last sixty years than any other event in the last century and quite probably more than any other event in history. This is no surprise; the tumultuous events of 1939 to 1945 were truly definitive in charting the course of our world into modern times, determining for millions how they lead their lives in the modern age. The Second World War has been examined from every angle, from the personal detailed recollections of individuals who participated or were affected by it, to sweeping strategic histories and all aspects in between. These accounts have covered politics, history, sociology, technology, and many other themes. Some have been written to try and justify individual decisions or actions and others to try simply to comprehend how mankind could descend into such tragedy and chaos. Like most wars, the Second World War goes beyond reason and logic and the explanation of what occurred reaches into every recess of why the human race has turned out how it has.

This addition by Professor John Philip Jones breaks new ground as it brings into the light for the first time the private record of one rather special participant. Peter Pettit's personal and contemporaneous notes detail his journey from the first encounters with a determined enemy in Tunisia, through the difficult invasion of Sicily, and finally onto the astounding events of Normandy in 1944 and the subsequent bitter fighting that led to the end of the war in Germany in 1945. To any student of military history and military matters more generally, these diaries provide a very rare and comprehensive record of how one thoughtful reservist soldier managed his part in a huge theatre of war.

This story is made much more interesting and accessible for the general reader by the accompanying succinct historical overview of the events of which Peter Pettit was part. This context not only provides the backdrop against which Peter Pettit fought his war, but also a concise reminder of the strategic and operational decisions and actions which shaped the course of the war and the destiny of nations. The combination of context and personal history conveys the sheer scale, effort and strategic risk of the struggle between states and it also succeeds in painting a realistic and sympathetic picture of how hard it is for the officers and men drawn into war who must do their duty in all manner of conditions – determined to succeed, paying the price, whilst at the same time longing for it to end and to go home.

For me, the small things that are recorded in the diary entries are the most poignant, touching as they do on familiar aspects of my own service. The death of officers as a result of not wearing the issued steel helmet but the same colourful side hat that I still wear in barracks. The constant interest in finding good sleep, decent food and shelter from the elements. The massive importance of serving with friends and the sadness of simply having to carry on when they die in battle. The randomness of events, where people are alive one moment and stone dead the next for the smallest of chances, and the pervasive uncertainty about what will happen next and how it will affect individual lives. For a field gunner like me, the drills employed by Peter Pettit and his regiment in deploying the guns and sending observers forward into the fight are directly relatable to those that apply today, with all the same frictions and challenges of finding the right places to go, the best route to get there and then performing well in action. All of us in this business remember long frustrating and tiring nights looking in vain for comrades who must be somewhere nearby in the same dark wood. And in typical fashion the diary underplays the gritty resilience of those who were manning the guns. Peter Pettit skips easily over the manhandling of equipment weighing several tons in the dark and the mud with the huge physical effort required to pass a thousand rounds of ammunition, each weighing 25 pounds, through each gun over a twenty-four hour period. For anyone looking for a rare insight into the hard business of field soldiering in the crucible of war, these diaries paint a very colourful, accurate and illuminating picture.

As the author points out, Peter Pettit was not a regular officer, but a member of the Territorial Army. He was a solicitor with a practice in London and his soldiering was a matter of duty and passion, never a full-time career. So the book also makes the vital point that major conflicts between states are fought and won by civilians. Responding to the call to arms, men and women from all walks of life join the ranks and commit to training and operating to the best of their ability until the job is done. They fight in armies that are led by regular forces and where there are regular counterparts alongside, but for much of the Second World War the regulars were very much in the minority. The fact is, after enough training and experience in battle the civilian soldier more than matches the skill and professionalism of the regular. Quite apart from making forces as big as they need to be, reserve service draws on the full spectrum of talents found in society at large and applies them to the limit in the pursuit of victory in war. Properly led and resourced, civilians who stand up to fight make Armed Forces not just bigger but better.

This quality applies in particular measure to the Honourable Artillery Company (HAC) which has been a pillar of Peter Pettit's life and service. The diary records the particular pleasure he had in encountering his friends from 11th HAC Regiment during the course of the War and his sadness at the news of the loss of many. The names of the members of the HAC who did not return are recorded and displayed with due honour in the Headquarters of the Regiment in its historic setting in London. It goes without saying that there are very senior veterans of today's HAC who remember Peter Pettit and his son Charles as prominent, dedicated and very highly regarded members of a military organisation that traces its history back almost five-hundred years. The diaries set out splendidly how much can be achieved when the brains and characters of people who make their lives in the City of London in all manner of ways are drawn into military service and fight for their country. And so it will be in the future.

Preface

Diary, 28 April 1943
Quiet day. Moved 10 Battery forward to behind Longstop. Saw Denis's tank, something very heavy hit it bang on the turret where hinges are, blew them off, bashed in top of turret and track shield and made a horrid mess inside the turret. He must have been killed instantly.

Diary, 30 April 1943
Cooler, found a lark's nest with four eggs in the middle of our Regimental HQ in a grassy fold in the ground. Big battle on 1st and 4th Division fronts.

Peter Pettit, whom I refer to as PP, was a major aged 34 and Second-in-Command of 17th Field Regiment, Royal Artillery. He was a Territorial officer serving in a Regular regiment, but his military experience and keenness had prepared him well for this appointment. At the age of 19 he had joined the ranks of the historic London regiment of part-time soldiers, the Honourable Artillery Company (HAC), having followed his father into B Battery. His brother later joined it, and much later so did PP's two sons.

Peter Pettit took his military training seriously particularly when, during the two years leading to the outbreak of war, the Territorial Army (TA) was increased in size and a great boost was given to the pace of preparation for active service. After twelve years of service, he had progressed from Gunner to acting Major in command of B Battery, now in 11th (HAC) Regiment, Royal Horse Artillery, the first of the gunner regiments that were formed from the ranks of the HAC. By this time PP had qualified as a solicitor and was a partner in his old-established family firm in Baker Street, London.

The TA was mobilized just before war was declared in September 1939, and PP spent more than three years of full-time service in Britain, first with 11th Regiment and later with the 17th. By the end of this period he was a seasoned and experienced field officer, ready to go to war. In December 1942, 17th Field Regiment was sent overseas to join the Anglo-American force that had invaded North-West Africa in November. The invasion was improvised, which is not surprising since the two separate national armies had been thrown together at short notice. Although victory was won in May 1943, the intervening months were characterized by unpleasant winter weather on the Tunisian battlefront, and little military movement except some setbacks.

One of the main obstacles on the ground to the eastward advance on the city of Tunis was a dominant feature that was less than 40 miles short of it: a position strongly fortified by the Germans that the British named Longstop Hill. Longstop was captured with considerable heroism on the night of 22/23 December 1942. Almost immediately, the relieving force was driven off by a German counter-attack, and an Allied effort to evict the Germans failed. The battlefront now congealed and a wintry status quo prevailed until April 1943. Then at last the Allied armies were strong enough in numbers and firepower finally to take Longstop and advance beyond it.

In the early stages of this last battle for the feature the North Irish Horse, an armoured regiment mounted in Churchill tanks, was supported by 17th Field Regiment. An intrepid young Forward Observation Officer (FOO), Captain Denis Higgins MC, one of the regiment's Troop Commanders, advanced forward in a Churchill tank. But it was unfortunately hit and Higgins was killed. Longstop was finally taken on 26 April by a Highland battalion, 8 Argylls, led by Major Jack Anderson who had taken over when his Commanding Officer had lost his life as a result of enemy shellfire. Anderson led from the front, firing his Tommy gun, and was awarded the Victoria Cross.

This in brief is the context in which the two diary extracts at the beginning of this Preface can be fully understood. Readers will also be struck by the sudden change of pace after the first extract. After contemplating the horrors of war, the thing that took PP's attention was a lark's nest. He was an Englishman imbued with an English love of the countryside. The diary reads well and this is helped by its abruptness, caused by the conditions in which it was written. Its unvarnished descriptions of military life – on occasions violent and on other occasions tedious – illustrate how words scribbled on the spot and in the midst of battle or resting from it can bring life and immediacy to a work of military history.

In the vast literature of war there has been no shortage of diaries and letters, written day-by-day by combatants of all ranks. They fall into two broad categories which are quite different from one another. The first is the diaries kept by high-level military decision-makers; the second is those kept by soldiers in or near the firing line, especially regimental officers, and men in the ranks. Of the two categories, I have always found the first the more interesting, because such diaries integrate the activities of armies into the broad framework of history. The issues can be recognized immediately, although the generals' diaries manage to introduce many unknown aspects. They also illustrate the oppressive loneliness of high command when a general is under pressure and – a related point – the usually difficult relationships between top generals and their political masters. Here are three examples to make the point. These come from very different wars.

General Wolseley, Commander of the Khartoum Relief Expedition,
17 February 1885
With Khartoum in the Mahdi's hands my present force is totally inadequate to meet him except under very advantageous circumstances.

I have telegraphed this home in a secret despatch. It will kill the Government I think: I am sorry for Hartington but I have no mercy on that most ignorant of *soi-disant* statesmen, Mr. Gladstone. He is responsible for Gordon's death and all the bloodshed and horrors attendant upon the fall of Khartoum.

Field Marshal Haig, Commander-in-Chief of the BEF,
29 March 1918
Met General Foch at Abbeville about noon. I told him that I thought the Allies were fortunate that the attack had fallen on the British and not on the French because the latter could not have withstood it. I also pointed out
(1) British infantry in France at the beginning of the battle were 100,000 less than a year ago!
(2) We now have three times as many Germans on our front as we had last year.
(3) We had also extended our front (by order of the British Government) fully one-fifth more than it was last autumn. This may have been necessary, because the French had inadequate numbers and the Americans had not arrived, but it rendered our front precarious.

Field Marshal Brooke, CIGS,
5 June 1944
Winston had returned on Sunday evening in a very highly-strung condition. He invited the Chiefs-of-Staff to lunch, which was a bore. I found him over-optimistic as regards prospects of the cross Channel operation and tried to damp him down. I knew only too well all the weak points in the plan of operations. First of all the weather, on which we were entirely dependent; a sudden storm might wreck it all. Then the complexity of an amphibious operation of this kind, when confusion may degenerate into chaos in such a short time. The difficulty of controlling the operation once launched, lack of elasticity in the handling of reserves, danger of leakage of information with consequent loss of that essential secrecy. Perhaps one of the most nerve-wracking experiences when watching an operation like this unroll itself is the intimate knowledge of the various commanders engaged. Too good a knowledge of their various weaknesses makes one wonder whether in the moments of crisis facing them they will not shatter one's hopes.

Brooke's chilling fears about D-Day are directly relevant to this book. Chapters 4 and 5 are devoted to the invasion of Normandy, and PP's most intense experiences of military action during the war are recounted in Chapter 5.

This brings me to the deficiencies in the diaries of top commanders. Generals live in a world above the battles, and they move formations and units like pieces on a chessboard. Their diaries do not therefore help us smell the whiff of powder or hear the whistle of bullets, which are what war is most obviously about. And they are indeed what PP's diary is all about. To balance the above three diary extracts from the stratosphere of command, here are three examples from soldiers much lower down the military pyramid. Again they came from very different wars.

Lieutenant Gordon-Duff, 1 Gordon Highlanders, Magersfontein, South Africa.
13 December 1899
The country is quite treeless with very little water, and scant grass and scrubby prickly plants on most horrid red sand and boulder-covered hills. There were all sorts of relics. Old bullets, cartridge cases, shells etc. Also a partially buried Boer, old saddles, helmets – every blessed thing in fact. We pitched our tents by the Seaforth and Highland Brigade lines. Numbers of them were absolutely crippled owing to the effect of the battle, when they were on their faces for hours with the backs of their knees being burnt off. They could hardly hobble with great bandages.

Captain Crofton, 2 Life Guards, Ypres, Belgium.
18 November 1914
At 7 o'clock we made a breakfast of rum and bully beef. The day got warmer later on and was very clear and bright. About 10 o'clock the first shells fell over our trench. These increased in number very shortly until about 10:30 when a perfect inferno was raging over the whole of our line of the trench. They were chiefly of the Black Maria and Lyddite types. It was all very shaky. We lay prone on the bottom of the trench, but from time to time looked out from the peep-hole to see if there were any signs of a German attack. The shells pitched very close in front, the Germans obviously had the correct range, and tore in the parapet, thus causing the sandy sides of the trench to silt in. We were half stunned, choked with sand and half buried in the debris. The explosions deafened us.

Trooper Merewood, The Queen's Bays, Mareth, Tunisia.
27 March 1943
Then the quiet was suddenly shattered by a terrific bang. Anti-tank guns hidden in the trees ahead opened fire. I saw Jim's tank hit and it immediately burst into flames. He and his turret crew bailed out, all three of them on fire. They ran about screaming . . . and all died. The other two crew members never got out of the tank. Then we were hit too. I

found myself covered with blood, but it wasn't mine, it was Nobby's. He'd been hit on the head and he dropped straight down into the turret beside me. Our wireless operator lay on his back on the floor in a state of terror, beating the floor with his fists and his heels. Colin, our driver, shouted over the intercom: 'My periscope's shattered, I can't see where I'm going.' Without stopping to think, I jumped up, took Nobby's seat and, half out of the tank, saw we were still heading straight for the trees. Shells were flying everywhere. Any minute I expected we'd be hit again. 'Jink, Colin, jink,' I shouted. Colin zigzagged but we were still going forward. I yelled at him: 'Pull on your right stick as hard as you can.' He did as I said and we made a complete U-turn: 'Put your foot down. Let her go.' Colin kept his head, did as I directed and we kept going until it was safe to stop.

The Battle of Mareth, which was eventually successful, opened the way for the advance of the 8th Army on Tunis from the south. Meanwhile, 78th Division, in which PP was serving, was making preparations for a major attack and then an advance on the city from the west. The pincers would before long be closing.

Readers may wonder why these six extracts from battle diaries, four of which are unrelated to the Second World War, have a place in a book about the campaigns in Tunisia, Sicily and North-West Europe. The answer is simple. The diaries illustrate a dichotomy, with three from the top of the military hierarchy telling one sort of story and three from the bottom telling another. Diaries written by generals seem detached and remote from the actual battlefield. They need the addition of something from the firing line. On the other hand, the diaries written by men at the 'sharp end' have too little background. The action described is an isolated event. The episodes in these diaries may be very exciting, but when they are read they inevitably raise questions: 'What is this battle all about?' 'What is the larger scheme of things?' 'Did the difficulties eventually get resolved?' 'Who won?' Such diaries need a strong injection of the 'big thinking' that comes from the generals.

This dichotomy has led me to construct the book from two elements. First, I have written an abbreviated work of history. The campaigns in which PP served – Tunisia, Sicily and the various phases of the invasion of Europe – are described in six chapters (numbers 2 to 7). I narrate the history of each campaign, with an emphasis on the overall command and the strategy. In every case the story is complex, with much evidence of differences of views at the top. I have done my best to write this history component both comprehensively and succinctly, and have based the narrative on the best of the vast literature published since 1945, supplemented with unpublished war diaries. These works are listed in the Bibliography. The second component is the diary itself. In the chapters describing the campaigns, the narrative begins with the history and is followed by the diary. But often afterwards I return briefly to the history in connection with episodes described in the diary. The two elements work closely together. Although the narrative is based on many published and unpublished sources, I decided to avoid endnotes flagged by numbered references in the text itself. A forest of numbers in the narrative would impede the flow too much, and in any case the Bibliography is detailed and comprehensive.

In Chapters 2 (Tunisia), 3 (Sicily), and 4 (the first phase of Normandy), the history contains more words than the diary. The opposite is true of Chapters 5 (the second phase of Normandy), 6 (the advance across north-west Europe) and 7 (the surge across the north German plain). In editing the diary I have omitted many daily entries when little was happening. But I have made very few changes to the text itself and kept the telegraphic style, with incomplete sentences and abbreviations (which are described *in italics* and also amplified in the Glossary).

Besides writing such a splendid story, PP deserves my thanks for yet another reason. He wrote his diary in tiny handwriting in a series of six-by-four inch blank notebooks made for laundry lists. One of them fitted into one of the breast pockets of his battledress, so that it was accessible for him to write a day's entry. (A typical page of the original diary is illustrated in Plate 13, together with a typed transcript.) PP's writing is unfortunately very difficult to decipher. Because of this, after the war he had the whole diary transcribed and printed in clear typescript and bound in four volumes that included various maps and ephemera: newspaper clippings etc. These four volumes have made life much easier than it would have been if I had had to wrestle with the handwritten notebooks. (I would probably still be at work making sense of them all!)

The book also has a 'top and tail': Chapter 1 and the Afterword. Chapter 1 is devoted to artillery. Since the diary describes the battles of Royal Artillery Field regiments during the Second World War, readers will benefit from some understanding of what guns can do and how they are deployed in action. I have tried to avoid technical language, and Chapter 1 is supplemented by a full Glossary (at the end of the book) which gives explanations of the more arcane aspects of gunnery and how it works in cooperation with the other engines of war.

The Honourable Artillery Company always retained PP's special loyalty. Chapter 1 gives a brief account of the long history of the regiment. It provided 4,000 officers, mainly to other regiments, during the Second World War, and PP's diary records the many occasions when he came across pre-war regimental friends on his peregrinations over the battlefields.

The Afterword describes the Territorial Army's major contributions to Britain's military effort during the two world wars. However, since it was re-formed in 1947, it has had a checkered history. Its members have maintained the old volunteer spirit and never lost their loyalty to their regiments. But the problem has always been too few men (and women) in the ranks. In comparison with the years before 1914 and 1939, when there was a threat of war, the TA since 1947 has been almost a shadow organization. In response to the problem, the military authorities have over the years attempted reorganization and rationalization but without long-term success.

In the recent past plans for the armed services have been constantly reviewed, in response both to reductions in the military budget and to different forecasts of future wars and how these would affect the rôles of the various branches of the services. In 1996, a major change took place with the introduction of a scheme for Territorial soldiers to serve on active service at times when the country has not declared general mobilization. Men and women were now encouraged to volunteer (and on occasions could be compelled) to serve for a year, with six months of intensive training, and six months abroad in the front line. Since 1996, 15,000 Territorials have served in this way. In 2013 the scheme was ratcheted-up in anticipation of the greater contribution that the Territorials (now called the Army Reserve) will be expected to make to the army as a whole. It is planned that, within a relatively short period, 27 per cent of the army's strength will be made up of Reservists. There are doubts about the practicability of this proposal, and it has generated a good deal of debate in the 'quality' newspapers.

This book, being based on a contemporary war diary, is concerned with facts and is a record of things that happened in the past. However, the very end of the Afterword makes a transition from the past to the future. One of the things we always know about the future is that it will be different from the past and that forecasts, no matter how imaginative and brave, generally prove to be wrong. Does this mean that planning – including the proposals currently on the table – will inevitably be futile? This is not necessarily so. The central problem that must be faced is how to make contingency plans for a range of possible but unknown emergencies. The army must be prepared. But prepared for what? What form is the army's training going to take? Can the TA reach the same standard as the Regulars? Top professional military planners have greater skills than anybody else for addressing these problems, and the 2013 plan is the result of their deliberations. Their willingness in the present difficult circumstances to think in radical terms deserves direct support, but one qualification is necessary.

In Britain, the system of politico-military decision-making is modelled on the method developed during the Second World War, when the chiefs-of-staff of the three services – three men including a chairman – answered to Churchill as Minister of Defence. He was an especially tough taskmaster; the scars from his bruising conflicts with his service chiefs can still be seen in Field Marshal

Alanbrooke's riveting war diary (which made him unpopular with the Churchill family). What Churchill demanded was complete justification for all recommendations, which meant that the chiefs and their immediate staffs never stopped working on assembling supporting data and exploring alternative plans that the Prime Minister constantly put forward. However, Churchill's understanding of the British political system was such that he always in the end accepted what his advisers had to say. He knew that he ultimately had to take their recommendations – or accept their resignations.

This relationship was a war-winner, because of the experience and powerful personalities of the men who ran military affairs at that time. This is not to criticize the people who have had this responsibility in later periods. But there is a point of principle that remains as important as ever. Plans must be constantly questioned; they must be (as it were) 'tested to destruction'. If they remain intact after this process, then it can be assumed that they are as sound as human judgement can make them.

As with all my books, my first thanks go to my wife Wendy, who can with difficulty decipher my handwriting, and (in generally good spirits) puts up with my dictation. She always produces immaculate typescripts of the manuscript on her computer, and she has the patience to handle endless amendments to the drafts.

I am extremely grateful to General Sir Richard Barrons for contributing the Foreword. It is a lucid and elegant essay that gets to the heart of the book, and will be an ornament to the work. General Barrons is a serving soldier who has had an impressive career. He joined the army direct from Oxford University and was commissioned in the Royal Artillery. He progressed through the regimental ranks, graduated from the Staff College, and in 1997 he was given command of 3 RHA and served in Germany and the Balkans. Thereafter he interspersed command and staff appointments of increasing responsibility in England, Northern Ireland, the Balkans, Iraq and Afghanistan. In 2011 he returned to Britain as Assistant Chief of the General Staff, then Deputy Chief of the Defence Staff responsible for military strategy and operations. In 2013 he was appointed Joint Forces Commander, as a four-star General and received the KCB. He also became Colonel Commandant of the Honourable Artillery Company and an ADC to HM The Queen.

I am also most grateful to friends who have read all or parts of the work and suggested amendments that have always led to improvements. They are James Colquhoun (HAC); James Gray, MP (HAC); Brigadier James Groom (ex-RHA); Charles Pettit (HAC); Richard Pettit (HAC); Valerie Pettit; Major David Robinson; Lieutenant Colonel John Ross; Professor David Rubin; Professor Roger Sharp (once an artillery officer in the United States army); Anthony Simpson (21st SAS Regiment – Artists); Justine Taylor (Archivist, HAC); James

Westlake (HAC); Lieutenant Colonel David Whiter (ex-RHA); Peter Womersley; and Lieutenant Colonel Geoffrey Wright. I was fortunate to have an excellent copy editor, Alison Miles. She is knowledgeable, punctilious, quick to respond and always helpful.

The handsome maps were computer-generated by Scott Bunting of Fresher Graphics, Syracuse, New York. Detailed work on the plates was carried out with their customary efficiency by Sharon Pickard and Collin Becker, of Industrial Color Labs, Syracuse.

Chapter 1

'Artillery, A Great Battle-Winning Factor'

The title of this chapter comes from the tribute that Field Marshal Montgomery paid to the artillery at the end of the Second World War. No one was better qualified to appraise the contribution of the Royal Artillery (RA) to British arms in defeat and victory. In land battles, success depends on synergy between infantry, armour, artillery, air and engineers: the whole becomes greater than the sum of the parts. This book concentrates on one of these factors, gunnery, and is written from the standpoint of a successful battery commander who was not a Regular soldier. The Royal Artillery expanded greatly during the First World War, and even more during the Second. One of its most serious problems was the shortage of junior officers. In both conflicts, a substantial number were commissioned from the ranks of the historic regiment of citizen-soldiers, the Honourable Artillery Company, universally known as the HAC. Peter Pettit, the author of the diary on which this book is based, joined the HAC in 1927 and had been an officer for seven years when war was declared in 1939. He had the temporary rank of Major.

'The Last Argument of Kings'

As war was fought in the middle of the twentieth century – conflict on a massive scale between national armies, navies and air forces – bullets and shell fragments in large numbers generally swept the battlefield. The largest volume of fire came from small arms; but small arms, particularly belt-fed machine guns, were essentially defensive weapons operating with deadly effect on the flanks to enfilade enemy infantry. In contrast, the contribution of artillery came from the destructive weight of each shell it fired. Artillery was effective in both defence and attack and it could perform tasks that were beyond the capacity of small arms; in particular it could neutralize armour and aircraft as well as troops in the open. In attack, artillery fire plans could make the difference between overall success and failure.

Complex fire plans were first developed during the siege conditions of the First World War. They set out a precise and elaborate web of fire tasks, with exact timings. These included: barrages on different enemy locations;

lifting/creeping barrages (i.e. curtains of fire falling 100 yards in front of advancing infantry and moving forward in pace with the rate of advance); counter-bombardment (CB) targets where enemy batteries were located; defensive fire (DF) tasks; and tactical support called for by Forward Observation Officers. Such plans could mobilize concentrations of sometimes 1,000 guns or more. At the Battle of El Alamein in October 1942, the artillery of the 8th Army was made up of 37 Field regiments (with a total of 888 guns) plus 33 regiments of other types: Medium, Heavy, Anti-Aircraft and Anti-Tank. The vast majority of these regiments participated in the fire plan, producing an unforgettable barrage that softened the enemy lines before and during the early part of the battle.

The success of artillery depended not only on the excellence of the guns and ammunition, but also on the organization, training and operational efficiency of the men in the batteries, and – very importantly – on totally reliable communications. These things are what this book is about.

Cannon, both guns and mortars, were originally employed by the Chinese during the late twelfth century, and their use spread slowly to the West during the late Middle Ages. They were large, heavy weapons, few in number; a typical example weighed 19 tons and needed sixty oxen to draw it. These early cannon were essentially immobile; they were smooth-bored and both inaccurate and muzzle-loaded, a process that meant a slow rate of fire. They fired at relatively short ranges, which meant that they could only be used for direct fire, described by gunners as 'over open sights'. Their projectiles were crude solid cannon balls, which could do a great deal of damage to the walls of fortresses, making it possible for infantry to force an entry. One of their effects was the important matter of shaking the enemy's morale. This is an extremely demoralizing result of artillery in all wars, especially the two big conflicts of the twentieth century.

During the two-hundred years between the early eighteenth and the early twentieth centuries, five technical improvements transformed artillery into the weapons used so effectively during the First and Second World Wars:

i.   Guns became smaller and more mobile;
ii. Rifling began to replace smooth bore;
iii. Breech-loading began to replace muzzle-loading;
iv. Projectiles were improved, with canister shot containing shrapnel (named after an officer of that name in the Royal Artillery); and, even more importantly, explosive shells;
v.   Increasing ranges, which made it possible to use guns for indirect fire.

The first of these innovations, mobility, transformed artillery during the eighteenth century. A typical 12-pounder (with a bore of about 4in) could be mounted on wheels and drawn by teams of horses across the battlefield, with groups of guns assembled in batteries. When these guns were in position they could fire at targets a mile away. A visit to one of the many well-preserved battlefields of the American Civil War (1861–1865), invariably shows such batteries *in situ*, normally on high ground from which they could fire on advancing enemy troops.

Napoleon, who was trained as a gunner and never forgot it, came into his own at the sound of the guns and in all his battles deployed his artillery with finesse and great effectiveness. After the Napoleonic War, Prussian guns were handsomely engraved with the motto *'Ultima Ratio Regum'*: an appropriately classical aphorism meaning, in English, *'The Last Argument of Kings'*. This was a succinct commentary on the many wars at that time between European nation states, mostly kingdoms and empires. Guns had become the single weapon of decisive importance.

The next three improvements, breech-loading, rifling and improved projectiles, were all introduced more or less at the same time, the middle of the nineteenth century. They were employed to a limited extent during the Crimean War (1853–1856) and the American Civil War, and widely rolled out afterwards in all large armies. The final improvement, extending the range of guns and the introduction of indirect fire, meant a major transformation of gunnery at the end of the nineteenth century. There was little opportunity for this during the Second Anglo-Boer War (1899–1902) because it was mainly a war of movement. But the Japanese practised indirect fire with great effect during the Russo-Japanese War of 1904–1906, using fixed Observation Posts (OPs), connected with the Gun Positions by telephone. European armies were not too aware of the details of this fighting on the other side of the world. Field Marshal Lord Roberts, the greatest British soldier of the Victorian era, was a gunner and even he was not au fait with this development. Although the Field Marshal had retired in 1905, he remained a *guru* whose views on military policy were widely respected, but he now devoted his attention to the controversial question of Compulsory Service.

In 1914 the British artillery was in general well prepared for a European war, which was universally expected in military circles. This war is, even today, often described as a conflict dominated by artillery.

The Royal Regiment

The Royal Regiment of Artillery has had a long and distinguished history. Artillery was first used by the British army during the reign of Henry VIII (1509–1547). However, it was first permanently established as a branch of the service in 1716, which was the official birth date of the Royal Regiment of Artillery. The Royal Artillery is one of the army's three (curiously named) 'teeth-arms', i.e. those in direct contact with the enemy. The others are armour (cavalry in its modern incarnation) and infantry. The RA's 'head count' has always been in total very large. And unlike most cavalry regiments and infantry battalions, the Royal Artillery was planned to have no affiliations with specific regions of Great Britain.

However, the Territorial Army has always been regionally affiliated, and many TA regiments became gunners after the First World War. One such regiment was the West Somerset Yeomanry, which became 55th Field Regiment, Royal Artillery, and whose active service in the Second World War will be discussed in this book.

There has been a long-established tradition for officers and other ranks to be cross-posted between RA batteries, which are small units that generate considerable *esprit de corps*. But in spite of the system of cross-posting, and also the absence of regional loyalties, the overall *esprit de corps* of the Royal Artillery has always been remarkable, even by the standards of the British army. It has invariably contributed to the operational efficiency of British regiments, and the gunners continue to gain special satisfaction that the RA has fought in every battle in which the British army has been engaged: hence their motto '*Ubique*': in English, 'Everywhere'. Infantry regiments have Colours which are in effect the distillation and point of focus of each regiment's *esprit de corps*. Cavalry regiments similarly have Guidons. The Royal Regiment has no embroidered silken banners. The guns themselves are the Regiment's Colours, and are accorded the proper respect. The beautiful Royal Artillery Slow March was composed by the Duchess of Kent, Queen Victoria's mother.

For more than two centuries, there were three branches: Royal Horse Artillery (RHA), supporting the cavalry; Royal Field Artillery (RFA), supporting the infantry; and Royal Garrison Artillery (RGA), mainly fortress troops, although during the First World War RGA batteries were in the field, operating the large-calibre Medium and Heavy guns that became so important during the years of siege warfare. The RFA and RGA were amalgamated after the First World War, but the RHA maintained its unique status, although cavalry now meant armour.

Up to the 1950s and to some extent even today, the British army has had an implicit 'social' pecking order, largely governed by the attraction of certain regiments to rich and well-connected officers. The regiments at the top of the list were (and still are) the Foot Guards and Household Cavalry, the Cavalry of the Line and the Green Jackets, who altogether account for about 10 per cent of the overall strength of the army. These regiments all have long and splendid fighting histories, but so have many less prestigious ones. For whatever reason, the officers in these regiments have always had a strong *amour propre*, which is transferred as if by osmosis to the men in the ranks. The Royal Artillery is a large force and has many historic batteries. But there is no inbuilt 'social' gradation between them. However, some of the cachet of the cavalry inevitably rubs off onto the Royal Horse Artillery, because they fight closely together.

Some RHA batteries were named, with great pride, after notable battery commanders and battles, mostly dating from the Peninsular War. Young subalterns are unable to join the RHA after they have been first commissioned, but if they show promise they may be invited to transfer: in gunner language, 'get their jacket'. Second Lieutenants are called Cornets, following the practice of the Household Cavalry. RHA uniform has a delightful idiosyncrasy. Nearly all British soldiers have buttons that are fairly flat but the surface is raised and stamped with a regimental 'sealed pattern'. However, in the RHA the brass buttons are shaped like small round cannon balls.

In 1914, the Royal Artillery had 279 Regular batteries, plus another 82 in the Territorial Force. The 25 Regular RHA batteries approximately matched the number of cavalry regiments in the army, and the number of 147 Regular RFA batteries was not far different from the number of infantry battalions. There was therefore a planned match of one cavalry regiment to one RHA battery, and one infantry battalion to one RFA battery. This held good until the Second World War, when the amount of gun support provided to the other 'teeth-arms' was boosted. Before the First World War, a group of three batteries was organized into a brigade, commanded by a Lieutenant Colonel. The name 'brigade' was always rather ambiguous, and Royal Artillery brigades were renamed Royal Artillery regiments after the First World War.

When the British Expeditionary Force (BEF) went to France in 1914, the average infantry division of twelve battalions was supported by four RFA brigades, containing twelve batteries. The one-to-one balance was firmly in place. The RFA was armed with the 18-pounder gun, an excellent weapon for its time, with a range of 9,500yd. It was directly comparable with the French 75mm and the German 77mm. All three had a reasonably high rate of fire, and they were mobile; a single gun and its limber, containing ammunition, were drawn by a team of horses. However, the British 13-pounder used by the RHA had very little 'punch'. These are the guns that are today fired on ceremonial occasions by the King's Troop RHA, and they are obviously military ornaments rather than effective weapons of war. The Royal Garrison Artillery had few Medium and Heavy guns, but the numbers of these increased greatly during the course of the war.

The siege conditions that characterized the First World War meant that virtually all gunfire was indirect. The concept of one battery supporting one battalion was predicated on the idea that battalions would engage in independent action. When this occurred, in particular when battalions were assaulting specific objectives as part of a large-scale attack, the Forward Observation Officer system was developed, with FOOs marching with Battalion Headquarters. But inadequate communication was a real problem. In the absence of portable radios, FOOs were accompanied under fire by sweating signallers unrolling telephone cables from large drums, and also using an array of other equipment, e.g. periscopes, trench ladders and semaphore flags. Aircraft were used experimentally for artillery spotting, but the radio sets available were very rudimentary. Air Observation Posts (AOPs) had to wait until the Second World War.

However, over the course of the First World War, independent unit action became less and less important. Very soon battles were being planned, not at a battalion or a brigade or even a divisional level. They were conducted by corps and armies, which meant inevitably that artillery would be concentrated. This was the genesis of the large-scale fire plan: a major innovation of the war. Field Marshal Brooke, a gunner, and Chief of the Imperial General Staff (CIGS) during the Second World War – and the most effective soldier ever to hold the post – made his early reputation devising complex fire plans for large formations. He did this job as a Major, later a Lieutenant Colonel, and a gunner staff officer with the Canadian army in the BEF.

In these ways gunnery evolved. But did the large fire plan for a set-piece battle make a major contribution to future victory? We now hit a roadblock. In the big attacks, notably at the Somme and the Third Battle of Ypres, the punctiliously prepared and powerfully executed fire plan was a method of waging war that did not work. One unfortunate effect was that the days of preparatory bombardment warned the enemy that an attack was imminent. The German lines were protected by dense entanglements of barbed wire, and parallel lines of trenches with deep and well-protected dugouts. The British bombardment mostly employed 18-pounder guns, which were not powerful enough for siege conditions. The projectiles were a mixture of high explosive and shrapnel. The result was that the wire was generally not destroyed because the shrapnel was useless and there were not enough high-explosive shells. The enemy troops manned the front line thinly, and then emerged from their dugouts and moved to the front-line trenches when the bombardment stopped. The result was that the unprotected British infantry, who were advancing in the open in broad daylight and soon impeded by German wire, were hit by enfilading machine-gun fire. In most cases the result was far worse than decimation.

The question that must be faced is: whose fault was it? The British army, including generals from all arms of the service, was totally unprepared for the new type of warfare. And the British were not alone, because every other country was equally unprepared. General Staffs everywhere followed their normal practice of preparing for the last war not the next one. Moreover, in the British army, not many of the top generals had come from the ranks of the gunners. In 1918, the six most senior generals in the BEF were three from the cavalry (Haig, Birdwood and Byng), two from the infantry (Plumer and Rawlinson) and only one gunner (Horne). The influence of the 'cavalry mentality' was felt during and after the First World War and had a long-range influence on British armoured tactics.

On the Western Front during the painful years 1915, 1916 and 1917, the British and French armies were constantly on the attack. Attackers always lost more men than defenders. Except for three major German offensives, the Second Battle of Ypres in 1915, the assault on Verdun in 1916 and the March 1918 attack at St Quentin, the German armies spent the time defending what they had won during the early months of the war. But the fact that the hated enemy occupied large tracts of French soil drove the French, with British support, to make constant and expensive efforts to evict them. This meant that the French and British suffered the greatest penalty from the failure of the deeply flawed tactics of artillery bombardment followed by daytime infantry assault. As the failures mounted, the only remedy from the military chiefs and their staffs was to apply greater force next time: with predictable results.

In the summer of 1916, after almost two years of war, the British unveiled and used on a tiny scale the first tanks: the crawling monsters that were the first major innovation of the war. (Poison gas, first used by the Germans during the Second Battle of Ypres, was an unpleasant surprise, but protective masks to counter its effect ensured that gas was never going to be a decisive weapon.) However, the British had not applied enough rigorous thought to how tanks should be effectively employed, and the attack on Flers on the Somme in 1916, and the larger offensive at Cambrai in 1917, gave no indication of the ultimately war-winning importance of this new weapon. The first major innovation to break the deadlock of trench warfare – the tank – was exploited for its weaponry more than for its mobility.

The second major innovation, developed by the German army, was based on new battlefield tactics. The dramatic use of these tactics, against the British at St Quentin on 21 March 1918, was considered after a few days to be the method by which the deadlock would be decisively broken. But this was not to be.

The technique, which can be described as 'crumbling', is associated with the name of General Ludendorff, the *de facto* Commander-in-Chief of the German army; but it was actually conceived by Colonel Georg von Bruchmüller, an officer who deserves to be remembered, especially since the techniques of the March 1918 offensive were echoed in the German Blitzkrieg of 1940. Von Bruchmüller's first principle concerned the point of attack. He was less interested in the long-term strategic value of the objective than in the fact that it was a weak spot in the British line; the first assault was on the thinly held front of the British 5th Army in front of St Quentin. The second principle was surprise, which was achieved by a very short artillery bombardment of unprecedented intensity, using high-explosive and gas shells fired on the British front line, and then quickly shifting to the rear areas to prevent reinforcements from moving forward. The third principle was the use of small parties of highly trained infantry named 'Shock-Troops', armed with machine guns, whose job was to find and exploit small patches of weakness in the British positions. They succeeded startlingly well, and the result was confusion in the British ranks, widespread infiltration and a rapid crumbling of the British positions. Within days, the 5th Army had virtually ceased to exist.

The first attack was followed later by two others on different parts of the long front in France and Flanders. Nevertheless, taking the long view, the Bruchmüller method was not a war-winner. By concentrating on tactics at the expense of strategy, the German assaults had no real focus, since the attacks led in different directions. The result was that the German effort ran out of steam despite the fact that it left huge dents in the Allied line. The Germans had shot their bolt and were therefore vulnerable to a major riposte later in 1918.

In the summer of 1918, the British gave birth to a third innovation, and this at last was the fighting technique that proved decisive. The underlying principle was *cooperation* between fighting arms that led to synergy (a point raised in the first paragraph of this chapter). The concept was developed by General Rawlinson's 4th Army and put into effect in August 1918. The attack saw the total integration of infantry, armour, air, engineers and artillery: the complete orchestra of war. The climax of the battle was, in Ludendorff's words, 'the black day' of the war for the German army. On top of all this General Foch, Generalissimo of the Allied armies, and Field Marshal Haig, British Commander-in-Chief, made planned switches in the Allied attacks on different parts of the long battle line. These disrupted German defensive preparations. Eventually Ludendorff lost his nerve and suffered a collapse, and victory came on 11 November 1918.

The contribution of the Royal Regiment was universally recognized, and the most visible tribute paid to it was the finest of all the monuments to British soldiers who had fallen in battle. This is the massive Gunner Memorial at Hyde Park Corner, near the Duke of Wellington's house in Central London.

However, the lesson from the British offensive in August 1918 – the vital importance of synergy resulting from cooperation between all arms, including air power – was all but forgotten by the British. The senior officers of the army continued to focus in a general way on mobility to overcome the curse of the siege warfare of 1914–1918. But the proven method of introducing mobility to break the deadlock, the all-arms offensive, was frustrated by at least four impediments. The first was the lack of a formal all-arms doctrine that could form the basis of planning and training. This is related to the second point, thinking in 'silos': something that in particular led to a lack of cooperation from the Royal Air Force. The third was a technical factor, the feebleness of tactical radio communications that were crucially important on a rapidly moving battlefield. The fourth – rather decisively – was the perpetual shortage of funds.

However, the Germans did not forget the lesson and it had a huge influence on the German tactics of Blitzkrieg that achieved dazzling results during the first three years of the Second World War. The success of Blitzkrieg also depended on the design of tanks, and in this the Germans were ahead of the British at the beginning of the Second World War, despite the fact that the British had been the original inventors. As the war progressed, German tank design continued to outpace the British and the Americans, and this meant that after the invasion of Europe in 1944, the Allied forces were faced with a number of formidable German machines: the Panther, the Tiger, the King Tiger and the *Jagdpanzer* anti-tank gun.

Blitzkrieg also depended on bomber aircraft that were small enough to support directly the army in the field. The reason that the British fell behind in tank design was also related to air power. During the 1930s, British politicians and military planners were fixated on air warfare. Fighter aircraft for defence, and heavy strategic bombers to attack the enemy homeland from the air, received the first call on funds: ahead of tank development. Aircraft took a large proportion of the meagre resources that were allocated to the armed services, and British expenditure on air armaments increased *eight-fold* between 1935 and 1939.

British sensitivity to the dangers of air attack had a direct effect on the fortunes of the Royal Artillery. It led to the foundation of Anti-Aircraft Command, a semi-autonomous organization that was connected with the network of fighter airfields and early warning radar stations controlled by the Royal Air Force. Anti-Aircraft Command deployed around many British cities, London in particular, batteries of formidable heavy Anti-Aircraft (AA) guns, with calibres of 3.7in and 4.5in. There were also batteries of searchlights, and even some of sound detectors constructed like giant microphones. Heavy AA batteries also formed part of British armies in the field. All these new gunner units meant a significant addition to the manpower of the Royal Artillery. At the same time, the artillery component of infantry divisions was maintained and eventually increased. For most of the First World War, each infantry division of twelve battalions was supported by twelve Field Artillery batteries. During the latter part of the Second World War, an infantry division (now composed of ten battalions: nine rifle and one of machine guns) was supported by fifteen batteries: nine Field, three Anti-Tank; and three Light AA (armed with Bofors, Swedish-designed 40mm guns). During the Second World War the Royal Artillery is said to have had more men in uniform than the whole of the Royal Navy (including the very large number of naval reservists who had been mobilized).

During the inter-war period, gunner batteries said farewell to their horses and converted to Mechanical Transport (MT). Increasingly efficient radio equipment was eventually introduced, and this made for reliable communication between observers in front – those in fixed posts and FOOs – and the Gun Positions. Also, as mentioned, many regiments of Yeomanry cavalry were converted to artillery. Most importantly, the 25-pounder field gun was introduced, to replace the 18-pounder that had given so many years of effective service.

Field Marshal Wavell made the following point in a lecture he delivered in 1939:

> Whenever in the old days a new design of mountain gun was submitted to the Artillery Committee, that august body had it taken to the top of a tower, some hundred feet high, and thence dropped on to the ground below. If it was still capable of functioning it was given further trial; if not, it was rejected as flimsy.

It is not known whether this remarkable testing procedure was used for the newly designed 25-pounder gun, but it was certainly built to last. This gun (Plate 2) became one of the best-known weapons of the Second World War. There were not enough of them to equip all the Field and RHA regiments at the beginning of the war, but they began to be delivered in quantity during 1940. The 25-pounder remained in use for more than thirty years, which was a tribute to its effectiveness. It had a range of 13,400yd, or almost 8 miles. An important feature was its maximum elevation, or upward tilt, of 40 degrees (compared with the 16 degrees of the 18-pounder). It could therefore fire like a howitzer, with shells going high in the air and plunging onto the target. In a later design improvement, the muzzle of the gun was capped with a brake, which dampened the strain on the recoil mechanism and made the guns more stable. The 25-pounder was operated by a close-knit and well-drilled team of five men, with Number One – a Sergeant or sometimes an experienced Bombardier – in charge. (However, depending on the strength of the battery, the team could be up to six or down to four.) There were twenty-four guns per regiment, eight per battery and four per troop.

The distinguished military analyst Basil Liddell Hart wrote the following about the 25-pounder in the North African desert: 'A gun's "long arm" is decisive, and here the British had the best of it. It was not pleasant to be exposed to the fire of their 25-pounder guns at extreme range and to be unable to make an effective reply.' Following traditional practice, during the Second World War a Field Artillery regiment supported an infantry brigade. A battery worked with a battalion, and there was an intimate relationship between the two. (Horse Artillery regiments, usually supporting armoured units, were organized in the same way.)

A gunner regiment contained a good deal of MT. In battle, this was organized into three groups: 'F' (or 'Fighting') Echelon: the vehicles used by the regiment when it was in contact with the enemy; 'A' Echelon, moving a 'tactical bound' in the rear: carrying immediate replenishments of ammunition, food etc.; and

'B' Echelon a further 'tactical bound' behind: a group of vehicles receiving supplies brought up from logistical depots and passing them upward to 'A' Echelon. In Normandy Peter Pettit, whose battle diary forms the skeleton of this book, commanded a battery of 116th Field Regiment, Royal Artillery. He used for his personal transport a half-track: a clumsy, partially armoured vehicle that moved well over difficult ground. It was big enough to carry signallers and a good deal of kit. He also had a Jeep.

Regimental Headquarters (RHQ), run by the Adjutant, was with 'F' Echelon, and contained the Commanding Officer (CO) and his immediate aides: the Second-in-Command, Adjutant, Intelligence Officer (IO), Signals Officer (SO), Medical Officer (MO), plus numbers of NCOs and other ranks. The CO often spent much time with his Brigade Commander, and had a reliable radio link back to RHQ.

Forward of RHQ were the three batteries, each relatively self-contained. Each battery was deployed in five functional groups:

i. *Command Post (CP)*, the main location of the Battery Commander (BC) and his small staff. It was run by one of the Captains because the BC was often away from his Command Post, with the commander of the unit he was supporting;

ii. *Static Observation Post (OP)*, often but not invariably set up; and established within reach of the HQ being supported;

iii. *OPs with the infantry*: one or more FOOs. The BC travelled with the Battalion HQ when major action was likely. The Troop Commanders were the FOOs and they were with (or within reach of) the commanders of the units they were supporting;

iv. *Gun Position*, normally where all eight guns were concentrated, although occasionally there were separate positions for each of the four-gun troops and its own Command Post. Gun Lines were usually sheltered, and established in the rear out of direct sight of the Forward Edge of the Battle Area (FEBA). During the Second World War, this area was called Forward Defended Localities (FDLs): separate positions occupied by infantry; there was mutual fire support between FDLs, with the gaps covered by fire and infantry patrols;

v. *Wagon Line (WL)*, where the battery's MT was parked; each of the eight guns needed its own towing vehicle, usually a QUAD, which was a truck with four-wheel drive and an enclosed cabin with a sloping top.

These five individual elements needed reliable radio nets (all using radio telephony, not Morse Code). Gunner communication was better than in the infantry because the artillery employed more powerful radio equipment. Where possible, static telephone lines – which were less open to enemy ears –

duplicated the radio links. Battery links were also established with RHQ and with neighbouring batteries: those both in the regiment and with neighbouring regiments. This made it possible for the FOOs to call in fire from a whole regiment (*Mike* Target); a division (*Uncle* Target); and (much more rarely) an Army Group Royal Artillery or AGRA (*Yoke* Target); a corps (*Victor* Target); and an army (*William* Target).

Changing a gunner regiment's location involved officers and warrant officers who had clearly defined roles which they carried out with practised skill. However, the process took some time, because of the need for batteries to reconnoitre OPs, gun positions and command posts; establish radio communications; sight the guns; then 'survey-in' the whole battery. The first job in sighting the guns was setting up a zero line. This was the centre line to the target, calculated from the map and put on the sight of a single gun with the use of a prismatic compass. This was done by aligning the compass bearing on an aiming post (a metal rod painted black-and-white) that was stuck in the ground in front of each gun; and it was on the aiming post that the gun sight was set. A ranging shot was observed and corrected, and all the guns in the Gun Position set their sights accordingly. When the guns were engaging subsequent targets, orders from the OP were given in switches from the zero line (X degrees right or left); and in changes of range (plus or minus Y yards). Range was not corrected by creeping up or creeping down, but by straddling the target in large jumps up and down until the target was found. When not engaged in a fire task, the guns in the Gun Position had their sights set on an emergency target, called a Defensive Fire (DF) target. If this was a particularly vulnerable spot, it was called a DF/SOS.

Surveying-in meant that the targets for the guns that were being set up were plotted on their battery grid (an overlay on the tactical map), enabling them to fire on the battery's targets. Then this was quickly integrated into a regimental grid alongside the other batteries, to enable them all to fire on the regiment's targets. The scale moved up progressively to target grids for the guns supporting larger formations: the division, and more rarely the Army Group Royal Artillery (AGRA), and sometimes even larger formations. The more quickly this setting-in was done, the speedier the opportunities for an officer in an OP or an FOO to call on extra fire on his own targets.

In changing a battery's position, the order of events was sighting and 'surveying-in', then camouflaging, then digging. While these jobs were being done, ammunition had to be transported. Each round weighed 25 pounds, so that eighty shells weighed almost a ton. There were also cartridges, containing bags of cordite, to speed a shell on its way. The number of these depended on the range of the target: one, two, three or (exceptionally) four, called supercharge. Time was then needed to lay static telephone lines. From PP's diary it is surprising how often 116th Field Regiment changed its positions. This meant an active life for the members of each of the three batteries. When the Regiment's position was established on the ground, PP was always on the move between Command Post and RHQ, and visiting OPs. The ten Captains and Subalterns in PP's Battery were fully occupied with gun lines and OPs, all of which had to be manned 24 hours a day. Officers' duties had to be staggered, to allow for rest periods. A battery also had many NCOs; every gun was, as mentioned, commanded by a Sergeant or experienced Bombardier.

Earning Rommel's Respect

It seems ungracious to question the performance of the British army in the Second World War. It had made a major contribution to victory in the West over a tough, experienced and professional enemy. Nevertheless, there has been no shortage of criticism of British leadership, and of the performance of individual branches of the service. British armoured tactics were for many years flawed, because tanks were encouraged to 'go it alone' without close infantry support. The tanks themselves were too thin-skinned to withstand the fire of the deadly German 88mm anti-tank guns. Until the end of the war the Shermans, the American tanks most widely used by the Anglo-American armies, were equipped with guns that were less powerful than those mounted in the huge German tanks. The British infantry was considered by the Germans to be brave, with great fortitude in defence, but the junior leaders and the soldiers were thought to lack initiative and forward drive when attacking.

The single branch of the service that was never criticized was the artillery. This chapter begins with Montgomery's tribute, and he had more to say:

> The gunners have risen to great heights in this war; they have been well commanded and well handled. In my experience the artillery has never been so efficient as it is today; it is at the top of its form. The contribution of artillery to final victory has been immense. The harder the fighting and the longer the war, the more the infantry, and in fact all arms, lean on the gunners.

Montgomery's last point has occasionally been given a negative twist. It has been argued that British infantry relied so much on the gunners that the result was 'stickiness', a reluctance to advance without overwhelming artillery support. Such support was however generally available and it managed to push the infantry forward, at least in the early stages of an attack. But advancing without artillery support was another story.

Two other top British leaders, Slim and Horrocks, paid their tributes in more personal terms, as might have been expected from men who were known for their sympathy with the dangers and hardships suffered by the soldiers in the ranks. Finally, it is particularly interesting to learn something of the opinions of

British gunnery held by Rommel, the legendary German officer who had been for long periods on the receiving end of the attentions of the Royal Artillery. He wrote about it on many occasions in the diary he kept when he was commanding the German Afrika Korps in the desert campaign of 1941–1942.

Field Marshal Slim:
I visited various units and stayed to watch a battery firing at Japanese reported to be collecting for an attack. One of the gunners, stripped to the waist, his bronze body glistening with sweat, was slamming shells into the breech of a 25-pounder. In a lull in the firing I stepped into the gun pit beside him. 'I'm sorry' I said, 'you've got to do all this on half rations.' He looked up at me from under his battered bush hat. 'Don't you worry about that, sir,' he grinned. 'Put us on quarter rations, but give us the ammo and we'll get you into Rangoon.'

Lieutenant General Horrocks:
I have often said in lectures since the war that, although I am an infantryman, I would say that the Royal Regiment of Artillery did more to win the last war than any other arm. Time after time their young Forward Observation Officers would step into the breach and take command of some forward infantry unit whose commanders had all become casualties, while the technical skill with which huge concentrations of fire were switched rapidly from one part of the front to another was never equalled in any other army. The Germans never succeeded in achieving anything like it.

Field Marshal Rommel:
23 November 1941
The attack started well, but soon came up against a wide artillery and anti-tank gun screen. Guns of all kinds and sizes laid a curtain of fire in front of the attacking tanks and there seemed almost no hope of making any progress in the face of this fire-spewing barrier. Tank after tank split open in the hail of shells. Our entire artillery had to be thrown in to silence the enemy guns one by one.

1 July 1942
Furious artillery fire again struck into our ranks. British shells came screaming in from three directions, north, east and south; anti-aircraft tracer streaked through our force. Under this tremendous weight of fire, our attack came to a standstill. Hastily we scattered our vehicles and took cover, as shell after shell crashed into the area we were holding.

23 October 1942

At 21:40, a barrage of immense weight opened over the whole line, eventually concentrating on the northern sector. Such drum-fire had never before been seen on the African front, and it was to continue throughout the whole of the Alamein battle. Apart from the divisional artillery of the attacking and holding divisions, Montgomery had concentrated fifteen heavy artillery regiments – representing a total of 540 guns of a calibre greater than 105mm – in the northern sector. The British bombarded our known positions with extraordinary accuracy, and enormous casualties resulted.

Report on El Alamein

The British artillery once again demonstrated its well-known excellence. A particular feature was its great mobility and tremendous speed of reaction to the needs of the assault troops. The British armoured units obviously carried artillery observers to transmit the needs of the front back to the artillery in the shortest possible time. In addition to the advantage given by their abundant supplies of ammunition, the British benefited greatly from the long range of their guns, which enabled them to take the Italian artillery positions under fire at a range at which the Italian guns, most of which were limited to 6,000 yards, were completely unable to hit back.

'Arms Are the Way to Preserve Peace'

The Artillery Garden comes as a surprise to a person who sees it but who was previously unaware of its existence. On the northern edge of the City of London is a 6-acre patch of well-mown grass enclosed by buildings, and which is not a public park. It is the home of the organization whose headquarters, an eighteenth-century building called Armoury House, is on the northern edge of the Artillery Garden (Plate 1). There are some handsome Regency houses on the west side, converted into flats (where I once lived). Most of the remaining buildings on the other three sides of the Garden are undistinguished office blocks. The body that owns Armoury House and occupies the ground is the Honourable Artillery Company, universally known as the HAC and often called the Company. It is composed of part-time soldiers and is the oldest regiment in the British army.

It was set up centuries ago, as one of a number of Fraternities or Guilds of St George, and the particular fraternity that became the HAC was formally incorporated by King Henry VIII in a Charter dated 1537. A document proving this has been preserved. The fraternities engaged in target practice with long bows, crossbows and hand guns. These weapons were known at the time as 'artillery', a word that has changed its meaning over time. Gradually, the word was altered to mean field guns, and the Honourable Artillery Company did not have any of these at the beginning. The Artillery Garden began to be used for target practice during the 1640s.

The HAC is an established military organization, but Armoury House is also a charity and a club for its members. Those who have spent a reasonable period serving as citizen soldiers can stay on as veteran members and still use the club. It is the only regiment that has an emblem beyond a cap badge: full armorial bearings that were registered (or, as it is thought, re-registered) by the College of Arms in 1821. The motto '*Arma Pacis Fulcra*' is translated literally as '*Arms, the Supporters of Peace*', but can be more freely rendered as '*Arms Are the Way to Preserve Peace*'.

As its motto implies, the purpose of the HAC is to defend the realm. But since there has been no invasion of Britain during the Company's existence, it did not engage a foreign enemy until conditions changed at the turn of the nineteenth/twentieth centuries. The HAC supplied officers for both sides during the Civil War (1642–1651), and was called out to suppress the anti-Catholic Gordon Riots in 1780. But these were the extent of its active military involvement during the first three-and-a-half centuries or so of its existence.

This book is concerned with artillery in its modern sense. The HAC, which had been infantry for almost 250 years, added artillery in 1781, when the City of London donated to the Company two brass 3-pounder field guns with a bore of under 3in. These still exist. The guns, on wheeled carriages, had axles too wide to be hauled through the doors of Armoury House to the drill hall, then at the front of the building. (A new drill hall was later built at the back and named the Albert Room, after Queen Victoria's Consort.) Two slots were therefore chiselled into the stone of the door posts to let the guns through. These slots can be seen today, although few people know what they were for.

The first call to arms came with the Second Anglo-Boer War (1899–1902), the largest conflict in which Britain was engaged since the Crimean War. Reinforcements were needed because the beginning of the war saw a number of British defeats. Conscription was out of the question, but many men volunteered to serve. The HAC Infantry supplied a company in the over-strength battalion raised by the Lord Mayor and paid for by the businesses of the City of London, the City Imperial Volunteers (CIV). The HAC Artillery provided the officers and NCOs for a gunner battery. In addition, sixty men volunteered to serve with other units. The members of the HAC performed well in the field and earned the respect of the Regular army. Six members lost their lives, and the HAC earned its first Battle Honour.

The early years of the twentieth century saw the Haldane reforms, which shook up the existing ramshackle and variegated organizations of part-time soldiers. The old Volunteer infantry and Yeomanry cavalry were reorganized into divisions in a new Territorial Force (TF). The HAC was in a special position because of its ownership of property and, by special Act of Parliament, its independence was maintained. All Volunteer battalions in the London area were organized into battalions of a large umbrella unit called the London Regiment; but not the HAC. The whole of the TF – with an overall strength of fourteen infantry and six cavalry divisions – was organized for home defence. This caused an immediate problem in 1914, when reinforcements were desperately needed for the British Expeditionary Force (BEF) serving in France and Flanders.

In 1914, the HAC comprised an Infantry half-battalion (soon increased to a full battalion of four double-companies), plus two Batteries, A and B. They were all up to strength. The Company's main source of recruits was well-educated young men who worked in the City of London and were introduced into the HAC by their friends, and this is still true to some extent. The HAC now also has women members. By long tradition, everyone had to enter the Company in the ranks, and officers were commissioned from within. This changed only recently.

Members of the Territorial Force did not have to serve overseas. Nevertheless, most of the members of the HAC volunteered to do so, and the call came quickly. The Regiment more than doubled in size, to two full battalions and five batteries. In both world wars, Territorial units needed a good deal of intense training before being committed to battle. In the First World War, most either spent months in Britain or were dispatched to Egypt and India to relieve Regular battalions on garrison duty. However, the demand for more men for the BEF led to the speedy departure to France of a few selected Territorial battalions. On 18 September 1914, 1 HAC sailed on SS *Westmeath*, whose bell hangs today at the top of the stairs in Armoury House.

The expected rôle of Territorial soldiers who agreed to serve abroad was to reinforce the Regular army. This was therefore the first purpose of the HAC. But within a short period, the Company was called to make a second – and even more important – contribution. It was put into the small category of 'class' regiments whose special duty was to supply junior officers to other units, initially Regular battalions in the BEF. This started in early January 1915, when twenty-one private soldiers in 1 HAC were given immediate commissions in Regular battalions and departed without delay, with a single subaltern's star sewn on the cuffs of their privates' tunics. NCOs could not be spared. There is a legend that the Commander-in-Chief, Field Marshal French, selected twenty-three men when he inspected the battalion. But since only twenty-one names appeared in the *London Gazette*, two men were probably killed before their promotions could be officially recognized. During 1915 the majority of members of 1 HAC were commissioned. (They included my wife's great-uncle.) They were replaced by recruits from Armoury House who had received some training, and this process continued until the end of the war. Another 'class' regiment was the Artists' Rifles. A third, the Inns of Court Regiment, supplied officers in the cavalry: a smaller task since this arm of the service was declining in importance as the war progressed.

1 HAC entered the battle line in November 1914 and began to suffer casualties and earn its first awards for gallantry. They spent the miserable winter of 1914–1915 in the trenches, often wading knee-deep through water. Meanwhile, 2 HAC was training in England and did not arrive in the BEF until October 1916. The Battalion was soon in action and began to suffer horrendous losses. It was transferred to the Italian front at the end of 1917, where it performed notably well under the command of Lieutenant Colonel O'Connor, a Regular officer in the Cameronians. He was to make his name in the Second World War, when he commanded the corps that won the first British victory in that war. This was the bold advance against the Italian army in the Western Desert at the end of 1940 that netted spectacular numbers of prisoners.

A and B Batteries left England for the Middle East in April 1915 and spent the war fighting the Turks in the blazing heat of the desert. They participated in the final campaign, when the force commanded by General Allenby defeated the Turkish army. (As mentioned), three additional HAC batteries were also raised: an RGA Siege battery and two further Field batteries. They all saw considerable action with the BEF on the Western Front.

The HAC made a significant contribution to Allied victory; 1,600 members of the Company lost their lives. The Regiment earned an impressive clutch of Battle Honours, and its members received 788 decorations, including 3 awards of the Victoria Cross. Most important of all, the HAC fulfilled its second task of providing officers. It handed over to the rest of the army the gift of 4,000 well-trained and highly motivated subalterns.

After the end of the First World War, the Honourable Artillery Company did not take long to return to business as usual, with an Infantry Battalion and A and B Batteries. Many members who had become officers during the war became Privates and NCOs again, a number wearing their Military Cross (MC) ribbons. (This also occurred after the Second World War. When the Infantry Battalion was re-formed in 1947, three of the Warrant Officers were former Lieutenant Colonels.)

During the 1920s, no immediate change was likely, but in the long term it was possible that the Batteries would be mechanized. Until now the life of the Batteries had revolved around their horses. Peter Pettit (senior) had served in B Battery before the First World War and commanded a battery of an RHA Yeomanry regiment during that war. He had found it a hard experience, since he received a bad leg wound that left him lame. In civilian life he was the senior partner of a firm of London solicitors, one that his two sons were later to join. His elder son Peter (junior) – whom I call PP, the author of the diaries that form the fabric of this book – was born in 1908 and joined B Battery in 1927; this became part of 11th (HAC) Regiment, RHA, in 1939. PP's younger brother Paul, who also joined B Battery, was commissioned and in 1939 joined the 12th (HAC) Regiment, RHA. Paul Pettit left a series of graphic descriptions of activities in the Battery during the 1930s. Here are three quotations from his reminiscences; the third, rather sad, extract dates from November 1937:

> Gunnery and gun drill, signalling (visual and telephone), deployment and, above all, management of the 'noble animal' occupied evening drills and riding school with the Household Cavalry or the RHA Battery at St. John's Wood. On several weekends or Sundays each year, we practised manoeuvres at Aldershot, Woolwich, Shorncliffe, or wherever Regular units could horse us.

> Camp always began on a Saturday in May. The first day or two resembled a rodeo. A typical day in camp began with Trumpeters sounding Reveille at 06:00. We had ten minutes to dress in old tunic, slacks and gum boots, to fold up blankets and ground sheet and double to the horse-lines. On fatigues we always doubled. Morning stables meant 'mucking out', clearing the lines of the night's droppings and a quick brushing if a horse had soiled itself. If the shovels had not arrived by the first morning, the BSM bellowed 'what are your hands for?' to get us going. The horses were then watered and fed. On frosty mornings we'd break the ice in the troughs with our boots before the horses drank. After breakfast, the next call was 'Boot and Saddle', a scene of frantic activity as the sub-sections raced each other to saddle up and harness the teams and get to the gun park to hook in.

> Military vehicles began to arrive at Armoury House in November, including six-wheeled tractors to pull the guns. Solid rubber tyres were fitted to gun and limber wheels so that they could be safely towed along the streets at 15 mph. Farriers went on courses for motor mechanics; and signallers, to get acquainted with wireless sets. Instead of the peaty smell and healthy exercise of riding school, we drove round the dark, deserted streets of the City, inhaling petrol fumes. The party was definitely over.

Discipline and Pride

The British government in 1937 began – very belatedly in view of the looming threat from the other side of the Rhine – to step up the pace of rearmament. In 1938 the size of the Territorial Army (no longer the Territorial Force) was doubled. And a law was passed to conscript young men: this was to begin in 1939. These decisions would directly affect the HAC.

In view of the Regiment's proven record in providing officers – and remembering the number of potential leaders who were lost as casualties when 1 HAC was in the firing line during the early part of the First World War – the

HAC Infantry Battalion was now classed as an Officer-Producing Unit, together with the Artists' Rifles and the Inns of Court Regiment. This meant that when war was declared the Battalion marched out of Armoury House, travelled by train to Salisbury Plain, and formed an Officer Cadet Training Unit (OCTU). The vast majority of members were commissioned within months into virtually every regiment in the British army. Meanwhile, the original A and B Batteries expanded dramatically. During the summer of 1939 three new units were formed: 11th (HAC) Regiment, RHA; 12th (HAC) Regiment, RHA; and 86th Heavy Anti-Aircraft Regiment, RA. (One of the battery commanders in this was to be Edward Heath, future Prime Minister.) The HAC had never before witnessed such enormous and rapid growth. Later in the war, yet another unit would come into existence: 13th (HAC) Regiment, RHA. There would also be some smaller units for home defence.

The 11th, 12th and 86th Regiments were manned by existing members of the HAC, plus those on the waiting list, and also recruits with a similar background to existing members. Peter Pettit was in the thick of things. In 1939 he was an acting Major, in command of B Battery, one of those in 11th Regiment. The pre-war Adjutant of the Batteries, Captain Richard Goodbody, became the Adjutant of 11th Regiment on its formation. He was posted away in May 1940 to enter the Staff College, and returned to command the Regiment in North Africa after the Battle of El Alamein. He eventually became a full (four-star) General, Adjutant-General with a seat on the Army Council, and during the 1960s Colonel Commandant of the HAC.

It was (perhaps surprisingly) a long time before the newly formed Regiments departed on active service. 11th Regiment sailed for the Middle East in September 1941; 12th Regiment for Tunisia in November 1942; and 86th Regiment for France in June 1944. 13th Regiment also went to France in June. There were a number of reasons for these delays.

Preparing a new unit for war is a slow, progressive process. The first impediment was that the training of the three newly formed Regiments was constantly interrupted as large parties of NCOs and Other Ranks were interviewed and quickly dispatched to OCTUs. (In total, the HAC produced 4,000 officers in the Second World War, to match the 4,000 that it had provided in the First.) The officer cadets who left in 1939 and 1940 were replaced by young conscripts from civilian life, including batches of young soldiers from infantry battalions who naturally had no knowledge of gunnery. When the newcomers arrived, the interrupted training had to start all over again. The second impediment to training was that from mid-June to mid-September 1940 11th Regiment was deployed as infantry, to man defences on the south coast of England in preparation for an enemy invasion.

The third interruption in what the HAC should have been doing – general and specialist training, field firing and tactical exercises – was a number of erratic time-consuming activities. These included regular changes of location; medical inspections and inoculations (from which the troops needed time to recover); demonstrations by other fighting arms; learning to use and service new vehicles and other equipment; changes of 'management', with officers coming and going; parades of different levels of importance; and visits from senior officers. These things are typical of what happened in a regiment on active service, although not yet on the field of battle.

Since life in uniform was a novelty for so many of the men who had just joined, they needed time to adjust to their new existence – learning to obey orders instantly, parade ground drill, polishing and shining equipment, digging, fatigues, guard duty, marching long distances, self-reliance in the field – but throughout these activities their morale was maintained by the comradeship of their mates in the ranks. Then, very slowly as if by osmosis, they began to absorb the *esprit de corps* of the Royal Regiment. The French poet Alfred de Vigny described the process, which is the lifeblood of armies in all countries, *Servitude et Grandeur Militaires*: which is more-or-less the same as the maxim *Discipline and Pride* that the Brigade of Guards considers the key to building a first-class military unit.

PP handed over command of B Battery on 23 March 1941. He transferred to 17th Field Regiment, RA, a Regular unit in which he was eventually to become Second-in-Command. His next eighteen months in England were to be in a sense a repetition of his time in 11th Regiment. The long process, of training initially reluctant civilians and turning them into an efficient and motivated body of men, was concluded by the time PP and his Regiment went to fight overseas.

Chapter 2

Tunisia – The Begining of the End

After the British victory at El Alamein, Churchill gave a memorable speech in which he said that it was not the end or even the beginning of the end, but it was perhaps the end of the beginning. The British battle in the desert was followed by the great Russian victory at Stalingrad in January 1943. The even greater Anglo-American triumph in Tunisia – to which this chapter is devoted – marked a further stage beyond Churchill's imaginative perspective on the El Alamein victory. Tunisia indeed was the beginning of the end.

The End of America's Isolation

The devastating Japanese air raid on Pearl Harbor on 7 December 1941 struck deeply into the psyche of the American public. Hitler's almost immediate and gratuitous declaration of war on the United States did not change greatly the American perception that Japan was their enemy, their main one at least. This feeling remained with some people for decades. However, within days of Pearl Harbor, Churchill was in Washington, DC, and an official agreement was reached that Germany had to be the Allies' first priority. The President and the Prime Minister remained loyal to the 'Germany first' decision until Roosevelt's death. But this did not prevent bickering among the American and British Chiefs-of-Staff (a committee that became known as the Combined Chiefs). The American Admiral King was never convinced that Europe was more important than the Pacific.

Just as seriously, the 'Germany first' decision was interpreted by the American and British Chiefs in different ways, and in these disputes the British showed a broader strategic vision. Jumping forward in time, the British – and Churchill in particular – had their eyes on the Eastern Mediterranean, something the Americans saw as a continued manifestation of imperialist ambitions. In reality, Churchill was foreseeing the dangerous post-war position of Russia in Eastern Europe, which was something that had to be contained. The British also constantly supported the arduous campaign in Italy. The Americans interpreted this as a British drive to attack Germany from the indirect and difficult southern route. What the British meant was that the Italian campaign was a demonstrably successful method of drawing Germany reserves away from France, where the German defenders always vastly outnumbered the Anglo-American invaders. The British arguments cut no ice with the Americans.

Leaving on one side the top-level disputes between the Allies, the military operations of the United States were conducted with great efficiency. A mighty army, navy and air force were planned, recruited, equipped, trained and committed to battle, where they learned practical lessons very quickly. (The number of senior officers who had seen active service during the First World War and could apply its lessons, was much smaller than in the British army.) In 1942, Roosevelt, as Commander-in-Chief of the United States armed forces, formed a small body to advise him and to coordinate and make decisions under his overall supervision. These were the Joint Chiefs-of-Staff, officers at the apex of the individual armed services. There were four members, of whom General Marshall and Admiral King were the most powerful. The others were Admiral Leahy, Chairman of the Committee and Roosevelt's personal adviser, and General Arnold who was head of the Army Air Corps. This was then part of the army, which made Arnold the subordinate of Marshall. The Joint Chiefs reported to the civilian heads of the services and then upward to the President. They exercised more independence than their British opposite numbers.

The British Chiefs-of-Staff Committee was made up of the three officers who headed the three services. The Chairman was General Brooke, who came from a prominent Ulster family and had been brought up in France. He had started his military career in the Royal Artillery, where he developed an extraordinary reputation as a gunner staff officer during the First World War. Brooke was a hard and experienced man with a first-class intellect. A highly talented strategist, he could expound his arguments powerfully and unrelentingly. (The Americans were always uncomfortable with his persistence.) The Committee reported, via the civilian chiefs of the services, to Churchill who was Minister of Defence as well as Prime Minister. Churchill was much more involved day-by-day than was Roosevelt, which meant that the members of the Committee had an extra-heavy load in examining in detail and satisfying (and often denying) the demands of their relentlessly energetic, imaginative, experienced and knowledgeable master. In Brooke's debates with Churchill, it was a case of Greek meeting Greek.

Grand strategy was planned by the two national committees, who for this purpose were amalgamated (as mentioned) to form the Combined Chiefs-of-Staff. Their headquarters was in Washington, DC, and the British Chiefs appointed a senior officer in the army and another in the navy to be their personal representatives. The frequent occasions on which the Combined Chiefs travelled the long distances to meet face-to-face marked important decision points and the discussions themselves were characterized by strong, often acrimonious, but generally constructive debates.

America had from the beginning two major allies, Britain and Russia. Britain's main enemy, and Russia's only one, was Germany. Moreover, Roosevelt and Marshall were convinced that the defeat of Germany first would almost immediately bring down Japan, while the defeat of Japan first would leave Germany not much less formidable than before. To the Americans, the decision to deal with Germany first meant that there must be an assault on Continental Europe across the English Channel. But it became almost immediately obvious that this would not be a feasible operation of war in 1942. There were too few trained troops and not enough landing craft; and the flow of weapons and supplies was as yet only a trickle although it would soon become a torrent.

Operation *Torch*, the invasion of North-West Africa, was therefore a second alternative, whether or not it would be followed by an assault on Continental Europe from the south (a matter as yet undecided). The Americans nevertheless tackled the job with their customary enthusiasm. In strategic terms, the invasion of North-West Africa was intended to squeeze the Axis forces in Tunisia against the advancing British 8th Army, and it was hoped to vanquish them in one big battle. The importance of this strategic plan was always implicit, but it became realistic and very important after the fortunes of the 8th Army had greatly improved after the Battle of El Alamein.

The 8th Army comprised British, New Zealand and Indian formations, and was controlled on a short leash by General Montgomery. It was made up of five infantry divisions and two armoured divisions, all highly seasoned troops. The morale of the 8th Army was high, which was a tribute to Montgomery's powerful personality. (When they got to Tunisia, they were patronizing towards the British 1st Army and had a very low opinion of the Americans.) During the long advance from El Alamein, fought in October 1942, there were two occasions during which the advance of the 8th Army was open to serious criticism. These were the delayed advance from El Alamein, and the initially unsuccessful assault on the Mareth Line. Nevertheless, this Army was run like a smoothly functioning machine. It covered the distance of well over a thousand miles from Egypt to Tunisia in less than six months, maintaining its huge flow of supplies over inadequate roads, while its opponents suffered substantial losses in men and materiel. The 8th Army became a legend to the beleaguered people of Britain.

The Commander-in-Chief for the invasion of North-West Africa had to be an American because the United States would eventually provide the largest share of manpower in the European theatre. It was also thought that the Americans would be more acceptable to the French in North-West Africa. Lieutenant General Eisenhower, a brainy staff officer who had never commanded troops in battle, was selected by Marshall over the heads of many more senior officers. Marshall displayed extraordinarily imaginative insight in making this appointment. In Tunisia, Eisenhower in his headquarters (which was often criticized for its elephantine size) had an efficient Chief-of-Staff, Major General Bedell Smith. Reporting to Eisenhower was a British subordinate commander, Admiral Andrew Browne Cunningham (universally known as ABC) whose naval headquarters was some distance from Eisenhower's.

Cunningham was a sailor in the Nelson tradition, fast in his responses and fiercely aggressive, with a fine feel for strategy and tactics. Although a demanding disciplinarian, he had personal charm and this made him popular. He had held high command in the Mediterranean for almost two years, since Italy had entered the war in June 1940. He had seen continuous action, winning two splendid victories against the Italian fleet at Taranto and Matapan; ensuring that the ever-important convoys got through to Malta and Alexandria; evacuating the British and Commonwealth troops from Greece and Crete; and bombarding the North African coast in support of the 8th Army. Cunningham's ships had suffered terrible losses, mainly from German air attacks, but their morale remained high. Cunningham never wavered in his demand for effective air cover for his ships. Cunningham joined Eisenhower after seven months in Washington, DC, and was appointed Commander-in-Chief of all naval forces in the Mediterranean. Under him he had a formidable naval force, with plentiful air support, and he was a proactive supporter of Eisenhower as Supreme Commander, although Cunningham was well aware of Eisenhower's extremely limited battle experience. But, like all Americans, Eisenhower was a fast learner.

The goal of the invasion was the French North African colonies: the enormous desert territory of Algeria, and the smaller and more compact colony of Tunisia. The ground on which the campaign was fought stretched for long distances, which meant that logistics were always going to be an important consideration. Furthest to the west, on the Atlantic coast outside the Straits of Gibraltar, the Americans landed at Casablanca and two other places. Inside the Mediterranean, British and American troops landed at Oran and Algiers. Algiers is 700 miles from Casablanca as the crow flies. The objective of the invading armies was the city of Tunis, more than 500 miles east of Algiers. From the Straits of Gibraltar, the North African coast line stretches west to east all the way to Tunisia, which terminates at the promontory of Cape Bon. Short of Cape Bon is the port of Bizerte; and Tunis is 20 miles south-east, at the base of the Cape Bon peninsula. From Cape Bon, the coast line stretches to the south in a ragged shape for 300 miles. It then turns a corner to the east and meets Libya. Montgomery's 8th Army would be advancing from this direction. See Map 1.

Convoys of more than 100 ships arrived from the United States without encountering any enemy U-boats. The British contingent arrived separately from Scotland. A total of 107,500 troops were landed on 8 November 1942, and overcame the opposition of the French defenders fairly easily. At Algiers two brigades of the British 78th Division landed, accompanied by American detachments made up of their 34th Division and substantial portions of two others.

The various individual elements of the Expeditionary Force were widely spread and had to be committed to battle piecemeal. In most cases the troops were quite inexperienced. This also went for the commanders, in particular Eisenhower, who had been sent to London in 1942 as Commander of the United States European Theatre, and was soon afterwards put in charge of the invasion in North-West Africa.

The force assaulting North-West Africa was assembled without a detailed organizational structure and run on an opportunistic basis. Little was planned before the event, mainly because the expedition had been mounted hurriedly, and the reaction of the French defenders of the provinces where the landings were to take place was totally uncertain. Would they fight? Would they remain neutral? Would they join the invaders to attack the Germans? At an early stage, Eisenhower did a deal with Admiral Darlan who commanded the Vichy French Navy. This was extremely unwelcome in London because Darlan was remembered for his refusal to resist the Germans in 1940. However, Eisenhower's arrangement paid a dividend because the French army in North Africa joined the Allies. They formed a corps of 50,000 men, which became an effective fighting force after they had been re-equipped by the Americans.

Eisenhower's command comprised three separate national formations, grouped together as 1st Army, whose operational chief was the British Lieutenant General Anderson. Anderson was an experienced professional, but he lacked the 'grip' and personal magnetism of Montgomery. General Alexander, who in January 1943 took overall command of all the land forces under Eisenhower, called Anderson rather pejoratively 'a good plain cook'. The British force was eventually built up to five infantry divisions and one armoured division. As mentioned in Chapter 1, Major Peter Pettit (PP) was a 34-year-old officer in the Honourable Artillery Company (HAC), and was now second-in-command of 17th Field Regiment, Royal Artillery, a senior Regular unit that supported an infantry brigade in the 78th Infantry Division. (However, as will be explained, PP's regiment did not join 1st Army until the end of December 1942.) The second national formation was the United States II Corps, which comprised three infantry divisions and one armoured division. At a later stage, Anderson's command was joined by the French XIX Corps of five divisions.

Throughout the campaign, an enormous benefit was provided by the Signals Intelligence (*Sigint*) that came from the *Ultra* code breakers in Bletchley Park, north of London. This vital information helped the military planners make their best moves on the ground, and was (as it had been for many months) a special bonus to Cunningham in countering the efforts of the Italian fleet and detecting and destroying Axis reinforcements to the Tunisian front. The source of all *Sigint* was invariably tightly protected. In the field, even divisional commanders were not told about this source, although they received the intelligence itself in a veiled form.

To some extent, 78th Division was different from most of the other invading troops. Although this division had been formed in June 1942 specifically for the invasion of North-West Africa, a high proportion of the individual units had seen action in France in 1940. Battle experience was always considered valuable. (In March 1943, the Division in turn had to send back to England twenty-two officers and sixty-nine NCOs, all battle-hardened men, to help train troops in Britain.) 78th Division was initially made up of three infantry brigades: 1st (Guards) Independent Brigade Group, of three Regular battalions; 11th Brigade, of two Regular battalions and one 'hostilities only' (made up of troops conscripted for wartime service only); and 36th Brigade of three battalions of 'hostilities only' troops. There were four artillery regiments, of which 17th Field, a Regular regiment, was the senior. As mentioned, PP was its Second-in-Command.

The 78th, known as the Battleaxe Division (because of its identifying sign), was commanded by Major General Evelegh (Plate 8), who was 43 years old. He had seen brief service at the end of the First World War, and much of his later career was as a staff officer, although he had briefly commanded 11th Brigade. He was a large, forceful man, who was well-liked and respected, and he deserves credit for building the division's formidable fighting reputation. He was relatively young, and two of his brigadiers were older and senior to him. One of these was Brigadier Wedderburn-Maxwell, the Commander Royal Artillery (CRA), with whom there were some face-offs, although the General and the Brigadier eventually built an excellent modus vivendi. The other officer was Brigadier Copland-Griffiths, who commanded the 1st (Guards) Independent Brigade Group, which was a reinforced formation. His relationship with the General remained prickly. The Brigade was not one of the two that landed on 8 November 1942. It joined 78th Division at the end of the year, and 'exchanged out' two months later. 17th Field Regiment supported 1st (Guards) Brigade, which meant that PP's entry into the campaign was delayed until the end of December 1942.

Deadlock

The terrain of Tunisia is very rough, with hills and mountains which are most unwelcoming in the wet winter weather. It was ground much better suited for defence than for attack. There are two mountain ranges that stretch from the base of the Cape Bon peninsula towards the south-west. Between them and providing a through route is the Kasserine Pass. These mountains were to be the American area of operations. In the north, the British were to attack east through mountainous country. Many individual bumps became important tactical features because of their command of the outlying country. In the east is the small town of Medjez el Bab, and beyond this towards Tunis is the important feature that the British named Longstop Hill (Plate 5).

Anderson's two brigades from 78th Division had landed at Algiers before dawn on 8 November. They and accompanying Commando units were pushed forward without delay, by road and also by small landings along the coast. On 16 November, the British force had advanced 400 miles against German air attacks. Command of the air was immensely important throughout the campaign. Before long Allied air power grew in strength so that it overwhelmed the Luftwaffe. But this was not the case at the beginning, as reflected in this order to all units of the 78th Division: 'All vehicles with removable hoods will travel with them down and a man will constantly stand up in the vehicle by day and night watching for enemy aircraft whilst on the move.' The troops in 78th Division moved forward through the hilly country in the north of Tunisia. They were organized in three columns. The race for Tunis was on. However, it was too little and too late. The advance was made by 6,000 troops, only a tiny fraction of the 107,500 who had landed. One of the major unknowns before the expedition was launched was the likely extent of the Axis response. This was much fiercer than had been anticipated, and heavy German reinforcements were landed in Tunisia from Italy, commanded by a seasoned professional from the Russian front, General von Arnim. His intentions were made obvious to all his soldiers: 'Behind us the sea! Before us the enemy! There can be no withdrawal!' The Germans had many of the formidable 88mm anti-tank guns which caused their usual havoc, and a small number of Tiger tanks that also carried the 88mm weapons. Despite Cunningham's tight blockade, supplies for the Axis armies trickled in, together with 16,000 troops by 5 December 1942, followed by another 30,000 by mid-February 1943, and a further 31,000 in March.

For the first four months of the campaign, 78th Division – which was becoming increasingly mixed – was engaged in small-scale but bloody fighting. In particular Longstop Hill proved too difficult an objective to capture, and here some British soldiers felt that the Americans, in their first experience of battle, did not hold their positions against German counter-attacks. During the course of December 1942, 78th Division's third major component arrived on the scene. This was the 1st (Guards) Independent Brigade Group, which was to be supported by 17th Field Regiment, Royal Artillery, in which PP was serving. The Regiment did not arrive until the very end of December. It was made up of 10, 13 and 26/92 Batteries (the numbering of the latter was changed); there were eight 25-pounder guns per battery. PP's specific job was to understudy the Commanding Officer, with particular responsibility for reconnoitring the ground to locate gun positions for some or all of the individual batteries.

17th Regiment travelled from Scotland to North Africa. As it was arriving, it experienced an exciting episode when the transport ship was bombed and crippled; 5,000 troops were on board but the casualties were surprisingly light.

The Regiment had to transfer to another vessel, and landed at the end of December at Bone. This was the major port nearest to the northern sector of the front, where there was continuous military activity but no sign of a breakthrough. The British force there was a mixture of infantry, parachute troops and armour, and it was fighting in places alongside American and French units.

On 2 February 1943, 1st (Guards) Independent Brigade Group was attached to 6th Armoured Division. The transfer was made permanent on 24 March, when 78th Division received in return 38th (Irish) Brigade. This was made up of three battalions: one Regular (1 Royal Irish Fusiliers), one Territorial (2 London Irish Rifles) and one 'hostilities only' (6 Royal Inniskilling Fusiliers). This meant that for the large, decisive engagements at the end of the campaign in which 17th Regiment played a role, it was supporting the Irish. The Brigade had been formed at the behest of Churchill, and it was to build a formidable fighting reputation in Tunisia, Sicily and Italy.

After it had landed at Bone, 17th Regiment moved by road for more than 100 miles to the Medjez el Bab sector. Here for the first time it fired its guns in anger. During the first four months of 1943, the Regiment was engaged in three periods of front-line action: Medjez, Bou Arada, then Medjez again. I have selected the diary entries that describe the most active spells, and I pay much less attention to the day-to-day routine of soldiering in the field. There is generally a good deal of rain during the Mediterranean winter and spring, and this made for discomfort for the soldiers who were living rough. But the riot of wild flowers and the ever-present nesting birds gave much pleasure to those Englishmen, like PP, who in their youth had learned to appreciate the simplest pleasures of nature.

The geographical area where the Regiment fought was very restricted. Between 4 and 13 January, the guns were at Medjez el Bab, which had become an important tactical centre for the British army. It is in mountainous country and 40 miles from Tunis (east by north). Longstop Hill is 10 miles along (and north of) the road to Tunis. After the Regiment had first fired its guns at Medjez el Bab supporting 1st (Guards) Brigade, it moved 25 miles south-east to Bou Arada and (8 further miles south) to Djebel Mansour. *See Maps 1 and 2.*

At Bou Arada, where the Regiment anticipated its first serious action, it was sharply alert and the officers and men did not leave their command posts and gun pits while they awaited orders. 1st (Guards) Brigade was now in 6th Armoured Division, and between 3 and 26 February the Regiment supported a mixed bag of units: battalions of 38th (Irish) Brigade, the North Irish Horse (in Churchill tanks), 1st Parachute Brigade and the (French) Schmeltz Regiment. The Americans were also coming onto the scene. As the diary shows, there was a good deal of sticky fighting and the Regiment suffered casualties.

Between 22 and 28 April, the Regiment was back north of Medjez el Bab, now in support of 38th (Irish) Brigade in 78th Division. April was to see the

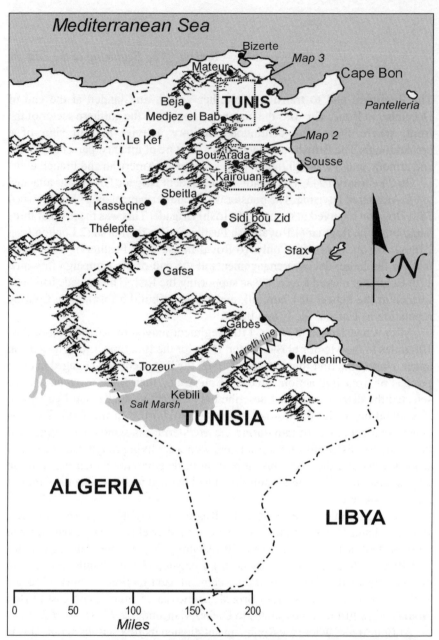

Map 1: Tunisia. The mountainous terrain of Tunisia made for tough campaigning, especially during the winter. In November and December 1942, the British elements of 1st Army advanced in the northern sector, up to Medjez el Bab; the Americans operated further south. Military operations congealed with the arrival of the cold, wet weather. The Americans were defeated at Kasserine during the third week of February 1943, and quickly learned some sharp lessons about the effectiveness of their German opponents. Thereafter parts of the different armies became mixed, but were reorganized for the final assault on Tunis at the end of April. Four converging attacks were made: by the Americans in the north; the British from Medjez el Bab; the French further south; and the British 8th Army that had advanced north after the Battle of Mareth. The Germans suffered an overwhelming defeat and were ejected from the African continent.

decisive battles that clinched the Allied victory. *See Maps 1 and 3.* The 17th Field Regiment was commanded by Lieutenant Colonel Tom Thomas, with PP as Second-in-Command. There were three Batteries: 10 (commanded by Major Ian Robertson), 13 (Major Dick Firth) and 26/92 (Major Bill Auld).

War is often described as short periods of intense and terrifying activity which punctuate much longer periods in which the troops lead a quiet life. The PP diary describes fully both types of military experience. However, I shall pay most attention to the periods of activity. In order to identify the diary extracts, they are indented in the text. The dated entries all refer to the diary although letters are sometimes included and indicated. In this and later chapters, the quoted extracts include some contemporary reports from PP's comrades, again all identified. The diary entries were obviously written in a hurry, and I have deliberately not smoothed the rough edges (e.g. incomplete sentences, interrupted flow, variable punctuation, military abbreviations). These contribute to the immediacy of the writing, which is always perfectly understandable. I have however cut out much material that I have judged to be of secondary importance, and in some cases I have added in italics some explanation of what was going on. Many military abbreviations are translated in the Glossary at the end of the book, although I have thought that some need translation in the text itself.

2 January 1943
Tom [*Lieutenant Colonel Thomas*] went off up the line not feeling too well. More air raids, they had better luck today, hit 10 Battery's ship just after they had got the last vehicle off, and dropped one down between *Ajax* and the freighter she was alongside, damaging both. They also set on fire a tanker in the outer harbour which burnt well for days, a collier and a freighter next to her in the inner harbour. Pretty good results. The cruisers belching orange and red flame from their many AA guns was a fine sight.

3 January 1943
Left AM in regimental convoy (less 13 Battery who had trouble with damaged vehicles due to a 3-tonner which had got loose in the hold during the gale). Into the mountains, twisting steep roads, cork forests and little *Wog* towns [*Wog is a soldiers' impolite acronym for 'wily oriental gentleman'*]. Bivvied for the night on top of the world it seemed, wet and high wind. Tom got a room in the Hotel Transatlantique where we dried out by a welcome fire aided by good red wine.

4 January 1943
Moved on to the White House, HQ of 1st (Guards) Brigade, a few miles

west of Medjez el Bab where Bill Pike (Brigade Major) and others gave us a great welcome. I shared his room and they fed us well. The regiment harboured in olive groves a few miles west of Teboursouk. Who should we take over from but John Barstow [*Lieutenant Colonel*] and the 12th (HAC) Regiment, RHA.

5 January 1943
Recce gun areas and 10 and 26 Batteries did a night occupation. Movement by day very restricted by enemy aircraft, every vehicle has had to have an air sentry. Stop and dismount when unidentified aircraft spotted. They can hit you first time.

13 January 1943
F Troop fired for effect. About 400 rounds in support of John Nelson's company of 3 Grenadier Guards who attacked towards point 620 and took a prisoner. They only found one dead after all that.

14 January 1943
Recce Bou Arada area with Tom. Farms and town very rural. We to come under command 6th Armoured Division to support attack on Two Tree Hill ridge. No trees there now, the Boche has removed them and put them up 1,000 yards further north. The farms the only cover at all, not even a fold in the ground so we put guns in six farms along the Goubellat road.

15 January 1943
Advance parties to Bou Arada, I return to White House and move the Regiment that night. We had to move via Gafour, rather roundabout and approximately fifty miles. Half way there I found Green (my excellent batman) had forgotten my maps so I had to go back for them. We thus left 78th Division and came under command of 6th Armoured Division.

16 January 1943
Digging in. We were to remain silent until the attack on the Two Tree Hill feature which was to take place on the 19th. RHQ was dug in in the Square with timbered roof piled with earth. Wireless sets dispersed and dug in, vehicles dispersed round the side roads and houses. A telephone wire was run under the road by tying it to the tail of a dog who was then persuaded to run through a drain with it. The Officers Mess was in a villa without water or lavatory, Tom and I slept there.

17 January 1943

Digging continued. Bill Auld made 26 Battery wear blankets when walking about so that they would look like Wogs. Tom and I did a peacetime reconnaissance on Grandstand Hill which was rudely disturbed by mortars. No damage to us but we bit the dust a number of times. Baptism of fire.

Lieutenant Colonel Thomas, report on Bou Arada and Djebel Mansour, written (with charming understatement) in October 1943, with its accompanying sketch map. The guns were facing east, with eight OPs on hilltops. See Maps 1 and 2.

Bou Arada is a small French town situated in the middle of a flat fertile plain and overlooked on two sides by rocky hills. North of the El Aroussa – Pont du Fahs road the hills are steep and bare. To the south they are steeper and covered with trees and scrub. Boche air was very much to be reckoned with. They liked farms and villages and were consequently unpopular as gun positions. On the other hand, the enemy had magnificent observation from the north and he could see anything that moved in the open in the Bou Arada plain.

Ordered south to Bou Arada to give additional support for a brigade attack (a big show in those days) upon the Boche positions round Two Tree Hill. We got into action on the night of 15/16 January and made ready for the great day. The attack was timed to start early on the morning of the 19th. [*The next gunner unit, some miles north, was 12th (HAC) Regiment, RHA, in 6th Armoured Division*]

Very early on 18 January things began to happen. We were most of us woken up by bursts of machine gun fire from the high ground on our left and as dawn broke we saw some thirty Boche tanks coming slowly across the plain and heading straight for our positions. There was a lot of small arms fire on our left and soon our neighbouring gunners started shooting away merrily. We heard later that they had done great execution on attacking Boche infantry from the famous Regiment Koch. Our own position was not too happy. We had no infantry in front of us. There was a troop of 6-pounders [*anti-tank guns*) also in the farms and it looked very much as if we were all that lay between the Boche tanks and El Aroussa. Our guns were in indirect fire positions behind the farms, nicely dug in, and were quite unable to shoot over open sights. In fact we were caught out and something had to be done quickly.

Detachments were ordered to manhandle their guns forward to the front edges of the farms and stay silent until the tanks got within range. Some of us got up to the roofs of the farmhouses and anxiously watched to see if the tanks would reach us before the guns were in position. Fortunately

they were moving very slowly over the muddy fields. Soon our anxiety as
to the guns getting in position was set at rest as detachment after
detachment sweated their way up. Our one thought then was 'will they
have the sense to hold their fire?' We've rubbed it into them often enough.
We had not been spotted yet, remember, and this was our very first action.

Of course it happened. Two guns opened up with AP when the tanks
were still about 1,500 yards away and then the rest joined in. The tanks
went back about 300 yards and then let us have it. Our rooftop became
distinctly unhealthy. Guns were hit. The Padre and the Doctor were
everywhere. The Boche gunners opened up on us. Casualties had started
to mount up. However, the Boche tanks were having an uncomfortable
time too and they withdrew, still very slowly. That afternoon RHQ
received the contents of fourteen Stukas and the MPI [*Mean Point of
Impact: the impact point of the average shell in a barrage*] was plumb
on the target. A decidedly eventful day.

PP diary, 18 January 1943
Woke up about 05:30 to the noise of gun and MG fire. The Boche had
attacked first. Found a good OP on roof of hospital. He dive bombed the
cross roads, they came very low and one was shot down by small arms
fire; apparently a new type with tank-busting cannon it was an object of
expert attention for some days. Roy Oddie [*who was in the HAC Infantry
before becoming a gunner officer*] killed, and Bill Auld [*commander of
26/92 Battery*] wounded early on Grandstand. About 10:30 I saw twenty-
seven tanks advancing up the plain quite slowly in line abreast towards
our farms. Everyone opened fire too soon with 2-pounders [*obsolete anti-
tank guns*], 6-pounders, 25-pounders. They came on to within 400 yards
in one place, halted, put out some ineffective smoke and withdrew to
rally in a fold in the ground. There they were engaged indirect by the
divisional artillery and mediums and more were knocked out. Total was
only twelve because we opened fire too soon. [*Officers in the Royal
Artillery did not normally wear steel helmets in battle, presumably for
reasons of pride. In 17th Field Regiment, they wore the bright Royal
Artillery blue and red side cap. Oddie was wearing this when he was
killed, and he died because his head was not well enough protected*]

Another dive bombing attack on the Town PM while I was at HQ 26th
Armoured Brigade. I returned to find the Town in ruins and full of blazing
vehicles, ammunition going off all over the place. RHQ had been bracketed
by bombs twenty-five yards away and aerials blown off for the second time.
Only casualty one driver who had not got into a slit trench. Sandy MacGill
[*Medical Officer*] did a fine job of work at the Regimental Aid Post [*first
stop for casualties*] in a hall, the roof was blown off during the bombing.

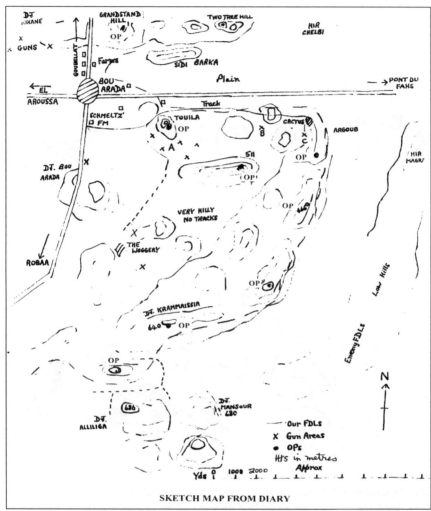

SKETCH MAP FROM DIARY

Map 2: Bou Arada. On 19 January 1943, 17th Field Regiment, Royal Artillery, of which PP was Second-in-Command, moved south of Medjez el Bab to occupy defensive positions around Bou Arada. The regiment was facing east, and established eight static OPs in the hills. There were a number of tactical engagements but nothing of strategic importance. This is an original sketch map from the diary.

Lieutenant Colonel Thomas, report, written in October 1943
During the night two batteries came out of the farms and went south to the Bou Arada – Pont du Fahs road; the attack on the 19th now being off. 26 Battery remained in an anti-tank role in case the Boche tried again. The 19th was a bad day. RHQ was heavily shelled and we saw little or

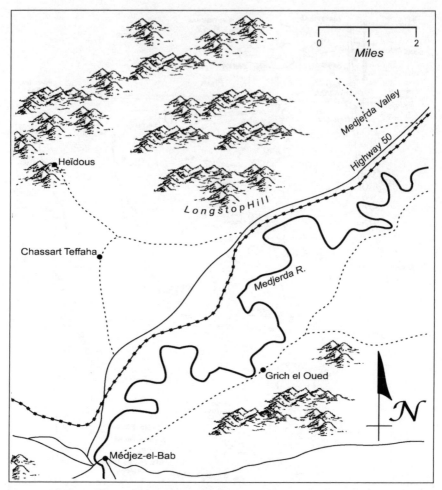

Map 3: Medjez el Bab and Longstop Hill. This is the mountainous sector in which 17th Field Regiment operated during the final offensive of the campaign in April 1943. Spring was coming, and the forbidding Longstop feature was taken at last, at a heavy cost in casualties.

nothing to shoot at. The Stukas also visited us again. We moved out on the night of 19/20 January and Bou Arada was voted by common consent to be an unsuitable place for RHQ. It also moved. The 20th was much better. As dawn broke and the mist cleared slight movement was seen on Gribana. During the day we shot away merrily and did some useful execution. By the afternoon of the 21st the Boche had had enough.

After this we had a very valuable ten days. We reconnoitered positions south of the road. The country further south was looked after by the

French. We selected OPs, tied up DF tasks with the infantry, got to know the country, improved our communications and our target drill. It was astonishing how quickly our powers of observation and OP drill generally improved during this short time. The French gunners were to teach us a great deal more later on.

PP diary, 23 January 1943
Saw some Goums [*French troops recruited from North African Arabs*] on the road, picturesque-looking cut-throats, could hardly understand them.

1 February 1943
1st Para. Brigade have now occupied Argoub making a salient about five miles deep down the Pont du Fahs road. This to deny the high ground to the enemy. [*Commanding 2nd Parachute Battalion was Lieutenant Colonel Frost, who in September 1944 led his battalion to capture the north end of the bridge at Arnhem, which he held until his battalion was virtually wiped out*]

2 February 1943
26 Battery being at Argoub and 10 Battery due to go, both a few hundred yards behind our FDLs, recced RHQ area there also. The track is in view nearly all the way and the enemy had a snipe target at a corner of the cactus just before you get out of sight. He had a go at my staff car and two shells missed us by 75 yards. Mr. Pritchard [*RSM*] and I ducked pretty quickly. He dropped the range for 10 Battery's truck half an hour later and hit Peter Sykes [*FOO*] in the head unfortunately. When they arrived at Argoub he was obviously in a bad way, the Paras gave him morphia and he died on the way back. [*Like Oddie on 18 January, Sykes was wearing a Royal Artillery side cap, and this did not give his head enough protection*] The tracks got like ice after a little rain.

Lieutenant Colonel Thomas, report, written in October 1943
On 3 Feb we heard about a proposed attack by us on the very strong German position on Djebel Mansour. It started as a battalion attack on the night of 3/4 Feb, which later became two battalions. We were to support it, but with one eye on the east all the time. This was to continue to be our main task, the defence of Bou Arada from the east.

Djebel Mansour was in the French sector and the country around was quite strange to us. Direct movement by vehicles between batteries was quite impossible. You had to come right round by Bou Arada and the journey took about an hour. RHQ was just behind Argoub. You could see

Mansour beautifully from Krammaissia, but it was covered with trees and small ups and downs. It was a mountain with a steep northern face and the only way to find out what happened the other side was to go up it and look; and when you got there you could not see more than 100 yards without climbing a tree. This practice the Germans objected to but it was later tried in desperation by most of the FOOs.

Our plan was to establish a regimental OP on Krammaissia, to register regimental fire plans etc. from there and to hold a pool of FOOs under cover. By the end of the operation we had three OPs still carrying out our main task, two on Krammaissia and five crawling about Mansour trying to find an open space in the trees. From Krammaissia you could see the tracer flying about Mansour, but no definite positions; the infantry not unnaturally unable to spot the exact positions of their FDLs and the FOOs seldom saw a Boche until he was too close to our own troops to fire at.

By 6 Feb. the second battalion had been committed and the order was given to withdraw. We were asked for smoke and we fired all we had. Groups of infantry started coming away by degrees. The enemy was only too glad to see them go and did not follow but two of his 5.9s did some accurate shooting as they came away. [*These were 150mm field howitzers. They and the 170mm guns were the heaviest artillery in the German armoury*] Our FOOs and their signallers – loaded up with all their wireless sets and kit – started appearing by twos and threes. Miraculously all but two signallers and an OP officer returned. Some of us gunners were giving a hand to the wounded as they came in. Not one but ten or twenty infantrymen came up to us and thanked us for our support.

PP diary, 6 February 1943
Straight to Para Bde. at a delightful farm miles away. A very welcome breakfast. Managed to get the 21 set [*an early model radio*] to work on speech at 20,000 yds. Saw the Col. Schmeltz, a little cock robin with a scarlet waistcoat and side hat who commands the Spahis. Hard as nails he is reputed to have shot two of his men who went absent for 48 hrs.

7 February 1943
CO explaining possibility of attack to French Colonel with map:
'Je crois que les Boches peuvent attaquer ici, et peut-être ici comme ça – but I don't think they will, we gave the buggers such a pasting last time.' All perfectly understood, the Frenchman once gave a lecture in English 'au Shop' [*Royal Military Academy, Woolwich*].

19 February 1943

Walked to Geoff Wright's [*17th Field Regiment*] OP and got very wet indeed. Visibility almost nil. French very helpful and offered food and drink. Glad to get even NAAFI whisky and a change at the farm. Met Virginia Cowles there, she and escort are staying at a nearby farm. Most intelligent and well up in affairs. Said she was not going to write another book. [*Virginia Cowles, 1910–1983, was a prominent American author and journalist whose work was published on both sides of the Atlantic. As a war correspondent, she covered the campaigns in Tunisia, Italy and North-West Europe*] Thunder and torrents of rain. Tents dry. Tracks foul.

24 February 1943

Hasty recce for a bty at 16:50. 450 Fd Bty (American) arrived during the night and I put them in for which they were very grateful and said they had never been looked after so well; not at all bad positions either. They had come from Kasserine [*described in the next section, 'The Framework of Command'*] in two days travelling and had lost their Battery Commander and both Troop Commanders there.

Lieutenant Colonel Thomas, report, written in October 1943

At first light on 26 Feb the enemy attacked again. He put in two battalions on the front stretching from just south of Paul's [*Paul Lunn-Rockliffe, who commanded 26 Battery*] OP on the Argoub. He came in just before dawn and overran Paul and Denis [*Denis Higgins, FOO*] almost at once but our friends the infantry were ready for them and had them off again in no time. Our OP parties joined in with a will with their tommy guns. From then on for the rest of the morning we and the infantry had some grand shooting. When the Boche got close up under the hills the infantry tickled them up with their mortars and chased them out to where the 25-pounders could get at them. They had no chance but to come on gallantly in spite of heavy losses. It was the answer to a gunner's prayer.

By midday the German attack was completely broken up, but an Italian battalion put in an attack on our right from the Mansour direction at about 16:00 hours and Peter [*PP*], who had had a most uncomfortable morning from enemy shell fire and had had to move his OP, had the satisfaction of giving the order: 'Target 39 – 10 rounds gun fire!' We had a battery of strangers under our command at the time who also joined in the fun and the result was electric. The attack broke up in disorder.

Not many of us had seen much of the results of our efforts but we fired 400 observed rounds per gun during the day and during that night 87 dead Germans were counted in front of Paul's OP alone. We were soon to move from Bou Arada. It was there that we started to learn to become real gunners.

PP diary, 26 February 1943

Noise of battle early; went to Bde HQ at farm. Enemy had attacked Argoub and the salient round to Krammaissia, had overrun two OPs in the dark and mist, but both areas were re-taken by midday and he had very heavy casualties. Denis Higgins was surrounded but they did not see him or his carrier in the trees and scrub so he carried on shooting all around and joined in the counter-attack when it came. MC awarded about April. Paul Lunn-Rockliffe had to abandon his carrier but took the telephone and teed in further back. He hadn't the heart to fire at an MG which was hiding behind it but he gathered some chaps and led a counter-attack which retook it. MC awarded September. All attacks were repulsed and over 200 prisoners taken by the Para. boys. One Italian said there were only five left of his section or platoon of 48 after a regimental concentration was put on them. They also attacked with tanks in the Goubellat Plain and broke through behind to our north. This put the wind up all the wagon lines in that area who had to move pretty smartly. However, they were held by a scratch force about five miles north and seven out of eight tanks were destroyed. The Churchills only lost one. Slept at the farm, well looked after.

3 March 1943

Tom feeling poor, tummy again. Saw acting CRA and learned that 1st Gds. Bde. are away from the Div. for good in exchange for 38th Irish Bde. from 6 Armd. Div. – bad. Also the Para. Bde. are going and the Americans are coming in with a Field Artillery Battalion in place of 450 Bty. Advance party of two came PM. We gave them the picture and grub. They seem alright: 'We can learn a lot from the British' which took us aback as we had been led to expect rather the reverse. Their jolt at Kasserine seems to have borne fruit already.

PP's 'home from home' on 8 March is shown in Plate 4. Meanwhile, the transfer of 38th (Irish) Brigade to the 78th Division, and the transfer out of 1st (Guards) Brigade, was unpopular. However, in response to an emergency, 1st (Guards) Brigade had already been dispatched further south to reinforce the Kasserine sector. The soldiers in both brigades were discontented, believing that they had been doing a good job where they were. General Anderson, the 1st Army Commander, issued sharp Orders of the Day to both formations:

To the 38th Brigade:

This change must be, for unavoidable reasons. Accept it as good soldiers. There is no need to be sad about it, as you are entering a fine Inf. Div. which is going to lead the way into Tunis. Thank you for your good work so far. There is hard fighting ahead, lots of it. So get on with the job –

which is to beat the Germans. You have hit them once – do it often again in your new division and do not worry about anything else.

To the 1st Brigade:
Chance has cast you for a new role. It will require all your skill and you have little time in which to learn many new things. Therefore, get busy.

To both Brigades:
Don't bellyache.

PP diary, 15 March 1943
Drying out. Now have a trench-round tent for drainage of rain before it sinks into the hole. Heaps of little flowers popping up, saw wild tulips and clumps of thyme. Sure we saw a pair of black redstarts the other day. Birds singing AM now, saw a jay today.

17 March 1943
St. Patrick's Day celebrated by U target (72 guns) at noon, Boche must think we are nuts. [*U-Uncle was the codeword for fire from all divisional artillery: three field regiments*] Boche shelled our valley PM and holed Gerald's car and Service Dress hat, put Sandy's pants up in a tree but he wasn't in them [*these were two officers in the Regiment*].

20 March 1943
Corps Commander visited, still very muddy. Saw some *Daily Mirrors* 14–19 Feb, we are out of touch with affairs at home e.g. Beveridge Plan debate. Soldier's idea of when to eat his emergency ration: 'When you've got f - - - all and f - - - all chance of getting f - - - all.' Easily the most overworked adjective in the army.

26 March 1943
US CO to Jock Wedderburn-Maxwell's 'Well what can you do for us?' 'We can shoot, we can observe and say boy we can commoonicate.' Decent. We are to be considered as resting and have nothing to do unless there is an attack. Only two OPs out and a general feeling of relief at the change and lack of the sole responsibility for a large area such as we had had at Bou Arada. No scrub or cover for miles that isn't occupied so we are nearly all in folds in the ground, except RHQ's sandpit.

2 April 1943
Showers. Recce gun areas south of Oued Zarga on foot. Rain outside, sweat inside after walking over plough. This and minimum numbers

necessary to prevent enemy noticing our added interest in that part of the world which up to then had been the prerogative of the Recce Regt only. Lots of our mines on the heights. HQRA afterwards, back at 17:00 to find the Regt moving. Took recce parties to old olive groves SW of Teboursouk, bed down 21:30, wakened 23:00 to find we were supposed to be in the groves just north of Teboursouk. Moved and found the Regt getting in without recce. Bed again 01:30. We have returned to 78th Div for the first time since 15 Jan.

In this way 17th Field Regiment went to war. The Regiment's operations played a small part in shaking the Allied forces from the stasis that had set in at the end of 1942 in the mountains overlooking the Plain of Tunis, 30 miles short of Tunis. In January 1943, the Allied forces began slowly to 'get their ducks in a row', to resume the offensive. At the highest level a firm organization was put in place, but it was more than two months before this began to pay dividends. I shall return later to PP's diary describing the role of 17th Field Regiment in the final battles of the campaign. This will be fitted into the chapter after I have given some details of 'The Framework of Command': the framework that prepared the Allied forces for victory.

The Framework of Command

After the campaign had progressed rather unsatisfactorily for some weeks, and following the conference between Roosevelt and Churchill and the Combined Chiefs at Casablanca in January 1943, two other British officers were appointed as Eisenhower's subordinates, for the air and land forces respectively. They were Air Chief Marshal Tedder and General Alexander.

Tedder was an intellectual, which Cunningham and Alexander were not. Tedder was a graduate of Cambridge University, where he had published a monograph on the seventeenth-century navy. He had built his career through command and staff appointments in the Royal Flying Corps and the Royal Air Force. A pioneer of army/air cooperation in the Western Desert with the 8th Army, Tedder ran such cooperation on his own terms, by following the traditional Royal Air Force doctrine that the air could win wars on its own. As a result, Tedder did not get on well with his colleagues in the other services, but Eisenhower liked him well enough to arrange for his appointment as Deputy Supreme Commander for the invasion of Europe in 1944. However, as a result of Montgomery's insistence, Tactical Air Forces were formed before the invasion to provide highly effective ground/air cooperation, and this made an enormous contribution to the campaign in North-West Europe. Alexander, who became Eisenhower's land forces commander in Tunisia, was an extremely experienced commander who got on well with the Americans. But he was to demonstrate certain serious professional deficiencies, and Cunningham considered him a lightweight at best.

Eisenhower now had three direct subordinate commanders, Alexander, Cunningham and Tedder, all British and all heading multi-national forces. This structure represented integration of a high order, although many Americans were unhappy with it. Discontent continued to grumble for the rest of the war.

In February 1943, Montgomery's 8th Army was approaching the Mareth Line, the last major obstacle on the long road from El Alamein. Rommel, who was conducting a skilful fighting retreat, saw the danger of being caught between the 1st Army in the north and the 8th Army in the south. He therefore took the opportunity to make an unexpected and savage – but typical – counter-attack. His objective was the Anglo-American forces in Tunisia and he originally planned an ambitious move to envelop them. This was vetoed by Kesselring, the overall Axis commander. However, between 19 and 23 February, Rommel managed to hit the American II Corps hard at the Kasserine Pass, the route through the mountains that formed the spine of Tunisia. The Americans suffered 6,300 casualties – 300 killed, 3,000 wounded and 3,000 prisoners – out of the total force of 30,000 men who fought there. They also lost 183 tanks, 104 half-tracks, more than 200 guns and 500 Jeeps. It was naturally a severe blow to the prestige of the American army. The Germans were shocked (and depressed) by the rich volume of supplies available to the Americans. Rommel's talents were greatly in demand and he was soon afterwards transferred, first to Italy and then to prepare the Atlantic coast of France for the inevitable invasion by Anglo-American forces.

As a result of Kasserine, Alexander began to lose confidence in the fighting quality of the American soldiers, although he had no idea how quickly they would learn. It was fortunate that at this time the American army threw up some demonstrably fresh talent: two officers who were later to build a formidable reputation in Europe. The first was Major General Patton who was already in French Morocco knocking a new armoured corps into shape. The second, Major General Bradley, had just arrived from the United States. When they moved up to the battlefront they had undefined appointments, but Patton was soon made commander of II Corps. (Not surprisingly, his predecessor who had commanded at Kasserine had been sacked.) Bradley was made Patton's 'shadow' and second-in-command, and it was intended that he would take over the Corps when Patton was given greater responsibility. This happened when Patton was detached to plan the invasion of Sicily, the next big Allied move that had been decided at the Casablanca Conference in January. During the final successful offensive in Tunisia in April/May 1943, Bradley commanded the American force, and his success confirmed that he had a promising future.

The reorganized command of the Allied forces, the stiffening of the Americans under the leadership of Patton and Bradley after the setback at

Kasserine, and the advance of the powerful 8th Army from the south were all leading to a climax: an organized all-out assault on the stubborn German defenders of the remaining square miles of the African continent that they still occupied. But important preparatory work was needed. This was to take a firm hold on the hills to the north of Medjez el Bab, in particular capturing at long last Longstop Hill. This was the job for which 78th Division was moved north.

6 April 1943

Moved down to RHQ in a small gorse wadi AM. Grand sunny day. Left the car out of sight until dusk, then Mathews [*PP's driver*] brought her up. I hope we have got it all buttoned up. We are the Centre group with 132nd Field Regt and a Medium Bty. supporting 36th Brigade. Who should arrive as the Left group representative with us but Warnock [*formerly with B Battery HAC*]. No grub so had to get him a box of Compo [*popular, newly introduced ration pack*]. Hear 8th Army have attacked this AM. Four hours sleep.

7 April 1943

Der Tag. Fire plan 03:50, recce parties forward 05:40 but no move till 10:20. Only odd enemy shelling. Very successful attack. Move guns into the only possible area, too close to Churchills so we were bombed PM. One bounced off the rise where Tom's party were and sailed through the air turning end for end over our heads to burst 200 yds. the other side. For the next attack I dived into a hole near Tom's carrier on the knoll and saw an Me. with bomb under the fuselage coming straight for me but he didn't let it go till he had gone over. Plenty of our fighters about and we heard that not one of the last attackers got home. Little cover so it was just as well the RAF were there. Achieved a shave in the back of the car 19:30. Weather turned colder and cloudy with stiff breeze. Four-and-a-half hours sleep.

8 April 1943

Recce for move forward 05:30. Mines all over the place and we drove over about fifteen twice – very lucky. They were within twenty yards of the track and when lifted the RE said one of them had the detonator pressed down but had not gone off. A scout car went up on them before our second crossing so we took our own wheel marks pretty carefully. We wanted to get guns up as far as possible so I ordered Rollo Wood [*Subaltern*] to go on in his truck as it seemed there was a clear lane. It went up as it passed mine and into the ditch. The driver was saved by the sandbags on the floor of the truck, wounded only. The rest had singing heads for a bit and Harold Denman's [*officer in 17th Field Regiment*] last pair of glasses were blown off leaving him as blind as a bat. Two of my windows were broken and my ears felt as if they'd been boxed. Decided on a safer area for guns behind the mines, they were thick in the verges and fields either side. Got into green crops, RAF still keeping most enemy air away. One hit-and-run bombing raid PM and two Me.'s machine gunning. Strong cold wind very uncomfortable. Battle seems to go well, three of us very busy all PM (after move) on U, Y and M targets up to three at once [*U-Uncle, fire from all regiments in a division; Y-Yoke, fire from an Army Group Royal Artillery: the massive concentration of a large formation's artillery under central control; M-Mike, fire from one regiment*]. Like Babel and very cold sitting still on radio, or phone or both. Brigade Major on rear link at HQRA very bad and the rest not much better. Very tired. Slept well 21:30 to 06:30, grand.

9 April 1943

Plenty more shooting, battle still goes well. RHQ is in long green corn which gives some shelter from the cold wind, when you lie down. We are near Y farm of ill repute; there are still some of the Guards carriers knocked out on the track which is mined so we have made a long detour through the corn. They say that attempts to open the farm door blew the roof off, it was for some time a sort of booby trap exhibition for both sides who tried to catch each other's patrols. Recce PM north of Bouneb.

10 April 1943

Moved forward 08:30 to positions recced yesterday. Saw three Jerry planes shot down, one landed in flames near F Troop. Confusion about command between 78th and 46th Divisions, anyway we had no orders all day so Tom quite rightly got on with it. 26 Battery went forward about 1,000 yards left front at dusk, we to follow AM. Six-and-a-half hours sleep.

11 April 1943

Moved 08:30. Recce parties at same time at Toukabeur in the other direction. Recce AM in fields of flowers of all sorts, most wonderful scents. Two raids definitely beaten off by AA. One down. CRA conference PM had to walk miles up to their quarry. We were nearly shot up by a Bren gunner shooting at aircraft. Fine tracer display at dusk. I went ahead to deal with dumping ammo in new positions. Guides got lost, twenty-four lorry-loads had to follow me up the mountain road and Dick Dobson [*Subaltern*], BSM Hamilton and I had to see to the unloading and assist the drivers and their mates. Bill Auld [*Commanding 26 Battery*] is coming back recovered. Btys. very late in and RHQ after them; appalling winding narrow road through the mountains, up and down and roundabout. No sleep, only just got 10 and 13 Btys.' working parties away down the road (which is in view by day from Longstop area). The shell holes stand out clearly and you can see the barrage on the ground.

15 April 1943

Still sleepy after ten hours. Counter-attacks AM, otherwise quiet before the next storm. Fire plan for recapture of three final objectives including Djebel Ang.

16 April 1943

Apparently our attack met a Boche attack, both at the same zero hour. Prisoner said our fire plan landed on their forming up position and caused heavy casualties. They were beaten off. We got Djebel Ang and Kef el Tiour. David Brown [*FOO*] had a party and had to use tommy guns and pistol, a grenade got his wireless. Dumping scale increased to five hundred rds. per gun.

20 April 1943

Talked fire plans AM. Five Field Regiments, one Medium Regiment and a Heavy Battery. Some crump. Conference PM to all officers of Div was addressed by Commanders of V Corps, 78th Division and 1st Army. All impressive except the latter. We have overwhelming superiority in air, men, guns, tanks and at sea.

21 April 1943

Rain PM and cool. Regt moved forward to battle positions at 19:00.

22 April 1943

The stage is all set for the final battle of the Tunisian campaign. 8th Army started two mornings ago. The Hun attacked 1st Division yesterday with three battalions or more and over 50 tanks. He was beaten off with a loss of 27 tanks and 500 prisoners. By the sound of gunfire from the south this morning, IX Corps have attacked at Bou Arada.

78th Division is concentrated in the mountains north of Medjez having been in the line since 7 April. [*See Maps 1 and 3*] The Infantry are tired and in many cases well below strength; they have already put up a magnificent show in capturing these mountains. Preliminary moves of Artillery and Infantry took place last night. All day the Boche has shelled our HQ area intermittently – there is a track behind us in full view which has been used at various times by mules, vehicles and infantry and even anti-tank guns. He has also shelled and mortared OP areas, unfortunately killing Tom Farr [*Subaltern*]. We lost an OP assistant in a similar way yesterday.

The RAF have sent over several sorties of bombers. All ranks have enjoyed the sight and sound of our own bombers at work on the defences of Longstop. There are thunder clouds and lightning in the sky, a haze and darkness over the view.

Gunners are completing gunpits and slits. Command posts are working out the gun programmes for two separate attacks, firing from 19:45 to 02:19. OP parties are preparing to join their battalions by daylight. There is a general air of battle and preparation about, almost a tension. You go around the Regiment, the gunners are tired after a night move and digging but full of fight. Hardly any vehicles remain in the area.

One talks to FOOs and Infantry, wishes them good shooting. No one talks much about the job in hand. You wonder whether you will see them all again, and in an idle way whether you may be unlucky yourself. Tea, the main meal of the day is over. The light begins to fade. CO moves off to Brigade in his carrier and you are left to run RHQ. Mepacrine (anti-malaria yellow pills) comes up with the rations. There is a rum ration which is taken in tea. You feel you are having it under false pretences anyway, staying where you are while the Infantry go forward.

19:45. The fire plan for 38th Brigade attack starts. MG fire is heard during this. At 22:00 the first part of fire plan for 36th Brigade goes off and lasts an hour. No news at 23:00. Quite a lot of MG fire and a lot of crumps – you suspect mortars. They should be on first objectives by now, foothills just west of Longstop. Next fire plan is a barrage 00:15 to 02:19 to get the Argylls along Longstop to its eastern end. Can't get news from OPs when they are humping 21 sets.

The Army Commander said: 'Never before has the British Army gone into battle with such overwhelming superiority, six to one in the air, command of the sea, almost ten to one in tanks, more men and very heavy odds-on in guns.'

23 April 1943

Good Friday – still no news. MG fire still going on, and crumps. Some aircraft floating around. 00:20 we hear Heidous is still held by enemy and our troops are still going slowly on to Tanngoucha. On our front, Buffs are on objective.

Complicated fire plan. As usual barrage is postponed half way through and has to start all over again an hour from original start time. Saw it off again at 01:15 – then to bed.

After several false starts barrage etc. went at 11:30 and the Argylls followed on to Longstop Hill with pipes playing. David Brown [*FOO*] killed on Longstop. He and Paul lost two killed and four wounded in their OP parties plus three missing. It's stupid to put valuable technicians in front where they are away from their communications and useless. It is all very well the CO leading the attack with his pipers behind him, but what is the use of taking his Gunners with him without their radio?

A hairy day for the Infantry. The Boche is fighting hard and the immediate counter-attack always comes, usually followed by others later. No risk of rain for two or three days. Expect hot dry wind with dust from the south. Rained PM and temperature dropped!

The Regt. fired 650 rpg. today; Div. Arty. fired over 42,000 rounds of 25-pounder from three Regiments.

24 April 1943
Situation confused. Bigger and longer bangs everywhere PM. We stay in the mountains and do our share. Premature in 26 midday caused by swelling in barrel by breech and no damage – whew! [*A premature was a dangerous accident caused by a shell exploding before reaching its target; if this happened shortly after it had left the gun, it could cause serious casualties in the gun position*] Guns get very hot on fire plan – gunners pour cold water over and down them and it comes out boiling! Kenneth Platt [*Subaltern*] killed PM with line party to Longstop. Now six officers down in Regiment. Last night's rum ration in tea at breakfast – ugh!

25 April 1943
Much quieter. Tanngoucha and Heidous taken at last. Ammunition suddenly restricted to 50 rpg. 23:15 – out of bed to hear Tom to do GI and new CO coming. [*GI is the abbreviation for General Staff Officer First Grade, Chief-of-Staff of a division. PP then held the fort for two days, until the new Commanding Officer arrived. He was Lieutenant Colonel Rollo Baker*]

26 April 1943
Saw Tom 06:00 and took over fire plan for Rhar. Plenty of enemy shelling from six to eight guns. Not pleasant on Longstop. Boche shelling the reverse slopes of the hill continually, lots of dirt flying about, rather uncomfortable. Went up to about 220 yards and saw tanks moving forward, then some infantry went over a crest, that brought ten rounds gunfire airburst from two guns which burst very accurately right over them but they went on and disappeared over the top. Battle went well, everything fine till I heard Denis [*Captain Denis Higgins MC, Troop Commander*] killed in a Churchill. The first of my own 26 Battery chaps to go. Peter Royle [*Subaltern*] had some very close ones. We've paid a heavy price for that beastly hill.

The final assault on Longstop was made by 8 Argyll and Sutherland Highlanders. The Commanding Officer was killed by shellfire, and the assault was led by Major Jack Anderson, who charged forward firing his Tommy gun, and displaying the heroism that won him the Victoria Cross. The Highlanders also took 350 German prisoners. Anderson survived, but he was alas killed in Italy some months later. There is a strange coincidence concerning Anderson's Victoria Cross.

In his last year at Stowe School, Anderson had shared a cramped study in Chatham House with a friend who would become an airman during the Second World War. The friend took his initial flying lessons with the Oxford University Air Squadron, and when he was mobilized and after further training, he became captain of a heavy bomber and soon saw action. By the end of the war he was the best known pilot, innovator and tactical leader in Royal Air Force Bomber Command. He was Leonard Cheshire, who after the war built an extraordinary career as a care-giver for sick and deprived people in many countries. He also won the Victoria Cross.

The Victoria Cross was awarded in the Second World War to fewer than *one in twenty thousand* servicemen, and their deeds were examined with punctilious care before the award was made. The American Congressional Medal of Honor is the only decoration that is in any way comparable with it.

27 April 1943
CRA said there would be no more 25-pounder ammunition in the country till 4 May. We are now rear-most and out of the hunt. However another 50 rpg. in the bank! Div. moved away to near Medjez.

28 April 1943
Quiet day. Moved 10 Bty forward to behind Longstop. Saw Denis's tank, something very heavy hit it bang on the turret where hinges are, blew them off, bashed in top of turret and track shield and made a horrid mess inside the turret. He must have been killed instantly.

30 April 1943
Cooler, found a lark's nest with four eggs in the middle of our RHQ in a grassy fold in the ground. Big battle on 1st and 4th Div. fronts.

Four months after Longstop Hill was taken, PP was in England and wrote an official report for the War Office on the fire plan for the battle, as it was executed by the four gunner regiments that participated. The plan was based on observed fire from static OPs and FOOs on the ground. PP wrote a one-page document, a model of succinct precision.

The Final Assault; a Precursor of Future Allied Firepower

While 78th Division was fighting its protracted battle north of Medjez el Bab, the rest of the Allied armies were now being drawn up, ready for battle. 78th Division was about to join the major attack, in conjunction with the rest of the very large Allied force. A French brigade was in the north, nearest the sea. Then there was the American II Corps, with three infantry divisions and one armoured. On its right were the British, with V Corps of three infantry divisions and one armoured brigade; and IX Corps of two infantry divisions and one armoured, to which XXX Corps from 8th Army was added temporarily. On the British right, the French XIX Corps, of three divisions, was in the mountains, linking up with the British 8th Army which was advancing north. There was now a full-scale attack on a 100-mile front, carried out by the whole Allied force: more than 300,000 men, with massive armoured and artillery support, and torrents of fire from 3,000 aircraft.

1 May 1943
78th Division pulling out of the mountains to go in between 1st and 4th Divisions for a push. Poor old 36th Brigade, at it again despite rumour that 'capture Longstop and you finish.' Cooler, cloudy, haze, cold wind at dusk.

2 May 1043
The whole area east of Medjez very crowded with guns, tanks and vehicles of every description. Could not do this without complete air supremacy. Very hot day. Rollo [*Lieutenant Colonel Rollo Baker, Commanding Officer*] always up at 5 and goes round the area before breakfast. We are right up close, about 1,000 yards or so behind our own FDLs. And only 24 out of about 650 guns being massed for the big show. Whew, who'd be a Boche? Tired, slept long and well.

3 May 1943
Movement everywhere, more and more stuff coming up. Very hot and dusty again. RHQ in glorious flower patch, grass, thistles, poppies, yellow daisies, mauve convolvulus, masses of larks, saw six new ones in one nest.

6 May 1943
This is the day. Attack by 4th Indian and 4th British Divs at 03:00, they are supported by the artillery of the 1st, 4th, 4th Indian, 78th, and 7th Armoured Divs. Nearly 700 guns. What a din. Barrage 2,700 yards wide and 3,600 yards deep. After the fire plan, little to do. Saw the armour going past at about 07:00 according to plan. About 100 bombers went over at 16:00, haven't seen anything like it since the Battle of Britain.

There were a number of difficulties at first with the main attack, which began on 23 April. But in the last and most powerful phase of the offensive on 6 May, the guns in the British sector drenched the enemy positions with one round for every 6ft of enemy line (compared with one round for every 30ft at El Alamein). Everything was over on 12 May, when von Arnim surrendered. He had been outfought on the ground and bottled in from the sea by Cunningham's ships. Before the surrender, the British army was closing in on Tunis.

8 May 1943
RV at La Mornaghia, about seven miles our side of Tunis, by 07:30. The traffic all the way was like the Brighton road. Hung about the main street and got some grub. Saw all the high-ups conferring, a girl with very short skirt passed by and every one of them turned to look. Found space for the Regiment to pull off the road into open fields by a farm. Also found a Boche Q store and heaps of stuff in the farm which was thereafter called Loot Farm. Terrific crowds, flowers flying all about, cheers and delirious excitement. Chaps loved it and emerged from the town with flowers all over their trucks, lipstick on their faces. Writing this diary on a huge Nazi banner which I believe they used for aircraft to identify own troops, makes a good tablecloth. A memorable day, six months exactly since the first landings in North Africa. Slept like a log.

Considering the unpromising beginning of the campaign, it is astonishing that victory came in six months, with inexperienced troops having covered long distances and fought bitter battles. At the beginning, Eisenhower introduced a remarkable double innovation: a complete integration of American and British military staffs, and overall command of land, sea and air. This was soon demonstrated to be the correct way of conducting grand strategy, and it became the pattern for future wars. But there were teething troubles, notably Eisenhower's inability to conduct closely the land battle because he was too distracted by quasi-political matters that demanded attention. Matters improved in January 1943 when Alexander was given command (under Eisenhower) of all ground forces, including the 8th Army. But the cooperation of 8th Army in Tunisia was in fact less than stellar. Many British soldiers by this time had grown sick of war.

As mentioned, Alexander because of his personality got on well with the Americans. But he lacked the force of character to control mavericks like Montgomery and Patton, and this problem was to grow worse in Sicily. The green troops who invaded North-West Africa, and their equally green commanders, learned fast: certainly more quickly than many British generals, especially Brooke, Alexander and Montgomery, gave them credit for. This improved performance was especially true of Patton and Bradley, although not of Anderson, who subsequently returned to England. He was scheduled to command the 2nd Army in the Normandy invasion, but this was vetoed by Montgomery. Anderson took command of a military district, and was not promoted further. (At the end of the Tunisian campaign, 1st Army – now British – was absorbed into 8th Army.) During the whole of the campaign, the Anglo-American forces had unlimited supplies, and superb cooperation from the navy although rather less from the air force. They also had the enormous benefit of accurate *Sigint*.

On 20 May 1943, Eisenhower and his main military subordinates and his American and British political advisers arrived in Tunis for an imposing Victory Parade. More than 30,000 troops of all nationalities who had fought in the campaign marched with considerable style past the reviewing stand. The British army contingent was led appropriately by the Royal Artillery. PP was the right-hand man in the front file, so that he can be said to have been the number one British soldier on that brief occasion. The appearance and bearing of the bronzed, victorious soldiers made an everlasting impression on Cunningham. He was not alone. Many people thought that this great Parade was a symbol of a change in fortunes: that the British army, with its Allies, would before long return to Europe, and win. The Parade (Plate 6) was filmed for newsreels, and PP was seen in cinemas all over Britain.

20 May 1943

The chaps were grand and marched as if they had been practicing for six months instead of fighting. The crowds clapped and cheered, cried 'Vive les Anglais' etc. and flung flowers at us some of which hit me in the eye. Some grabbed our hands as we marched by. Some of the troops who were watching boo-ed good naturedly and some cried 'Bull' as our guns went by. They were all painted up and white-washed wheels etc. and produced one remark 'When are you going to use them?' No one would have dreamt that they had fired on average about 4,000 rounds of effective fire out here. Very hot, sweated like a bull, glad really when the four-and-a-half miles was finished, the water content of my body having dried up much earlier. Returned to our olive grove.

How Marshall's Judgement Was Correct: Eisenhower Takes the Reins

Despite much fashionable opinion that Eisenhower was an inadequate commander, being thought of as the military equivalent of the non-executive chairman of the board, this underplays his importance. He made four major contributions.

First, he was an extraordinarily fast learner. Within months he had become an authoritative figure who was listened to by politicians and senior commanders.

Second, he was able to provide leadership to an unruly crowd of talented subordinates. He kept the peace and gave them their instructions. And his personal presence among the troops acted like a tonic. He was responsible for the historic innovation of integrating American and British staffs, and joint planning of the three forces of land, sea and air. The vigorous support he received from Cunningham in particular made a great contribution to making this system work.

Third, he had excellent military judgement. He had to have exceptional qualities for the shrewd Marshall to have been persuaded to appoint him over the heads of large numbers of senior officers to important staff jobs in Washington, DC, and then to commands in Europe and North-West Africa. One indication of his military ability was that when he considered the initial plans for the invasion of Europe in 1944, he knew instinctively that the assaulting force was too weak. This judgment coincided with the views of Bradley and Montgomery. Montgomery, who commanded all the ground forces at the time, changed the plan accordingly. A year or so later, Eisenhower was one of the very few people 'in the know' who opposed dropping the atom bombs on Japan. And when Eisenhower was President during the 1950s, there were four occasions when international tensions called for a military response. On all four occasions, President Eisenhower's decision – which was invariably successful – differed from the advice given by the Joint Chiefs-of-Staff. It is a good bet that if Eisenhower had been in the White House instead of Kennedy and Johnson during the 1960s, the United States would not have become embroiled in Vietnam.

Fourth – and most important – Eisenhower was a winner, which was remarkable enough when one considers American military history after the end of the Second World War. Since the late 1940s, the United States became engaged in five armed conflicts. In only one of these, the first Gulf War, was there clear victory, and this was anyway a much more modest affair than Eisenhower's victorious campaigns.

The ultimate achievement of the Anglo-American Army in Tunisia was to overcome the highly professional Axis forces. The bag of prisoners – 250,000 men, plus large quantities of equipment and supplies – was greater than at Stalingrad. An event of historical importance is that Colonel von Stauffenberg, the officer who made the attempt to blow up Hitler on 20 July 1944, was desperately wounded in Tunisia. He was the Chief-of-Staff of the 10th Panzer Division, and was at the receiving end of a vicious fighter-bomber attack on 7 April 1943. He had seen at first hand the weight of the Allied forces, and it would be very surprising if he had not concluded that Germany would inevitably be defeated and something had to be saved before that catastrophe occurred.

Bradley, like most Americans, was initially unenthusiastic about the invasion of North-West Africa. But the campaign, which provided such strong evidence of the capacity of the German army, made him change his mind: 'In Africa we learned to crawl, to walk – then run'.

Chapter 3

Sicily – Europe at Last

The invasion of Sicily was strategically even more important to the Americans than to the British. The commitment to Sicily – to attacking Europe from the south – was a decisive confirmation that the cross-Channel invasion that the Americans so earnestly wished for would be put 'on the back burner' until 1944. On the other hand, to the British, Sicily represented a natural prolongation of the victorious campaign in Africa: the continuation of an established and successful strategy.

Storm from the Sea

The campaign in Tunisia had not spared the 78th Infantry Division, including the gunners who provided so much effective fire support: five Royal Artillery units, of which the 17th Field Regiment was the senior. For the next phase of military operations in the Mediterranean, the invasion of Sicily, 78th Division was to be kept in reserve in North Africa, and sailed to Sicily more than two weeks after British and American troops had landed on the island and seen hard fighting.

Although invading Sicily was a logical next step after the conquest of Tunisia, it was not until the Casablanca Conference of January 1943 that the decision was taken to proceed. The American Joint Chiefs-of-Staff were still fixated on assaulting Germany by the shortest route, through an invasion of Western Europe, and it took hard persuasion by the British Chiefs-of-Staff Committee on the grounds that there were simply not enough trained troops or large enough numbers of landing craft available in 1943 for a successful assault against Hitler's Atlantic Wall. The large but unsuccessful Commando raid on Dieppe in August 1942 that attempted to capture the port had been a bruising experience. Nevertheless, the eyes of the Americans remained on Western Europe, and it was not until the campaign in Sicily had almost come to an end that the decision was made to invade the Italian mainland. However, invading a greatly more hostile shore than North-West Africa, Sicily and Italy was going to be a very serious proposition. Western Europe had to wait.

For the landing in Sicily, codenamed Operation *Husky*, Lieutenant General Eisenhower was confirmed as Commander-in-Chief, with General Alexander as his land forces commander. Planning was soon put in hand, although this process lacked urgency and there were false starts. The Americans, the British, and the naval and air forces all had different ideas. The various planners were also in different locations, which made coordination extremely difficult. Alexander's lack of a firm 'grip' was the first of the deficiencies in his leadership that were revealed in Sicily. The more-or-less agreed initial plan to attack Sicily proposed multiple landings around the island in such a way that effective air cover could not be provided. Montgomery described it as 'a dog's breakfast'. In despair, he finally took the planning in hand personally and prepared a simple and workable scheme for an assault that was to be the largest seaborne invasion in history up to that time. A total of 160,000 troops, 14,000 vehicles, 600 tanks and 1,800 guns had to be put ashore. Montgomery planned two landing places. In the background, *Sigint* from the *Ultra* code breakers continued to provide information of vital importance.

In preparation for the assault, the British developed a diversionary plan called Operation *Mincemeat*. This was the brilliant deception – the brainchild of Ewen Montagu, a British lawyer and Lieutenant Commander in the Royal Naval Volunteer Reserve – that employed a corpse in the uniform of a British officer with a briefcase chained to his wrist containing false plans for landings in Sardinia and Greece. The body was dropped off the coast of Spain and the contents of the briefcase were soon in the hands of the Germans. As a result, the German army reinforced the places that were not the real Anglo-American objectives, and the German generals' eyes were temporarily taken off Sicily. On 4 July, the Germans were misled into believing that landings were possible in Sardinia and Greece as well as Sicily, and their dispositions were made accordingly.

Preparing for the Next Round

A secret instruction circulated within 78th Division on 1 June 1943 stated explicitly: 'There is no attempt to disguise the fact that the Allies are to take part in a combined operation this summer against Southern Europe.' But beyond this cloudy generalization, total secrecy prevailed. The last time that the British army had assaulted a hostile shore was at Gallipoli in 1915, and one of the reasons for its tragic failure was that the Turks knew that the invasion was coming. An important element of Operation *Husky* was that no breach of security was going to be permitted. The troops were even discouraged from speculating about their next task. The objective, the date, the strength and order of battle, and the tactical methods to be employed, were pieces of knowledge tightly restricted to a small number of officers. The majority of the troops who would carry out the job would only know the details when they were on board ship.

After the German defeat at Tunis and von Arnim's surrender on 12 May, the Allied Armies were to have more than seven weeks before the landings in Sicily.

78th Division was to have over nine weeks (as will be explained). All the soldiers felt some euphoria after their victory, but the weeks before *Husky* were put to good use. First, reinforcements were absorbed into the different units. 8 Argyll and Sutherland Highlanders, which had lost so many men, received eighty-two replacements from the Welch Regiment, which made for an interesting and surprisingly successful fusion of two different Celtic cultures. Second, all the Allied formations and units carried out some serious training: TEWTs (Tactical Exercises Without Troops) for the officers, and field exercises for all ranks, with much marching and digging. Third, there was rest and relaxation, mostly well-organized.

Four months' active service, including a good deal of battle experience, encouraged PP to dwell on the lessons he had learned as an artillery officer. On 13 June 1943, he composed a brief summary, organized under thirteen headings:

> The work of the FOO
> Gun areas
> Fire plans
> Rates of fire
> Ammunition
> Stores
> Fire for effect
> Target records
> Air sentries
> Location of enemy fire positions
> Anti-tank defence
> Need for urgency in handling messages
> *Binge*: the word favoured by Montgomery to describe the drive and
>   enthusiasm needed for success in battle

PP put these points in a letter to his younger brother Paul, also a member of the HAC and a Battery Commander in another Royal Artillery Field Regiment. To illustrate the practical value of PP's conclusions, this is what he said about fire plans.

> **Fire plans**. Usually laid on at very short notice entailing speed of distribution. Then there was plenty of time to do sums: slow the distribution and there isn't.
>
>   Must be simple and practice in hatching them is needed by Artillery and Supporting Arms. They ought to send officers on every artillery scheme for that very purpose. Is it practical? Ammo? Will it do the trick? What have we omitted to paste [*i.e. cover with heavy fire*]? Joint recce whenever possible.

Quick barrage is popular. Inf. prefer a barrage to concentrations, then it is up to them and the closer they are behind the shells the less distance between bayonet and Boche when it lifts. For this the guns *must* shoot together and in operations always keep an eye on them for that. Can't have all three batteries asking to be superimposed because they cannot guarantee their calibration. The barrage on 6 May for 4 Indian and 4 Brit. Divisions was 2,700 yards wide (giving overlaps on flanks) by 3,600 yards deep.

Lifts. I have read that 50 yards a minute was popular in 1916. In the mountains we did 100 yards in four minutes – 50 yards should be covered by the zone of the gun. At Longstop we did 200 yards in eight minutes, and it was said to be popular. I believe the last one was 100 yards in three minutes: it was merely undulating.

I am now including a few more of the diary entries relating to Tunisia. There is just enough here to tell the story of what PP was doing during his nine weeks of preparation for the next phase of his war.

9 May 1943
Back through Tunis at about 07:00; at one place a mass of people all over the roads and pavements, smart gendarmes cleared it for us and they all cheered and waved and clapped like mad. In many other places smaller groups including Wogs clapped us, rather like country house cricket. A fine start to my birthday. Liaison Officer arrived from Brigade in the shape of Douglas Seymour [*HAC Infantry, now 2 London Irish Rifles*].

10 May 1943
Likely to be here about two weeks, we are non-operational now. Bath very welcome, I was thick with dust, clothes ditto. Tunis crammed but only odd wine shops open and no hotels. Ten percent allowed in on pass now, French troops there now and Yanks arriving. Many got very tight by 16:00 and lay about the gutters and pavements until taken away in lorries. Nothing else to do and men unused to wine who drink it like beer are apt to get sudden results after a bit. Saw one very smart French officer on a grey followed by a groom, Spahi I think.

14 May 1943
The band of the 47th Panzer Grenadier Regiment having been captured complete with instruments came over from Div. under escort and played very well indeed for an hour. Non-controversial music, the whole show was done as a drill – on signals from the Officer or Warrant Office in charge they all became rigid, presented instruments, played, stopped,

lowered instruments and stood at ease. Met a French officer who explained that every Frenchman in Tunis had experienced the Axis heel and they looked to 'le jeune Général' [*de Gaulle*] as leader of Free France because he had from the very beginning set up the standard of liberty and rallied them all and given them hope. Giraud seemed to be viewed with some suspicion as a collaborator.

17 May 1943

Drive to Bizerte, wreckage all along the road and bridge down, think we must have bombed and machine-gunned it pretty thoroughly. Had an excellent lunch with Tom and Robin [*Robin Smith, an old friend of PP and an FOO with a formidable reputation; 11th HAC Regiment RHA, 8th Army; MC and bar. See Plate 3*]. Best lunch I have had in the country.

23 May 1943

Thanksgiving Service in the Amphitheatre at Carthage AM. Rollo [*Lieutenant Colonel Rollo Baker*] went with a delegation. Gerald [*Gerald Solomon, Chaplain of the Regiment*] took a service in the same form among the olives. I read the lesson. More Italian ammo. went up during and after the service. Small arms stuff, grenades, some very attractive signal lights and then some AA shells.

26 May 1943

Went over to Philippeville for the night. Had a meal *en route* and looked over an American M7 (we call them Priests), 105 mm. gun on a tank chassis and no head cover [*used by 11th and 12th HAC Regiments, Royal Horse Artillery*].

3 June 1943

Saw Brigadier Kent-Lemon who brought 36th Brigade out. He was very busy as usual but said that we could go east of the river Safsaf. Had a good look and selected two sites for bivvies. A marvellous evening. Strong breeze reduced the mosquitoes. Now gather we'll not be here very long, hope all my efforts not wasted. Troop football league going strong. Training from 06:00 to 12:00, on the backs down till tea and training from 17:00 to 19:00.

9 June 1943

Passing out NCOs AM, gun drill for four hours, very hot. Lovely bath PM. Very pleasant evening. New sand fly nets issued in place of mosquito nets. More room inside.

11 June 1943

Announced at 15:00 that Pantelleria had surrendered. 1 Div. were due to assault at 12:00 so there couldn't have been much fighting.

19 June 1943

Visited Chassart and Longstop, all queerly quiet and unreal. Crops all burnt flat. Drove up the tank tracks almost to pt. 220, terrific view from even there all over our original FDLs in Medjez and beyond. David's [*David Brown's*] grave on the hill surrounded by thyme and sweet flowers and the litter of battle, the others in Chassart Churchyard but not one of the crosses put there by the Regiment is left. Wogs I suppose. Country is getting very parched but trees still a welcome green.

30 June 1943

Ran and walked again, grand bathe before breakfast – that's the time. Also PM. Monty came after tea, drove up in an open car, didn't get out. Shook hands and asked about service etc. Then called the Regt. round the car, terrific stampede, officers trampled underfoot, asked them odd questions, they loved it and him. He got right under their skins at once.

1 July 1943

Monty gave a lecture to all Officers of 78th Div. PM. We are now in his mind – a good thing. He said he planned on three principles: that he would not move until he was ready, that objectives would be limited, and that he would not ask formations to do something they could not do. We all sat on the sand under a huge canopy of car hoods put up by the engineers, 100 yds. from the sea.

3 July 1943

Exercise with the Irish Bde. Started down the Bou Ficha road but too far as we didn't get the orders for the assembly area in time. However all well and into action near our bathing place for the night. Masses of aircraft over, we must be hotting up some place before action – Sicily the news says. Foot aches from running, very tired. Very dusty along the road.

7 July 1943

Saw 36th Brigade returning from endurance exercise, twenty-eight miles and a hill climb or something. Royal West Kents going very well in sections and step, some sang. Argylls headed by a piper in threes in platoons apparently going twice the pace, some hats off, it seemed not so many men as the Kents. A very fine brigade. Buffs had come back last night having done the whole trip both ways in twenty-four hours or something [*5 Buffs were commanded by Lieutenant Colonel 'Ginger' McKechnie, DSO, HAC Infantry. He commanded the HAC Infantry when it was re-formed in 1947*].

10 July 1943
Up at 02:00 for a moment, air full of craft coming and going. Heard later in the morning that Sicily had been invaded by air and sea – it was Der Tag. Good show indeed, I wonder when and where we join in.

11 July 1943
Less breeze and a quiet hot day in camp. More transport planes seen at dusk. We are Corps reserve apparently and unlikely to move for seven/ten days. Now off shallow trenches and on fly-proof deep trenches but the seats are only half-height.

16 July 1943
Maps of Sicily arrive today.

Into Battle

Sicily is roughly triangular in shape. Its western tip is less than 100 miles from the Cape Bon peninsula in Tunisia. *See Map 4.* And although the sea passage from Tunisia to Sicily was dominated by the Anglo-American fleet, enemy submarines were still waiting to pounce, which meant that the passage was not totally secure.

From the western tip of the island, the coastline stretches east for 50 miles to reach the largest city, Palermo, and from there a further 150 miles to the Strait of Messina, which is separated from the toe of Italy by only a couple of miles at its narrowest point. From Messina, the coast follows a concave loop to the south for about 150 miles. From the south-eastern corner, the coast then continues north-west for about 200 miles to reach the western tip of the island. Sicily is rugged, with mountains, valleys and rivers, and it is baking hot in the summer. It is good defensive country, as the Anglo-American troops were shortly to find out. The island's most striking feature is the massive volcano Mount Etna, 11,000ft high, 50 miles south-west of Messina. Catania is a coastal port 20 miles south of the volcano, and to the west is the Catania plain: an obvious route to Messina, the main Anglo-American objective. The capture of the port would block the retreat of the defenders if they attempted to get away to the mainland of Italy.

Allied Headquarters assumed correctly that Sicily would be strongly garrisoned. The number of Italian troops on the island was accurately estimated to be 200,000, but the number of Germans who were likely to arrive after the invasion was of course unknown. But this enemy strength meant that the attackers would not have numerical superiority. There was however an important caveat. The majority of defenders were Italians, and most had lost faith in their cause and eventually put their hands up in large numbers, although the Italian artillery often performed well. The only serious opposition came in the event from two German formations, totalling 32,000 men and 160 tanks. The German garrison received reinforcements during the campaign, but its total strength never exceeded 65,000 troops. These manned a division of Luftwaffe infantry and armour, which did not perform impressively against the Americans; plus a Panzer corps of two divisions, which fought ferociously to impede the advance of the British 8th Army south of Catania, and continued to fight aggressive defensive battles when they were being pushed back by the British divisions, including the 78th.

The timing of the invasion was determined by the moon and the tides. The earliest suitable date was 10 July 1943, which to the planners was disappointingly late because of the need to forestall German reinforcements. The invading force was made up of two national forces. In Montgomery's 8th Army, the most important formations were Lieutenant General Dempsey's XIII Corps, and Lieutenant General Leese's XXX Corps. The British force numbered four infantry divisions, one airborne division, an independent infantry brigade and three armoured brigades. In addition, 46th and 78th Divisions were to follow sometime after the original landings. In Major General Patton's 7th Army, the most important component was Major General Bradley's II Corps, of three divisions, one being extra-strength. There was also a 'floating' reserve, which was shortly to be committed to battle, of one infantry, one armoured and one airborne division (which was commanded by Major General Ridgway, who was soon to make a name for himself). On the night of 9/10 July 1943, the Allied forces landed on twenty-six beaches, Montgomery on the south-eastern tip of the island, and Patton about half way along the southern coast, about 125 miles from the British. Surprisingly, Alexander did not formulate an overall strategic plan and was prepared merely to exploit local opportunities. This was to cause serious problems.

Although Eisenhower was in command of land, sea and air, the air commanders fought their own war. They provided plentiful air cover throughout the campaign, but there was no attempt to coordinate this with the land battles. This was a lesson that still had to be learned, and the invasion of France in June 1944 was planned more effectively.

An even more serious problem concerned the airborne soldiers who provided components of both Montgomery's and Patton's forces. Because of the inexperience of the pilots of the aircraft dropping the parachutists and tugging the gliders, the drops were tragically inaccurate. Troops landed all over the countryside, and in the British sector large numbers dropped into the sea and were drowned. As a result of the initiative of two strong local commanders, Colonel Gavin in the American sector and Lieutenant Colonel Frost in the

British, the airborne troops made important contributions, although these fell far short of what had been planned. (PP had encountered Frost in Tunisia in early February.)

Patton met serious, although not prolonged, opposition from the Luftwaffe division's infantry and armour, but before long he had established a strong foothold on the south coast; he managed to capture airfields (which had been important objectives). Montgomery had much less initial difficulty, and it did not take long for 8th Army to move north for 60 miles, to close in on Catania. Confident that his success would continue, Montgomery asked Alexander to allot Patton's army to him for the rather tame purpose of protecting the west flank of the British army. The Americans did what they were asked to do, but were extremely angry at being given such a job. During the operation, Leese's corps without warning moved west across the front of Bradley's troops, which caused undisguised outrage.

Patton now decided to take the initiative, and persuaded Alexander to let him surge forward north and west with the aim of taking Palermo. Bradley's II Corps remained on Montgomery's left. But on 19 July, Patton led the rest of the 7th Army forward. He did this with great panache and was accompanied by considerable publicity, but it was from the beginning unclear that the venture had any strategic objective beyond capturing territory.

By 21 July, after a number of days of fierce fighting, 8th Army was blocked south of Catania. The Germans occupied what became known as the Etna line, a 50-mile dog-leg stretching from the south of Catania north-west to the coast. Montgomery's initial attacks had been made by his XIII Corps on the right. He now had hopes for the success of a sharp attack on the left by XXX Corps, but this also did not manage to break the deadlock.

It took a double impact to break through the German positions: the rapid arrival of Patton's 7th Army and the entry of the 78th Division into the battle. After his colourful adventure in the west, Patton turned east towards Messina and the appearance of 7th Army was welcomed by Montgomery. There was much speculation about the greater effect Patton's army would have had if Alexander had directed him to cooperate with Montgomery before he embarked on his expedition to Palermo. (Major General de Guingand, Montgomery's Chief-of-Staff, believed that without Patton's diversion, Messina would have been taken much more quickly.) Patton continued to operate aggressively along the coast, and in parallel along the motor road some way to the south. Here he fought a bitter five-day battle to capture the mountain town of Troina. 78th Division arrived with the aim of striking forward, village by village, along the formidable Etna foothills: appropriate topography for troops who, from their experience in Tunisia, had become skilled in mountain warfare.

The Last Drive

Peter Pettit, still in Tunisia, heard on 22 July that 78th Division was bound for Sicily, with 12 hours' notice to move. They sailed on 27 July and arrived two days later, near the south-east tip of the island, and moved north by road.

78th Division was soon firing its guns in anger, and bringing fresh *binge* to 8th Army. The role of 17th Field Regiment was still to support 38th (Irish) Brigade, made up of three battalions – one Regular, one Territorial and one 'hostilities only' – with a strong national identity. PP, working with the infantry in a moving battle, was mostly with the guns. However, he had time to enjoy the countryside, with an English eye for small details, and to talk to many people. These included his regimental comrades, both officers and men, and many officers in neighbouring units, a surprising number of them members of the Honourable Artillery Company.

27 July 1943
Up at 05:30 and bathe in the twilight. Called forward and loaded in LST 424 [*Landing Ship Tank, a craft large enough to carry armoured vehicles*], much alteration in the loads as on the loading table. (I was OC troops.) Left quay at 15:00 to anchor outside the harbour. Sailed by midnight, slept fairly well, lots of bumping and rolling.

28 July 1943
Had a go at all meals and iced water but couldn't even keep that down. Pity because the food was good and plentiful. Skipper gave me gin in cabin while we discussed affairs of state. Kept on feet till 19:00, then slept well.

29 July 1943
Arrived G Beach about three-and-a-half miles north of Avola, Sicily at 08:30. Unloaded the ship in forty-five minutes (sixty-odd vehicles on two decks and 200 souls). To our Div. assembly area, lunch and lots of tea. Found plenty of almonds (not bitter). Country very like Tunisia. On to Div. concentration area west of Mineo, found George Condy [*17th Field Regiment*] there with a balance to light scale [*minimal equipment needed for battle*]. Terrific thunderstorm on the way through the mountains, streets in Vizzini and Palazzolo running like torrents. Mountains again, bad roads and bends. Heard guns again and smelt the peculiar odour of dead men.

30 July 1943
On to Castel di Judice area, very bare, very hot. Late orders to advance, moved right up north side of Monte Scalpello and found just room for one battery in the olive groves. 10 Bty. came in later. Glad to get to bed but sleep rudely shattered by heavy gunfire.

78th Division went into action on 29 July. During the following two weeks there was much hard but successful fighting. The first major objective was Centuripe, a small town perched on a precipitous hillside, and a key to any further British advance. *See Map 5 and Plate 7.* In preparation for the assault, 11th Brigade and 36th Brigade worked with two other divisions, one Canadian and one Scottish, to take the small town of Catenanuova. Then followed the attack on Centuripe itself, 5 miles to the north-east. This began on the evening of 31 July. 36th Brigade went in first, then were joined by 38th (Irish) Brigade. The town was taken on 2 August, following desperate close-quarter fighting. It was a classic soldiers' battle, supported by the whole weight of the Division's guns.

During all the fighting around Etna, the ground was extremely difficult for artillery, and this made PP's job especially difficult. The major problems were the lack of clear ground large enough for the gun positions of a battery's eight 25-pounders, and the steep winding roads. These were a major challenge for the heavy transport, in particular the 3-ton trucks carrying artillery ammunition.

31 July 1943

Ginger [*Lieutenant Colonel McKechnie*] called, his Bn. [*in 36th Brigade*] spread out among our guns and RHQ. While here Eric Riseley [*HAC Infantry*] and Lionel Cranfield [*HAC Infantry*] turned up, Eric now commands 40 LAA Regiment in Highland Div. and says he is a war-substantive Scotsman. Lionel commands a Beach Group. Put the other two Btys. in PM down almost impassable wadi but no other good positions available. Lots of close support bombers over and four Me.109s tried a little on their own account. Very tired.

1 August 1943

Advance proceeds slowly towards Centuripe, we recce almond groves on steep hillside and move in after dark. Very difficult country, rocks, bad roads and worse tracks cratered or landslid. Infantry must be finding it worse than Tunisia, going up and down hundreds of feet from one crest to the next. Fire plan soon after we get in.

2 August 1943

Centuripe (the key to this front) taken and we move up as far as we can towards the town. No chance of getting a vehicle off the road beyond our gun positions. It is cut out of mountainsides with hairpin bends galore and steeply terraced almond groves on either side. Go over and you drop for hundreds of feet. Considerable competition for space in our area, infantry bns. resting and Bde. HQs (to say nothing of the man who wanted to make an ammo. dump), the mediums and other field regiments.

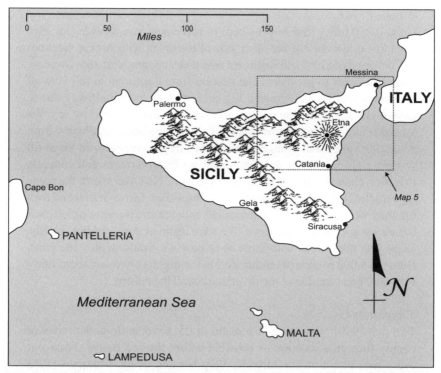

Map 4: Sicily. On the night of 10/11 July 1943, Montgomery's 8th Army assaulted the south-eastern tip of Sicily, and found little enemy resistance. But Patton's 7th Army had a more seriously opposed landing to the west, at Gela. Montgomery then advanced north, with the Americans protecting the British western flank. However, Patton persuaded Alexander to allow him to make a bold thrust north-west to capture Palermo and then fight along the northern coast of the island towards the Strait of Messina, which he eventually reached before Montgomery.

The loss of Centuripe caused the Germans' Etna line to crumble, which made it the decisive battle of the campaign. After the capture of Centuripe, a continuous and contested advance began towards the north-east. XIII Corps captured Catania on 5 August, while 78th Division was skirting the west side of Mount Etna. It had to fight for small towns – Centuripe, Adrano, Bronte, Regalbuto and Maletto – all the time moving through difficult country, over poor roads impeded by battle damage. (The little town of Bronte has some unusual historical connections with England. Admiral Nelson had performed valuable work for King Ferdinand of Naples, who as a reward in 1799 gave him the title of Duke of Bronte, which meant ownership of the town and the duchy surrounding it. Unfortunately, Nelson never managed to visit his Sicilian possession. Sometime later, the Revd Patrick Brunty decided to change his name to Bronte because of its connection to Nelson, although he was not related to him. Patrick Brunty became the father of Charlotte, Emily and Anne Brontë.)

4 August 1943

Up at 04:30 (after four hours sleep) to recce new gun areas in our own front line down the hill the other side of the town, with Archer, Second-in-Command of 57th Field Regiment now under command of 78th Division. Took two hours to get there. The descent from Centuripe in full view of the enemy and he had blown a big culvert clean away half way down. Only night work possible on that, too many casualties to RE by day. We looked at all the almond groves spread out on the slopes in full view from across the valley and orange groves down by the river also in view, till you get right in among the close-growing trees, terraces and concrete irrigation channels that form obstacles to guns. No cover worth the name for vehicles. Return about lunchtime for breakfast. Move in first and then off, then recce parties from Batteries left with me and we were called back before we got through the town. We went again at dusk and put the Bty. chaps into their areas with hints as to how we would deploy the guns. Dumped 6,000 rounds of ammo. during the night, convoy of about thirty very late, great trouble at the diversion round the culvert.

5 August 1943

Two-and-half-hours sleep. Up again at 05:30 to settle actual sites of twenty-four guns as soon as possible before the sun really shows our every movement on the hillside. Very hot and tiring. Mathews [*PP's driver*] got some peaches, grapes and green pears – a bit rough. Dumping another 6,000 rounds for the Regiment after dark. Head of convoy got hit and three lorries went up, giving a fine display of fireworks. The whole column of about sixty halted all down the long descent, the Boche threw his hat into the air and pasted the culvert in the hope of getting something else. He wasn't so lucky, so returned to the fire to warm it up.

After that we came half way up the hill and caused some casualties among the infantry. One shell slightly wounded Sgt. Summers in RHQ and punctured the Doctor's lorry in several places. In the meantime the drivers of the other lorries in the first part of the column thought it wasn't good enough and sugared off into the hills. Our half of the column had arrived close to RHQ before being halted. We couldn't get the lorries down to gun areas of 10 and 26 Batteries owing to jam so we packed them up even tighter than they were already, and got 2,000 rounds off in the 13 Battery/RHQ area away from the road. There followed a terrific turning round and I took the bull by the horns and sent them off home one by one, chancing the possibility of a jam further up. Nothing much happened, so I had the rest of ours unloaded in the ditch at the side of the road and go home likewise. We could pick it up tomorrow in trucks and ferry it the odd quarter-mile to the guns.

The night was going and we could not afford to have the column on the road at daylight or there really would be trouble. Behind the ammo. lorries were a Brigade HQ and the transport of two or more bns. who had to get down and through the river at the bottom in darkness. John Sibree, DAQMG at Div. [*Deputy Assistant Quartermaster General, a Staff Officer's appointment, normally held by a Captain*], came along in a jeep and went to sort out the leading lot [*a field regiment often needed thirty RASC trucks for its heavy lifting*]. Three loaded lorries came up and they are going to take the ammo. back so I had that put at the side of the road too. Then a trip down the road to the head of the column discovered it moving again; the Boche packed up after about an hour-and-a-half. The RASC officer i/c. my platoon of vehicles was most helpful when we started sorting out, and volunteered to take over the leading lot and see them to their destination if I could see his lot off on the way home, which worked out well. But he had to lie up all next day in the 57th area as they weren't unloaded in time to get back over the hill before day. Brigade HQ and bn. columns disappeared by magic as soon as the road was clear, and all ended well.

6 August 1943

Slept flat out. Boche seems to have gone back, no contact but shells early in river valley. Adrano regularly bombed by us all AM (and yesterday), a dozen machines at a time fly sedately over, round over the target and back over us; just as they get to us on the way back the whole town seems to jump up in smoke and dust and nothing is seen but the huge dust cloud for some minutes. The amazing thing is that when it clears away the whole town is still there and looks from this distance just the same as before. Mostly no AA but I saw four guns firing once and the silly little bursts up in the air near our bombers. Recce Regiment reported in Adrano PM and bombers shifted onto Bronte. Later it turned out that Recce were not in the town and I was called personally by the officious IO at HQRA to get a fire plan (he only said CRA wanted to see me and all the way I wondered what I had done wrong or whether I was to be promoted). Shocking drive in the dark. Only got back at 21:40, zero being midnight. However, all went well and they got it all worked out in time. Slept right through it for nine hours. [*See Map 5.*]

The Adrano fire plan is included in PP's diary, in his own handwriting. The infantry advance was slow: 100yd in 5 minutes. There was no smoke. The concentrated gun fire was prolonged: 170 minutes before the infantry advanced; 180 minutes to accompany the infantry; then 195 minutes from the medium guns firing on the back of the town. Adrano turned out to be a walkover.

7 August 1943

Very dopey at 08:00. Recce ordered at 14:30. Went to see new area in valley west of Adrano and then returned, but traffic jammed all along the road due to the diversions at both bridges which are one-way. Everybody trying to move forward, traffic from our way and traffic from Regalbuto meets at the bottom of the hill. Thick orange groves, walls, narrow gates and lava all over the area made it very difficult to find gun positions, but we did after much head-scratching. Cratered roads didn't help but we got over them. Map is nothing like the country just here. Regt. moved at 18:30 so we didn't go back. Green [*PP's batman*] had to cadge a lift with our stuff on other trucks. Drummed up M&V [*a tinned meal based on meat and vegetables; popular in the First World War*], in the radiator of the Humber, tin just fits if you take the filter out.

During the meal there were some big bangs and we got out to see; apparently the enemy were firing three of the six-barrelled mortars at the area, eighteen bursts came almost at once. They are fired by some sort of rocket because there are six red flashes from behind a crest and in the centre of each flash is a bright white streak like a rocket. You hear nothing for half a minute and then there is a rushing as of express trains in the air and these things burst with a shattering roar one after the other. Not very accurate, bursts were fairly well apart [*this was the first time that PP experienced the* Nebelwerfer, *the terrifying German multiple mortar*]. Slept well for six hours.

8 August 1943

Off again 09:00 up the Bronte road leaving two Canadian battalions behind. Adrano is a sort of Guernica, bodies still on the pavements, ruins everywhere and they had to use bulldozers to clear a way through for wheels. Half way to Bronte came to our front line. Craters ahead, no decent positions yet so went to see ahead. Found remains of enemy canteen supplies, and collected some packets of tobacco and a bottle of Weinbrand. There were also some cigars but the RE Sgt. had these and I saw him trying one while looking at the first crater. While looking at this with Ronnie Denton [*OC Royal Engineers Field Company*] Brens fired from behind us towards the ridge in front so it didn't seem too safe for guns yet. Much delay and congestion on the one road and you can't get off it without knocking a lava wall down. Saw A Battery, 11th HAC Regiment, RHA, and heard of John McAllum's [*Captain; MC*] death from burns a few days ago. Met Robin [*Robin Smith*] in a jeep looking for information. Progress slow but about 18:00 own infantry seen on the ridge. (IO of 11th Brigade did not know they had got there and couldn't see.) Guns came in after spending most of the day by the roadside. Some strafing by guns and mortars. All vehicles sent back to odd corners down the road. Went back to A Battery, 11th Regiment, to sleep; had a drink with Chrimes [*Major, later Lieutenant Colonel*], the Bty. Commander and slept very well.

9 August 1943

Dudley Smith arrived during my shave [*now Bty. Capt. of A Battery, 11th Regiment*]. 38th Brigade held up 1,000 yards beyond Bronte. 57th Regiment have put a troop just behind our RHQ, which is very noisy apart from being up very rough steep lava in the loop of a hairpin bend. Buck [*late of B Battery, 11th Regiment*] being the GPO; rather unfriendly but there was nowhere else for them. Sorted out RHQ five hundred yards back down the road, and most of our vehicles went two-and-a-half miles back where they broke down walls and got off the road and dispersed. Was told that Regalbuto is in a worse state than Adrano. This is the most awful artillery country. We are the furthest-forward guns and have had fifteen to twenty hit by shells or mortars so far. Steep slopes, lava walls and loose lava make it a nightmare for me, finding gun positions and places to get vehicles off the road. Most of the strafing is away to our left where no one is.

Fetched fire plan from CRA at 19:00 at 38th Brigade HQ; went on bike, less conspicuous going over the crest. While there, Jerry strafed again, great swooshing through the air as the big mortar bombs went over, most seemed to go down the hill as before but he swung them about and some were obviously close to our guns and RHQ. A few bits fell around. Delayed return until it died down, you cannot hear them coming on a bike. On return found that one officer and three men had been killed and another officer mortally wounded by one of the German mortar bombs which landed in 26 Battery gun line. They had gone to see if a wounded LAA chap was alright in the corner of a wall by a stone building, they had heard it coming and crouched against the wall but the bomb landed almost on the wounded man and got them all. BSM Fowles was with them but dived behind a trailer wheel five yards away for cover and was not touched. Three more fell round my staff car, which Mathews thought had gone, but it was only covered with black lava dust in and out, a few holes to add to the collection, headlight holed and aerial shot away. Two of them were within eight and three yards respectively of the MO and the cookhouse but they were in a slight hollow and no one was hit. Two more fell within thirty yards. One man ran off and was found eventually miles back in a carrier, very badly shaken (he was hit in Tunisia) and one or two others slid off too. Little Stinton, the mess cook, very cool and collected helping clear up the mess. A bad day for the Regt.

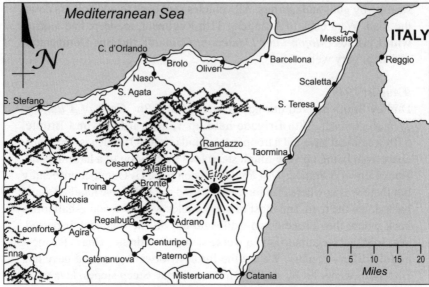

Map 5: West of Mount Etna. 78th Division, which included 17th Field Regiment, Royal Artillery, was in reserve at the beginning of the invasion. It was committed to battle at the end of July 1943 in the difficult mountainous region west of Mount Etna. 17th Regiment supported the 38th (Irish) Brigade as it fought forward to capture the small towns of Centuripe, Adrano, Bronte, Regalbutto and Maletto. These were soon in ruins but were held stubbornly by the Germans. 78th Division then returned to reserve, and the remainder of 8th Army advanced to the north on both sides of Mount Etna.

PP's diary includes a handwritten fire plan for the attack on Maletto which he had collected from the CRA. There was concentrated fire from four field regiments, thickened by occasional fire from medium guns, covering a beaten zone 600yd wide and 1,000yd deep. The planned infantry advance was very slow, 100yd in 5 minutes.

10 August 1943
Beautiful sunny morning, not a sound, last evening seems unbelievable. Must have been his usual farewell 'hate' before withdrawing. Hear Ginger [*McKechnie*] is wounded; later that he's gone back for a rest.

11 August 1943
Visited various sub-units, out all day. Went for some tomatoes where we were before, almost over but we scraped up a sandbag full. Div. HQ moved in ahead of 10 Bty. and wouldn't let them fire. So recced a position NE of Bronte for them and returned by moonlight. Up this one road there is much scrambling for space, with a whole Div. using it. The GOC has said that he is satisfied if two of the four field regiments are

able at any given moment to fire in support of the infantry [*17th Field
Regiment had clearly demonstrated its ability to carry out such a role*].

The division led the way to Randazzo, another mountain town which was in
ruins when it was captured. From here, the division made contact with the
Americans. Randazzo was taken on 12 August, and this marked the end of
78th Division's active fighting in Sicily.

12 August 1943
Joint recce with Archer of 57th, his Jeep very useful again. Moved 10 Bty.
forward and returned for late lunch and the night. Orders at 16:30 to
move the rest. Went off to see Rollo and on to Monte Rivoglia. The
Germans shelled the crest and the road their side of it, two battalions had
gone over into the thick scrub beyond the pleasant valley the other side.
But no one knew where they had got to. Avoided road and walked bty.
recce parties over the crest and down the valley, strung out in the
vineyards so as not to give away what we were up to. Found one OP
where enemy had guns by the refuse about, squeezed the others in by
breaking down walls. RHQ back over the hill on the almond terraces.
Moved 02:00. I slept all out.

13 August 1943
Getting right out of range despite our move forward, seems to be end of
exercise for us. Moved RHQ into the valley, and then 10 Bty., but they
did not get into action. Saw another fighter plane dive into the deck from
a low height as at Hammamet, also on his back but did not see how he
started it. Feel very tired, glad it's over for a bit. 22:00 wakened to hear
that recce parties to be ready at 06:00 – damn!

14 August 1943
Ready by 06:00 hours but no orders. Drove forward with RSM. Long US
column coming into Randazzo from the west, and we couldn't get on at all
(nor could they). Walked on nine miles. No sign of enemy at all. US pouring
through, very slowly with many halts. Our battle obviously over. Had some
wine out of a US mess tin. Traffic held up by mines ahead they said, and
we saw casualties coming back. Some story of a man pulling bunch of
grapes and getting blown up by the mine he thus set off. This anecdote came
rocketing down the column with an order not to pick any grapes.
　　Mathews not yet caught up so we started walking back. Found some
small tomatoes in the garden which we picked. While eating one a local
came up and said it was all his and would we like some wine. He only
said two words we understood, 'mio' and 'vino' but his gestures filled

the gaps. He took us to a sort of village post office which was quite like one of ours, where Madame gave us some reasonable white wine, much better than the rough red stuff. She had been in the United States thirty-two years ago and spoke a little American. She said that the Germans were all bad, had taken everything and broken the place up. She and her family were Sicilian and not Italian. Randazzo very badly knocked about indeed. Bulldozers needed to clear even single-line traffic through the town, not a building untouched, and a foul stink everywhere. Roads full of craters and mines and a very tortuous and narrow way through. The main road was hopeless, the big bridge over the river blown utterly.

The campaign now became a race for Messina between Patton's 7th Army advancing along the north coast and Montgomery's 8th Army moving forward around Mount Etna. The 8th Army's advance omitted 78th Division, which was recuperating from the tough fighting it had experienced since its arrival in Sicily; and XIII Corps to the east was still moving sluggishly. The relentless Patton got to Messina first, perhaps to settle scores with the British. In early August, Patton, an extremely volatile man, was accused of abusing verbally and physically two private soldiers, and came within inches of being sacked. Because of his emotional temperament, he took the race to Messina more seriously than Montgomery did.

By 10 August, the defenders were tightly packed into a triangle of land 30 miles long, with Messina at its peak. But the Germans were not trapped, as they had been in Tunisia. They conducted a gradual retreat to the Strait of Messina, which they crossed with the benefit of carefully formulated plans, underpinned by ferocious discipline: threats of immediate death sentences. By 17 August, 70,000 Germans, 40,000 Italians, 10,000 vehicles (including 47 tanks), and 17,000 tons of supplies and equipment had been evacuated, and lived to fight another day. The struggle for Sicily was over for 17th Field Regiment. They were later to cross to Italy, but PP was by then no longer with them.

After 12 August, the tension throughout 78th Division was relaxed, but PP had enough to occupy his time. The cohesion and efficiency of 17th Field Regiment were maintained and the Regiment was still at readiness. The CRA visited the Regiment. PP did some travelling, calling on the medical stations where the wounded and sick were taken. PP's batman Green was in a Casualty Clearing Station with an infection that incapacitated him, and PP was himself struck with serious 'tummy troubles'. Blood-sucking mosquitoes had appeared on the scene. PP managed to make an interesting trip to Lentini and Syracuse, over a road with 'very bad hills and bends'. He noticed that 51st (Highland) Division was much in evidence, wielding paint brushes (by 17 August their symbol, the acronym HD, was often interpreted as 'Highway Decorators'). Some of PP's comrades got to the top of Mount Etna, 5,000yd in a vehicle, followed by 5,000yd on foot. On 22 August, the Regiment held a church service under a large elm tree. The Divisional Concert Party afterwards gave its first performance on the same spot.

78th Division also embarked on further serious training. In particular the infantry were taught how to use the newly introduced PIAT. [*Projector Infantry Anti-Tank, a dangerous contraption constructed from a metal tube from which a heavy grenade could be fired from extremely short range to disable an enemy tank*) The PIAT would be part of the infantry platoon's repertoire of weapons during the campaigns in Italy and North-West Europe.

Hail and Farewell

PP's diary and a letter he sent home contain an unforgettable description of the massive artillery preparation for the British landing on the toe of Italy on 3 September (the fourth anniversary of Britain's declaration of war on Germany).

Letter, 3 September 1943
I got up at 03:30. It was dark but starry and I joined the CO and others on the road where we could see the water in the Straits, dull silver between black land. At 03:45 our side from Faro (the tip where one expects to see Charybdis on the map and doesn't), far down towards Taormina, burst into flame with a roar of hundreds of guns: British and American; field, medium and captured heavies (manned by a Battery of 11th HAC Regiment, Royal Horse Artillery). They fired series of concentrations on the beaches and beach defences, known coast defence guns and hostile battery positions while 17-pounders fired tracer across the Straits to guide the assault craft in. There was no reply. We moved down the road to our OP which gave us a view from Scilla to Reggio had we been able to see.

This fire continued with short pauses until 04:30, which was Zero hour, the time when the first flights of assault craft were due on their respective beaches. One saw the bursts in the black of Italy and occasionally a big red flame showed that something inflammable had been hit. Several fires were started and burned with varying intensity well into the morning.

At Zero all eyes were strained to spot ships on the water but the Straits had filled with smoke and the coast line was obscured so that none were seen. The shelling went on, the bursts appeared further inland but it was difficult to tell because of the smoke.

Just after 05:00 a faint lightening of the sky behind the Italian mountains gave a promise of day but it was 06:00 before it was light. In the meantime the shelling had ceased and all was quiet. It was most extraordinary watching the invasion of Europe proper in absolute silence, there was no reply at all.

A chatter of machine guns was heard beyond Faro point at about 05:15. After much discussion it was decided that they were Brens. Shortly after, we actually saw the flashes of machine guns firing across the Narrows from the edge of the water at Faro.

The smoke was dense and only a narrow strip of water on this side of the Straits could be seen. There was no wind but the smoke drifted and gaps appeared. At about 06:15 the first ships were seen, first two approaching Catona and over twenty round the spit to the south between Catona and Gallico. As we watched shells fell on the spit among the craft, not a lot about two or three guns we thought, and the dull boom of the guns was heard behind the mountains hiding Fiumara, out of our range. The craft sheared off a little into the smoke and then approached the beaches south of the point. None appeared to be hit although we saw a near miss on an LCI [*Landing Craft Infantry*]. One of our heavier batteries engaged the enemy guns who ceased firing shortly after. We saw two landing craft moving south in the Straits opposite to us but smoke closed in again and prevented our seeing north of San Giovanni.

We had been given long lists of light signals to look out for but we only saw two lots of green Verey lights and these weren't on our lists! There were a few shots from Giovanni but otherwise the landings appeared to be totally unopposed. Later in the morning escort vessels passed through the Straits unchallenged. All day the landing craft of all sorts and sizes came and went, Ducks, LCI , LCT, LST and no doubt others [*Ducks, or DUKWs, were floating trucks; LCI, Landing Craft Infantry; LCT, Landing Craft Tanks; LST, Landing Ship Tanks*]. Gradually reports came in of advances inland and no Germans seen. The enemy tried several hit-or-miss air raids during the day, probably with fast fighters, but a terrific barrage of AA bursts (they seemed all over the sky), and the ships' kites kept the enemy high and few bombs were dropped over a wide area.

The view of Italy in the afternoon with the sun revealing every building and fold in the ground was very clear from north of Scilla to well south of Reggio, landing craft came and went at will, our transport was seen moving up the hills towards Rosali and Villa. We really had got a large foothold in Europe. An historic occasion marked by the almost complete absence of opposition.

Admiral Cunningham was impressed by the display of firepower, although he also had serious doubts about whether it was necessary, because the actual crossing of the Straits by the Allied troops was so easy: by far the easiest part of the forthcoming bitter struggle for Italy. On 8 September, PP began a complicated journey to England, something that was made more difficult by an infected foot that impeded his walking. The reason for his return home was to spend three months at a senior officers' course at Brasenose College, Oxford, to prepare him for his next military appointment by studying higher strategy and military organization. This next appointment was to another gunner regiment in the army that was to invade Normandy in June 1944, and eventually to command a different field artillery regiment.

Sicily had been taken after less than forty days, despite the difficult topography and the fierce German opposition in the Mount Etna sector. After the event, enemy generals were highly critical of Montgomery's lack of audacity in creeping up the island from the south. The distinguished naval historian Samuel Eliot Morison also made the same point. The key objective was always Messina, and Anglo-American sea power would have made it possible to attack Messina and end the campaign by a *coup de main*. Montgomery's plan was, however, a typical example of his desire to control risk (echoed in his speech to the officers of 78th Division on 1 July). In almost every one of his battles he would err on the side of caution despite the attraction of enormous rewards for boldness. The single occasion in which he abandoned this strategy – 'a bridge too far' at Arnhem – was to demonstrate the danger of taking a gamble while the German army remained undefeated.

One of the most pregnant lessons of the campaign was Alexander's disappointing performance. He had not formulated the initial invasion plan; he had not dictated a strategic follow-through for how the campaign should develop; and there was no plan for an end game to annihilate the last defenders and prevent their escape. It was apparent to the senior Allied strategic planners that the invasion of France in 1944 needed a strong and energetic land force commander. Montgomery was well cast for this role, although his abrasive personality was to cause its own raft of difficulties.

Sicily cost the Allied forces 22,811 casualties, including 5,532 killed. Many officers thought that this was a high price. But Bradley admitted, as he had done at the end of the Tunisian campaign, that Sicily produced a hidden benefit to the American troops. It gave them additional 'hands-on' experience that would pay dividends during the larger operation to invade France in June 1944.

PP, handicapped by his septic foot, was eventually given an uncomfortable space on a Dakota transport plane that left Algiers on 14 September.

15 September 1943
Land Ho! about 08:00. Landed at Portreath at about 09:30 (08:30 BST), had breakfast and on to Hendon by 11:40. Rather more bumpy over land than sea. Swiftly whisked through Customs (who were very decent), Security Officer and MO, and then to good old 65 Baker Street in a luxurious limousine by 13:00 hours. Seemed very dangerous driving on the left of the road. Joy [*PP's wife*] in town. WHOOPEE!

Chapter 4

Normandy – 'The Majestic Plan of Forcing the Channel'

This quotation, interpreted with some freedom by Churchill, came from Stalin's message responding to the news that D-Day had at last arrived. In Operation Overlord on 6 June 1944, Anglo-American forces assaulted the Normandy coast. This meant that the most important milestone on the way to victory in the Second World War was passed. The long-awaited Western Front was now opened, and – perhaps more importantly – German resources began to be sucked away from other battlefronts to shore up the west, with the result that the Russian steamroller would soon begin to gather massive momentum.

'The Longer He Knew Montgomery, the Less He Liked Him but the More He Respected Him'

'What is your most valuable possession?'

'My rifle, sir.'

'No, you fool. It is your life. And that is why I am going to look after it for you.'

This true anecdote about General Montgomery, the commander of the invading armies, reveals two important things about him. First, he made himself personally known to his troops; and second, he did not waste their lives heedlessly, and his soldiers knew this. The men in the ranks and the junior officers who led them had much affection for him, and were rather amused by his public persona. This wiry, abstemious, intense figure, small in stature and dressed in eccentric semi-uniform, travelled widely among the troops and was noticed everywhere. Peter Pettit had seen and heard Montgomery in Tunisia, and was forcefully struck by the way he managed to penetrate (in PP's words) 'under the skin' of the soldiers and young officers. However, more senior officers, Lieutenant Colonels and above, viewed him with some trepidation because they knew perfectly well that he would sack them without hesitation for what he considered to be incompetence.

One of the reasons for Montgomery's remarkable success was that he was a rigorous planner and kept a tight 'grip' on the formations he commanded. As an army group commander, his operational plans laid down details of all the jobs to be carried out by his armies and corps, leaving little opportunity for the senior generals commanding these formations to display their initiative. He was nevertheless prepared to sack them when he believed that they were not doing their jobs well enough. Many battalion/regimental, brigade and divisional commanders were relieved; and even two corps commanders, Lumsden in the Western Desert, and Bucknall in Normandy. Their departure, *pour encourager les autres*, had an effect, and Montgomery's surviving generals built formidable reputations.

Montgomery was a driven, single-minded student of war. He was the first British general to realize that, despite the soundness of British army thinking after 1918 regarding the importance of mobility and all-arms operations, a doctrine based on it was not imposed strongly from the centre. Senior officers were allowed to interpret it in their own fashion. Montgomery had the brains, experience, vision and determination to impose his will on his subordinates, no matter how much he would ruffle their feathers.

It is impossible to deny his success, described in the words of a shrewd military analyst, David French:

> Unlike Haig he kept a tight 'grip' on the battle, attacked on narrower fronts but in greater depth, and developed the machinery of intelligence and deception in such a way as to be able regularly to employ surprise as an effective force-multiplier. British ground-air cooperation and artillery support techniques were far in advance of German practice. The British had also developed techniques to cross both man-made and natural obstacles in the shape of rivers and minefields. And they had become increasingly skillful at mounting large-scale offensives under cover of darkness . . . Even the Germans were impressed.

After the success in Normandy and as the campaign developed further, a few officers came to occupy positions equal to Montgomery's in authority. These men, Lieutenant General Bradley, Major General Patton and Air Chief Marshal Tedder in particular, grew to detest him because of his arrogant, unbending and abrasive personality, as well as the immense care he took in his military planning which inevitably slowed the progress of military operations. Their attitude rubbed off on the Commander-in-Chief, General Eisenhower. Although he was less easy-going than he appeared, Eisenhower devoted himself to cementing the Anglo-American alliance. But by the end of 1944 even he was well on the way to loathing Montgomery. On the other hand his British army superior, the Chief of the Imperial General Staff and former artilleryman, General Sir Alan Brooke, was his patron and supported him continuously, despite the frequent need to rap him over the knuckles for personal crassness. This support dated from 1939 and 1940, when Brooke had been Montgomery's

Corps Commander in France and was at that time instantly and permanently impressed by his military ability. This chapter is substantially devoted to Montgomery, because the Normandy campaign revolved around him. Despite the appalling flaws in his personality, he was the greatest general to emerge from either side during the Second World War. This anyway is my opinion, and is not a universally accepted view. I shall try not to let it colour my evaluation of the events that I shall describe.

Peter Pettit's experience of battle in Normandy was the most dramatic episode of his military career. Appropriately, the description in his diary is the most graphic episode in the work; Chapter 5 is devoted to it. However, to provide a proper context to the events, the fascinating history of the Normandy campaign must be described in fairly full although not superfluous detail. A great deal of high-intensity activity occurred during the two months of the fighting, in which the Allies outfought a tough, ruthless and well-prepared enemy. Victory was won because the Allied forces had a brilliant strategic plan; powerful leadership; the enormously valuable *Sigint* that continued to arrive from Bletchley Park; vast amounts of equipment (although much was not of high quality); endless supplies of gasoline and ammunition (despite logistical bottlenecks); and – not least – intrepid soldiers, sailors and airmen, whose morale remained high, although the troops on the ground were less well trained than their opponents.

The arrival in London of Eisenhower and Montgomery in January 1944 marked the final confirmation that the British as well as the Americans were committed to the cross-Channel invasion of Europe. Churchill and Brooke had fought a series of delaying actions to concentrate Allied resources on Italy, the 'soft underbelly' of Europe (an 'underbelly' that proved anything but soft). Brooke was brutally realistic about the demands that the invasion across the Channel in the face of desperate German resistance would make on the human and physical resources of the Allies. Churchill (who never forgot the Gallipoli disaster in 1915, for which he was partly responsible), had frightening visions of the English Channel turning red with the blood of fallen soldiers. The firm commitment to the invasion of France as the direct route to Berlin was the first signal that in the Great Alliance American influence had become more important than British. By the autumn of 1944 the balance had tipped further and the Americans, with more and more troops on the ground, became the dominant partners.

Important lessons had been learned from the Sicily campaign. First, there had to be an effective overall land forces commander to master-mind the strategy of the Normandy campaign. He had to be a man with a stronger personality than General Alexander, who was anyway not available because he was fully occupied in Italy. Nigel Nicolson, the well-known man of letters who had fought in Italy, said that the longer he knew Alexander, the more he liked him but the less he respected him. But the longer he knew Montgomery, the less he liked him but the more he respected him.

The second point is that air power had to be integrated into the overall offensive, and controlled by the generals and their subordinates on the ground. Most importantly, this also meant there had to be far better management of the air landings of the American and British airborne divisions. There were still problems with the airborne landings during the operation, but as a whole, the Allied air cover over Normandy was overwhelming.

It was essential for the Commander-in-Chief of the whole enterprise to be an American, because the American contribution in men and resources was expected to become much greater than Britain's before many months had passed. Churchill had initially promised the job to Brooke, but he had to withdraw it, to Brooke's intense disappointment. General Marshall would have done well, but Roosevelt insisted that he should remain in Washington, DC. Eisenhower was not an absolutely automatic choice. When Roosevelt and Churchill met Stalin at Teheran in November 1943, Stalin had pressed to learn the identity of the commander of the cross-Channel invasion, because he was still unsure that the Western Allies meant business. This forced Roosevelt's hand, and after some prevarication, he nominated Eisenhower.

Eisenhower was the best man for the job, not least because of his remarkable personality. He had learned a great deal from his experience in the Mediterranean, and he would now be free of the political entanglements that had enmeshed him in Africa. He had demonstrated his ability both to control a multinational force comprising land, sea and air, and to get the best from talented mavericks, the most important of whom was Montgomery. Nobody but Eisenhower could have done the job of making strong national armies pull together so effectively, although his American subordinates constantly criticized him for being pro-British.

Montgomery commanded three national armies, Bradley's 1st American, Lieutenant General Dempsey's 2nd British and Lieutenant General Crerar's 1st Canadian (formed after the campaign was under way, although one of the Canadian infantry divisions landed on the beaches on the first day). During the planned break-out phase, Patton's 3rd Army would enter the battle alongside the American 1st Army, whose command would pass to Major General Hodges. The two American armies would then form the 12th Army Group under Bradley. However, all four armies would still be under Montgomery. Much later in the campaign, when the size of the American forces on the ground would be much larger than the British and Canadian, Montgomery would command the 21st Anglo-Canadian Army Group, while Bradley would command all the American armies, which would include yet another American Army Group, formed later. Eisenhower at that time would direct the strategy of all Army Groups, a situation that provoked a crisis of command, during which Montgomery came within an ace of being sacked.

Eisenhower's most prominent field commanders were Montgomery, Bradley and Patton, between whom there was considerable antipathy. Montgomery was by far the most experienced but all three were highly competent, and they were all old enough soldiers to know the importance of obeying orders. The two Americans thought Montgomery patronizing and unable to accept any opinion except his own. He was also considered too slow and painstaking, although his longer acquaintance with the German army had taught him the danger of taking too many risks. Montgomery was a *thinker*. He did not read documents, nor did he wait for plans for his consideration drawn up by his staff. He pondered at length all aspects of the military problem that was his immediate concern, and once he had made up his mind about a course of action, he made sure that his orders were punctiliously executed and he relied on his staff to make sure that this took place. When – as happened at El Alamein and in Normandy – his plan encountered road blocks when the armies were in contact, he reconsidered his options and adjusted his existing plan, while remaining within his original strategic parameters. Montgomery was astonishingly single-minded and unyielding, which was one of the causes of his personal difficulties with other generals.

In contrast, Bradley and Patton were different from Montgomery and also from one another. Each was very much his own man and each has carved a niche in military history. Bradley was thoughtful, introverted and (from the evidence of his personal diaries) rather sour-tempered, while Patton was a caricature of a tough, profane and aggressive leader (despite his curiously squeaky voice). There was an inevitable problem with the three men's personal chemistry.

For the invasion phase, the American and British forces were approximately equal in size. The air forces, commanded by another Englishman, Air Chief Marshal Leigh-Mallory, were also approximately equal. Allied airpower for the invasion was massively greater than that of the Luftwaffe, most of whose strength had to be deployed in protecting the Reich from air bombardment, in keeping the Russians at bay on the Eastern Front, and in grappling with the Allied forces in Italy.

The navies – the British larger than the American – were commanded by the experienced and highly competent British Admiral Ramsay. Ramsay's greatest problem, which he handled with skill, was to protect the landings from U-boat and E-boat incursions. These vessels were notoriously slippery and able to infiltrate between naval defences. However, the British and American navies were enormously strong, with defences so thickly stacked that the landings were protected and very few ships were lost.

The air command was problematical. Eisenhower's deputy, Tedder, was a British Air Chief Marshal (four stars, the same rank as Eisenhower). He was closely involved in the air, thus making Leigh-Mallory rather superfluous. Air Marshal Coningham, in command of the tactical air forces (i.e. providing direct cooperation with the armies), was closer to Tedder than he was to Leigh-Mallory because they had served together in Africa, and as a result Coningham shared Tedder's intense dislike of Montgomery. Below Coningham, the individual tactical air forces worked very well, and Air Vice Marshal Broadhurst (a Royal Air Force officer who had once been in the army), whose squadrons supported the British and Canadian troops, was able, cooperative and popular. The aircraft, notably the rocket-firing Typhoon fighters, made an immense contribution to the fighting on the ground, and were only impeded by the frequent bad weather. Montgomery recommended Broadhurst for a knighthood soon after the fighting began, but this was obstructed by Tedder and Coningham, with the result that Broadhurst did not receive his elevation until 1945.

The underlying plan for the invasion of Western Europe had been worked out by a senior British staff officer, Lieutenant General Morgan, another former gunner, who had spent more than a year with the title of Chief-of-Staff to the Supreme Allied Commander, or *COSSAC*. (This was well before there was a supreme Allied commander.) Morgan correctly concluded that the factor determining where the assault from the sea would take place was its proximity to airfields in Britain, from which air support would be provided. Only the Pas de Calais and Normandy qualified; more outlying locations like the Bay of Biscay and Scandinavia were too far from Britain for effective air cover of the beaches.

When Eisenhower and Montgomery arrived on the scene, they accepted the main *COSSAC* recommendation, although Eisenhower, Montgomery and Bradley wanted a stronger landing force on the beaches. Montgomery made his own plan, which developed into an eight-division assault, including three airborne. By now the invasion had been codenamed Operation *Overlord*. Morgan was eventually appointed Deputy Chief-of-Staff in Eisenhower's headquarters, where he joined Tedder (Eisenhower's own deputy) as a leading member of the anti-Montgomery faction. Another influential member of the anti-Montgomery cabal was Admiral Cunningham, who had cooperated remarkably well with Eisenhower, but had worked unhappily with Montgomery in the Mediterranean. He was now the First Sea Lord, the professional head of the Royal Navy.

The south of England is separated from Normandy by 100 miles of often rough water, so that the transport of men and supplies was to be an immediate and continuing problem. Bad weather was a feature of the whole period of the Normandy campaign: it even caused D-Day to be postponed from 5 to 6 June when the troops were already on board ship. What made the situation particularly difficult was the absence of ports. Cherbourg was the only good one on the Normandy peninsula, and was an important early objective for the

American 1st Army, but the German defenders made every effort to destroy the port facilities. The town was taken within three weeks of the landing, and American engineers, with their customary energy, got the harbour working three weeks after its capture. But this was six weeks after D-Day.

The planners realized at a very early stage that the armies could not wait for Cherbourg to be opened. With dazzling powers of improvisation, during the period leading up to the invasion two concrete harbours called Mulberries were constructed in pieces, which were towed across the Channel once the Normandy beaches had been secured. One of them, in the American sector, had only a short life and was washed away in a massive storm on 19–22 June. But the other, in the British sector, survived despite damage and did its job very well. Its remains can be seen today off the beach at Arromanches. The artificial ports were before long supplemented by a pipeline under the ocean (codenamed *Pluto*), that carried gasoline from Britain to the fighting front. This came into operation in mid-August, when gasoline was very badly needed for the great Allied advances that were about to begin.

Improvisation did not stop with artificial harbours and the pipeline. Major General Percy Hobart, another maverick as abrasive as his brother-in-law, Montgomery, formed the 79th Armoured Division of 'funnies'. These were tanks that swam (Duplex Drive/DD); operated flails for destroying minefields and wire ('Crabs', Plate 17); carried fascines for filling trenches; were mounted with bridging equipment; laid mats to cross sand and shingles ('Bobbins'); worked as flame throwers, shooting out napalm ('Crocodiles'); and were armed with heavy mortars ('Petards', shooting 'Flying Dustbins'). These curious machines were not the least important contributors to the success of the Normandy invasion. Except for the swimming tanks, which were Shermans, the 'funnies' were not used by the Americans because they were nearly all constructed from British Churchill tanks, and the Americans believed that using foreign tanks would cause vast logistical problems. Hobart, who was unpopular and had been forced to retire as a Major General, was a corporal in the Home Guard when Churchill summoned him for greater things.

The Normandy peninsula juts north-west into the Atlantic. *See Map 6*. It is shaped like a narrow pyramid with a flat top. From the mouth of the Seine, the coastline stretches for 60 miles east to west. Then comes the dog-leg beginning at Carentan, at the south of the Cotentin peninsula, where the coast follows a 30-mile path north-west to the flat top of the pyramid. This is 30 miles in length, with Cherbourg two-thirds of the way to the west. At the western corner, which juts out into the Atlantic, the coastline turns and descends for 70 miles to Avranches, where an estuary divides Normandy from Brittany. Normandy is rich farming country and is enclosed. It is called the *bocage*, with small fields, tall hedges and sunken lanes. It is excellent for defence, particularly when manned by small parties of infantry supported by armour and artillery. But it is dangerous for assaulting troops and is bad tank country. To make matters worse, the country inland from Carentan is also marshy.

During the course of the fighting, the Americans made their tanks more effective through a typical piece of on-the-spot technical improvisation. A 29-year-old NCO in a fighting unit, Sergeant Curtis Culin, found a way of welding metal tusks to the prows of the tanks to uproot the hedges, and these cut directly into the ground so that the tanks did not have to rear up, exposing their vulnerable bellies to enemy fire. On 14 July, Bradley himself ordered all tanks and self-propelled guns to have these ugly but effective devices fitted, and the engineers went immediately to work. As a result of an astonishing feat of logistics, with metal parts being flown from England, within only a week 60 per cent of Bradley's tanks had been fitted with tusks and called Rhinos.

Cracking the Crust

The success of the invasion depended most of all on the German army and how quickly its divisions could concentrate to block the assault. The Germans had an estimated total of fifty-eight divisions in France: a mighty force, although these were not all equal in quality. The German Commander-in-Chief was Field Marshal von Rundstedt. Field Marshal Rommel, who reported to him, commanded Army Group B. This comprised fourteen divisions, and was responsible for the so-called Atlantic Wall. Rommel had spent the early months of 1944 frantically reinforcing this barrier with obstacles, mines and artillery emplacements. He anticipated that the main battle would be on the beaches, but this was not to happen, because of the strength of the assault and in particular the fire support from sea and air.

During the whole time of the invasion, von Rundstedt believed that the invaders would most effectively be defeated by armoured counter-attacks. The most formidable elements of the German army were the SS Panzer divisions. These were aggressively led, all at full strength, and manned with highly trained, fanatical and experienced troops. Their equipment was better than anything possessed by the Allied armies. It comprised the Mark IV, Panther and Tiger tanks, and the *Jagdpanzer* tracked tank destroyer, plus the incomparable 88mm anti-tank gun (a powerful flak weapon with a carriage adapted for horizontal fire: an inspired innovation that was mechanically not possible with the otherwise excellent British 3.7in anti-aircraft gun).

The Allied tanks were mostly Shermans (Plate 16), but the British also had Cromwells ('cruiser' tanks) and the heavy Churchills. All these were less well armed than the German machines, although a quarter of the Shermans, which were named Fireflies, were fitted with British 17-pounder anti-tank guns, excellent by Allied standards although outclassed by the 88mm German anti-tank gun that was also mounted on the Tiger and *Jagdpanzer*. All the Allied tanks were less well protected with armour than the German machines, and the

Shermans, despite the advantages of their reliability and speed, were high off the ground and had a horrible tendency to catch fire if hit. This was because they were gasoline-powered, and the fuel tank and ammunition racks were just inside the outer skin of the vehicle.

The German infantry were also better equipped than the Americans, British and Canadians. The German battalions had large numbers of Spandau Model 42 machine guns, which were belt-fed and had a very high rate of fire; they were also easily portable, unlike the American and British medium machine guns. The German mortars, particularly the six-barrel *Nebelwerfer* (which PP had encountered in Sicily), outclassed the Allied weapons. And the infantry on the ground had better sub-machine guns, stick-handle grenades, and the lethal *Panzerfaust* hand-held launcher that threw a heavy anti-tank bomb: much more powerful than the British PIAT and the American Bazooka.

Perhaps most importantly, the German troops – especially the junior leaders – were better trained than their opponents, and the majority had seen action in Russia. The only Allied troops who had seen shots fired in anger were the airborne divisions – two American and one British – plus three divisions that Montgomery had brought over from the 8th Army. These 8th Army divisions started badly because they were uncomfortable in the *bocage*, which was so different from the open spaces of the desert, although they got their act together after they had seen some action in France. In the American sector, Bradley implemented training programmes for small bodies of infantry to work in cooperation with tanks.

The sole fighting arm in which the Allied forces on the ground excelled was the artillery, especially the field guns. Hence Rommel's tribute that can be found in Chapter 1.

Well before the invasion the planners developed a deception plan, the originality and success of which can still hardly be believed. Before and for some weeks after the invasion, Hitler and the majority of German generals were persuaded that the main assault would be in the Pas de Calais and that Normandy was a feint. A phantom army was set up in south-eastern England, transmitting a high volume of radio traffic, and using imitation tanks, aircraft and landing craft, which could be photographed from the air. Patton commanded this army, and was widely featured in the British press. Reports of the assembly of the troops were transmitted to Germany by the leading German spy in Britain, who was in fact a double agent (and was awarded a German – and also a British – decoration!). As a result of this dense web of deception, the formidable German 15th Army remained in the Pas de Calais and was kept away from Normandy, where its presence might have been decisive. Normandy witnessed for a month or more a race between the Allied divisions arriving by sea on the beaches, and the German divisions arriving by land from the hinterland.

There was yet another brilliant Allied plan, focusing on the flow of German reinforcements. Professor Solly Zuckerman, an academic anatomist and protégé of Tedder, had studied the effects of air bombing on the ground in Sicily and drawn firm conclusions. He developed an interdiction plan for bombing rail networks, junctions and bridges in France during the period before D-Day. British Bomber Command pressed constantly for all effort to continue to blast German cities, and the American argued strongly in favour of attacking German oil production and supplies. However, Tedder, who knew Zuckerman well and had great faith in his scientific insights, personally pushed through the transportation plan. This was implemented and impeded the movement of German reinforcements to Normandy, and was shown after the event to have been amazingly successful. Zuckerman ended his career as Chief Scientific Adviser to the British government and became Lord Zuckerman.

Making a grand slam in the field of deception, the Royal Air Force carried out a remarkable ruse in the Pas de Calais immediately before D-Day. In the continued effort to persuade the Germans that this was where the invasion was going to take place, squadrons of aircraft flew from Dover to Calais in a tightly controlled formation dropping *Window*, the codename for strips of metal that were known to confuse the signals on radar screens. The plan simulated the imminent arrival in France of the large armada, and whose non-arrival caused great confusion.

The most striking feature of the months, weeks and days that led up to the Normandy invasion was the range and depth of the planning. Eisenhower's bold decision implemented in Tunisia to integrate the American and British staffs deserves to be remembered. The D-Day assault would put many lives at stake, and the planners knew it. The plans themselves were the end-product of the dedicated work of many first-class brains. These plans included but went well beyond the complex logistics of delivering eight divisions in an organized fashion to the beaches, supported by heavy, well-directed volumes of naval gunfire and unending air cover. They included a secret nocturnal reconnaissance of the beaches by a Commando, Sergeant Bruce Ogden Smith, who had been a pre-war member of the HAC Infantry and who (unlike his two brothers) had declined a commission. His family business was the manufacture of high-quality fishing tackle, and his firm produced a special type of strong fishing line which Ogden Smith took with him to make measurements on the beaches, where he also took samples of the sand. His work was a vital supplement to the tens of thousands of low-angle oblique photographs from the air that had been taken over all the beaches along the Atlantic coast. (Normandy was not singled out for extra attention, for obvious reasons.)

The most outstanding plan of all was Montgomery's strategy for the battle itself. It was one of two strategic plans during the Second World War in Europe that changed history. The other was von Manstein's *Sichelschnitt*, the rapid armoured advance in 1940 that cut off the British and French armies from their bases, providing the Germany army with its victory in the Battle of France. (Arnhem might have been a third, but it was tragically not to be.)

Montgomery realized that the key to the Battle of Normandy was the Falaise Plain, to the east and south, because this is the direction from which the Germans would be able to assault the left flank of the invading army. Montgomery was therefore determined to establish a firm block. The British army would provide this and would attract all the attention of the SS Panzer Divisions. By holding the Panzers in this way, Montgomery would liberate Bradley to take the Cotentin peninsula and capture Cherbourg, and then take the city of St Lô as a springboard for the main Allied assault into France. In other words, the British would hold the Germans in the east while the Americans would swing out from the west.

Montgomery never wavered from this strategy, although he had to make a number of tactical adjustments because the Panzer opposition was so strong and Montgomery therefore found it very difficult to capture ground. But he needed to be continuously aggressive because the Panzers had to be kept fully occupied. The most important German position in the east of the bridgehead was the ancient Norman city of Caen.

The First Gruelling Month of Battle

On the early morning of 6 June, five infantry divisions hit the beaches. They were landed and supported by 5,000 ships of all sizes. A few hours before, two American airborne divisions had been dropped at the western end of the landing area, and one British airborne division had landed to the east. This total of eight assaulting divisions (and there was also some armour plus Commandos and American Rangers) was twice the force committed to the Sicily landings in July 1943, which had until then been the largest invasion in history. See Map 6.

In the British sector of the Normandy bridgehead, two British divisions and one Canadian landed on three beaches. And in the west, two American divisions landed on a further two beaches. Of the five beach landings, the only one which was brutally contested was that on the American beach codenamed *Omaha*, which was dominated by cliffs from which the German defenders poured heavy artillery and small arms fire. *Omaha* extended out to sea through shallow water for 3 miles, which meant that the thin-skinned landing craft had to be loaded with troops and the DD tanks had to be launched into the water for a long trip to the shore. In the words of the celebrated naval historian Samuel Eliot Morison: 'Altogether, the Germans had provided the best imitation of hell for an invading force that American troops had encountered anywhere. Even the Japanese defenses of Iwo Jima, Tarawa and Peleliu are not to be compared to these.' Nevertheless, as a result of the heroism and determination of the American troops who landed there, this beach was more-or-less secure by the end of the day, and by this time all the other landings were firmly established.

It took a few further days for the forces on the different landings – which stretched for 50 miles – to be joined up. During the early weeks, supplies were often very limited because of the bad weather and the lack of port facilities. Artillery ammunition in particular had to be rationed.

Montgomery planned to capture Caen on the first day, but German counter-attacks made this impossible. From now on, the British slugged it out in and around Caen, while the Americans were capturing ground: the Cotentin peninsula and Cherbourg and then a hotly contested advance through the *bocage* and the marshes to St Lô; and after this, Operation *Cobra*, the American breakout and sweep south and east which started six weeks after D-Day.

The British made three large planned assaults on Caen. These were codenamed *Epsom* (on 25–30 June); *Charnwood* (on 3–8 July); and *Goodwood* (on 18–20 July). *Charnwood* and *Goodwood* were preceded by heavy bombing from British-based aircraft, and fire from ships offshore. This weight of fire devastated buildings, which in turn impeded the armour and even the infantry. Despite heavy casualties among the attackers, these operations yielded little ground. Although most of Caen fell by 11 July, vicious fighting continued in the southern suburbs and countryside 6 miles south of the city. It was during Operation *Charnwood* that the 59th Division entered the battle.

The Last British Reserve

The 59th (Staffordshire) Division was a Territorial formation that had not yet seen action. It was the last of the sixteen British and Canadian divisions that were to join 21st Army Group: evidence that Britain's resources of manpower were running dry. Britain was manning armies in the Mediterranean and the Far East, besides various overseas garrisons away from the firing line. She was also providing airmen and ground crews for the Royal Air Force for their continuous attacks on Germany and the occupied territories, as well as seamen for the Royal Navy and the Merchant Navy in their never-ending battle to keep the sea lanes open for supplies to beleaguered Britain. Further reinforcements to 21st Army Group had to come in 'penny packets', and it was not long before 59th Division, being the newcomer, was itself broken up and cannibalized.

These long-term problems were not however evident in early 1944, when 59th Division was preparing for war. The Division was formed in January 1944 and was soon at full strength, although under a temporary commander. Its ten infantry battalions (three in each of three brigades, plus 7 Northumberland Fusiliers, the Machine-Gun Battalion) contained no Regular units. Most were 'hostilities only', with some Territorials, although it was officially a Territorial Division. And although it was, again officially, based in Staffordshire, only five of its battalions came from the Staffordshire Regiments, but it included a battalion of the Warwickshire Regiment (from the neighbouring county). The remaining four were from other parts of England. 116th Field Regiment, Royal

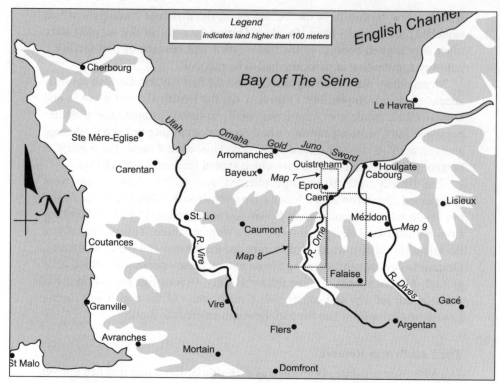

Map 6: Normandy. The D-Day invasion took place on 6 June 1944. The Americans landed on *Utah* and *Omaha* beaches to the west; the British landed at *Gold* and *Sword*; and the Canadians at *Juno*. The major problem facing the Allies was to establish a foothold in enough strength to hold off the formidable German armoured reinforcements that would soon arrive. The landings were successful, although during the first hours the situation was touch-and-go at *Omaha*, where the American beach was at the foot of steep cliffs which the troops stormed up with great heroism. Montgomery, the overall land forces commander, determined the strategy of the invasion, which was to attract the weight of the German forces onto the Anglo-Canadian sector in and around the ancient city of Caen. With this deliberate diversion of the German effort, the Americans would be able to take the port of Cherbourg and clear the top of the Normandy peninsula. Then, when the American strength had been built up, they could sweep out of their bridgehead and race to the west. This strategy was triumphantly successful although it needed six weeks of heavy fighting to bring it off.

Artillery, supported 176th Infantry Brigade, comprising 7 Norfolk, 7 South Staffordshire and 6 North Staffordshire Regiments. 481 Battery, which PP commanded, was attached to the Norfolks and the two units developed a warm and successful cooperation.

The Division, still with its temporary commander, got to work energetically in January and began a rigorous programme of exercises: a total of seventeen before the Division sailed for Normandy. A few were indoor 'cloth models' to test the efficiency of the different levels of command, but they became increasingly full-scale 'schemes' carried out in realistic tactical conditions in the field.

Montgomery visited the Division on 3 February to judge its quality, and was obviously satisfied. The King came on 2 March, always an event that boosted the morale of all ranks of any formation or unit he visited. On 29 March the permanent commander, Major General Lyne, arrived. He had come from the fighting in Italy, and immediately took a firm 'grip' on the Division. He was to have a successful wartime career. As mentioned earlier, Montgomery had brought from the Mediterranean three prestigious British formations to stiffen 2nd Army that was to invade Normandy. But in the initial fighting their performance was disappointing because they were uncomfortable fighting in the *bocage*, which was so different from their previous battlefields. Of these three formations, 7th Armoured Division (the celebrated 'Desert Rats') had a particularly difficult time, and two divisional commanders were quickly sacked. After 59th Division was disbanded at the end of the Battle for Normandy, Lyne was given command of the 7th Armoured Division, which fought splendidly through the whole course of the campaign, the advance from Normandy to the Baltic.

On 4 April, Lieutenant General Dempsey, Commander of 2nd Army, came to meet the senior officers of the Division. He was 'a safe pair of hands' (an appropriate metaphor for a noted amateur cricketer, which Dempsey was). Dempsey had earned his military reputation as a Corps Commander in Sicily, and was much respected by Montgomery, although he was often short-circuited when Montgomery gave orders directly to divisions from his Tactical Headquarters.

On 5 April, General Ritchie, Commander of XII Corps, gave a pep-talk to the officers of the Division. Ritchie was a talented Scotsman who had fought in the desert under Auchinleck. He had made his reputation as a staff officer, but as a mere Major General had been given – prematurely and unsuccessfully – command of 8th Army. Although 59th Division was in XII Corps during the months leading to its arrival in Normandy, it was transferred to 1 Corps at the end of June.

On 24 April, Lyne himself addressed all the officers. And on 13 May he talked to all company commanders and above about his experiences in Italy. 59th Division finished its last exercise on 30 June and immediately prepared to move to Normandy. The War Diary was appropriately optimistic about how the troops visualized their forthcoming baptism of fire: 'All ranks are glad that the period of training has now changed its character and are full of optimism, ready for whatever operation they may be required to undertake. Morale is high.' Secret Operational Instructions for 59th Division's initial tasks in Normandy had been prepared and distributed on 10 June. A first Intelligence Summary, also secret, was distributed on 29 June. This was accurate in detail and obviously derived from *Sigint* (but naturally without attribution). A sketch map was included showing the dispositions of seven German divisions in the 2nd Army sector of Normandy. The Summary also included detailed assessments of various types of German tanks. 59th Division would soon encounter them. On 27 June the Divisional Battle Log had been opened, recording events before, and leading up to, the first clash of arms.

To return to PP's role in 59th Division, he had finished a three-month Senior Officer's course at Brasenose College, Oxford, in December 1943 and received a good rating. In January 1944 he joined the 59th Division and was posted to the 116th Field Regiment. Shortly after the Regiment's arrival in France, it received a new Commanding Officer, a Regular, Lieutenant Colonel 'Streak' Corbett, whom PP had met before the war. (He was called 'Streak' because he was exceptionally tall and thin.) As mentioned, PP took command of 481 Battery. His many months of front-line action in Tunisia and Sicily made him obviously valuable in a job involving the direct command of troops. By this stage of the war, the British army was following the policy of enriching inexperienced units with men who had seen shots fired in anger.

The first months of 1944 were spent in training for war, tidying up the affairs of the Battery, and – most importantly – providing time for PP to get to know the officers and men. A total of nine officers reported to him, three Captains and six Subalterns. This was the full establishment to provide two Troop Commanders, officers in charge of gun lines and OPs, and officers marching as FOOs. This total number allowed for rotations when the Battery was in action for long periods, which it usually was. There are three group photographs, Plates 9, 10 and 11, that show all the men in the Battery. The officers are identified, and also some of the men who appear in the diary.

The Battery was stationed in Kent, within easy distance of London. When news came that the invasion had started, and the V1s began to fall on south-east England, it was clear that 116th Regiment would soon go to war. The Regiment was commanded (as mentioned) by Lieutenant Colonel 'Streak' Corbett. The three Batteries were 243 (commanded by Major John Brazier, who was killed on 9 August 1944, and succeeded by Major Tom Whitehead), 244 (commanded by Major Johnny Kell) and 481 (commanded by PP). 481 Battery had a strength of 10 officers (including PP) plus 174 Other Ranks. The names that appear most often in the diary are Captain Dick Plant, Captain Basil Johnson and Captain Martin Tonge. The other six were Subalterns, and John Sherren and Derek Farr are mentioned fairly often. (After the war, Farr who was an actor appeared in a number of popular films.)

Before getting to the extracts of PP's diary written when he was a Battery Commander, here is a reprise of some of the description from Chapter 1 of how Field artillery batteries were organized and their fire was controlled. As a general rule, a Field battery supported an infantry battalion, and there was an intimate relationship between the two. PP used for his personal transport a half-track: a clumsy, partially armoured vehicle that had wheels in the front and tracks in the rear. It moved well over difficult ground, and carried signallers and a good deal of kit. He also had a Jeep.

Regimental Headquarters (RHQ) controlled the three batteries, each of which was relatively self-contained. Each battery was deployed in five functional groups:

Command Post (CP); Static Observation Post (OP); OPs with the infantry; Gun Position (GP); and Wagon Line (WL). Although the battery commander's position was in his CP, he was for much if not most of the time with the battalion he was supporting. During the operations of a battery, reliable radio communication was immensely important. Radio was the contact between CP and Battery Commander; battery and RHQ; battery and other batteries; battery and higher formations; and of course within the battery: from CP to guns, static OPs to guns, and FOOs to guns.

From PP's diary, the batteries in 116th Field Regiment changed their positions surprisingly often, and this meant much planning work for officers and warrant officers, and a great deal of labour for the NCOs and men. In a battery, the order of events was sighting the guns and 'surveying-in'. Then there was camouflaging, followed urgently by digging. While these jobs were under way, ammunition had to be transported – eighty shells weighed almost a ton, and there were also cartridges, containing bags of cordite to fire the shells. While PP was constantly on the move, his Captains and Subalterns were occupied with gun positions and OPs. These had to be manned 24 hours a day, and officers' duties had to be staggered, to allow for rest periods.

As in earlier chapters, the diary and other excerpts are dated and indented.

PP letter to his father, 6 June 1944
It's started – and seems so quiet that one can hardly visualize the scrap and the noise that must be going on at the places invaded. Not for some days yet shall we hear anything like a full story, the situation must sort itself out, but I feel sure that it cannot fail, with the experiences of Africa, Sicily, Italy etc. to draw on, and the tried and experienced planners and leaders we have now.

I was delighted with the alert and flashing eyes of the men this morning, they really are delighted at the prospects and work with added verve and vigour because the long years of training and waiting are over. I always knew that they would all liven up a lot once over the water, but they have caught it already! War is a tonic when you are in it [*as mentioned, the same optimism was recorded in the Divisional War Diary on 30 June*].

PP diary, 21 June 1944
Up 05:30 and back before camp astir. Fly bombs in the night, they are a

long procession rather than a concentrated raid. People hate them, blast effect terrific but little penetration. Back to Kensington Close for dinner.

22 June 1944

As I looked out of a first floor window at the school [*where he was billeted*] I was fascinated by a fly bomb coming straight for me 'between the eyes'. When the engine cut out I ducked and in due course there was a terrific explosion. It had come down on a goods train, bits flying all over, several wagons on fire, windows out three hundred yards or more away. Kensington again PM.

As a celebration of his forthcoming adventure, PP had lunch on 23 June and also on 25 June at Scott's, one of the premiere old-established London restaurants (which moved to grand premises in Mount Street, Mayfair, during the 1970s). PP and his guests ate lobsters on both occasions. Food during the war was strictly rationed, but fish was available fairly freely during the season, and lobsters, crabs, oysters and salmon could be obtained although at high prices. Wine was scarce and expensive because supplies from France had stopped in 1939. On 26 June, the Battery left for war.

26 June 1944

Left 17:30 and embarked in *Empire Pickwick*. Men and officers crowded in holds with either hammock or palliasse. Five of us in sick bay for two! Slept nine hours and didn't hear a bomb close by.

27 June 1944

Left Victoria Dock at about 08:00 and lay up off Southend behind the boom. Masses of ships everywhere. Odd flying bombs about. Slept all PM and we sailed about 20:30. Whole estuary full of ships; brilliant sunset. Had some self-heating soup which was very good. Slept nine hours.

28 June 1944

Sea kind, hardly any movement, saw Beachy Head and the Seven Sisters in the haze. Second in starboard line, but after lunch began to drop back and nearly everyone passed us. Own cookers on steel decks. Channel full of ships once we turned south. Slept PM. As we neared France caught up to our place in the convoy which slowed down and came to rest about two miles off shore by 22:00. Slept well, air raid hardly heard. Saw doodle bombs fairly scooting over the Channel, lads saw some hit by Spitfires but I only saw puff of smoke in air. Saw *Royal Ulsterman* again – spent Christmas Day 1942 on her in the Med.

PP letter to his father, 2 July 1944
This invasion is a grand sight, the sea is full of ships and the sky full of aircraft – all ours of course – and Normandy seems to be full of our troops too. The enemy is in a bad way if he can't do a single thing about it, at sea or in the air.

PP diary, 29 June 1944
Up at 08:00, no Royal Engineers to unload us till about 13:00. I was first ashore of our party from an American LCT about 16:00 at Asnelles-sur-Mer and on to concentration area by 08:30. Sky full of own aircraft, sea full of hundreds and hundreds of own ships and land full of own troops. Green and wooded, heaps of magpies and pigeons. Sleep under apple tree full of mistletoe and small caterpillars. Heavy rain and thunderstorms.

30 June 1944
Battery gradually arriving all day, complete by about tea time less some transport which was put into too deep water. Went to find it in a Jeep and they were getting on well with it and I hope it will be in this PM. Saw 150 heavies bomb to the south east about 19:00, little flak and none down as far as I could see. Clouds of fighters. It was Villers Bocage. The twenty-four hour [*Compo*] ration very good indeed. Much less noisy here at the moment than with the doodle bugs. This is quite unlike previous invasions. I never imagined there could be so many hundreds of ships in the same area and the sky full of aircraft – as we only saw towards the end in Sicily. Sometimes you can't hear yourself think.

As PP was soon to discover, the battle ground was much more densely crowded than in Tunisia and Sicily, with large numbers of troops – Allied and German – packed into a relatively confined space. This meant a greater volume of artillery and small arms fire, and more casualties. The summer countryside and the local inhabitants were welcoming. The troops were surprised at the plentiful amounts of dairy products, which were a change from strictly rationed Britain.

Although it was a luxury to buy occasionally some of the produce of the local farms, a small and unsung innovation of the Allied invasion of Normandy was something that significantly improved the food that the soldiers took into the field. When troops are concentrated in battalions or regiments, food preparation is centralized: in cookhouses for the privates and junior NCOs, and separate messes for the senior NCOs and the officers. This is also generally possible when companies, batteries and squadrons are operating separately. But when soldiers are in contact with the enemy in small sub-units of platoons or sections, individuals do their own cooking, using ingredients issued to them.

The innovation introduced during the invasion was the Compo ration pack, which PP mentions in his diary on 30 June and 5 July. During the early years of the war, the troops received canned food in reasonable quantity, although they quickly got bored with the lack of variety: corned (bully) beef, meat & vegetables (M&V), bacon and sausages: basic foods chosen without imagination and typical of the rations provided to the armed forces in earlier years. Bread was rarely available, and the main source of carbohydrate was 'hard tack' biscuits, which could be digested only if they were slowly mashed in hot water to make a type of porridge. (The German army food was just as bad, if not worse. The Germans greatly enjoyed British bully beef when they captured British food supplies.)

The Compo ration pack, first issued on a small scale in Tunisia, was based on the American K Ration. One box provided a day's food in the field for one man. It contained cans of various ingredients, also dehydrated vegetables, chocolate, biscuits and other things. It was enough for two well-balanced main meals plus a snack, with plentiful calories to support an active life. Every soldier had a portable 'Tommy Cooker,' a small metal frame that could hold a metal mess tin, under which was a small block of solid fuel that could be lit with a match. Water could therefore be boiled for tea and for cooking dehydrated vegetables. An important feature of the Compo ration packs was that the menus varied. The boxes came in quantities that could be shared out between a number of soldiers, so that they had a choice of which box to select. Compo rations were very popular, and an instruction leaflet from one of PP's own ration packs is shown in Plate 12.

1 July 1944
A welcome day, to clean off waterproofing, charge batteries and generally get ready for the battle – lucky. Saw a green woodpecker in our orchard-cum-hayfield. Started on the farm butter (three shillings a pound), milk and eggs, cream cheese demi-sel, and Camembert (one shilling) not quite ripe yet. All very good, we shall make the most of them whilst we are in this area. Spuds, meat, green veg. and bread not allowed. Crops have suffered and there will not be so much corn, but then the Boche won't be here to pinch it so it balances out probably. They simply help themselves, the locals spit and say 'sales Boches!' with venom. Very wet evening, played Crap and won three hundred francs. Bath in bucket.

2 July 1944
Holy Communion after breakfast; we are put at six hours' notice from 12:00. Conference HQRA 21:00. Arranged to do recce for PM occupation tomorrow. Plenty of time, all laid on nicely before bed. We're living on Compo rations.

3 July 1944
At 01:20 message that we receive 400 rounds per gun at 07:15. Laid it all

on for 05:00 and had another two hours' sleep. Left at 05:30, poor area, chock full already, but used cornfields and folds in the ground. Very wet all day till late, heavy rain, much traffic, much mud. We are to fire barrage, no OPs, for Canadian attack on Carpiquet airfield. Met Bob Rowland Clark [*late A Battery HAC*] coming out of a one-holer in a garden I got my eye on. He is now in 153rd (Leicester Yeomanry) Field Regiment, Guards Armoured Division. He had seen 13th Regiment [*HAC, Royal Horse Artillery*], but direct hit on Command Post had prevented him getting information he wanted. All dug in ready to sleep after 20:00, when Regiment detailed to send CO's representative to meet Colonel, General Staff, of the Royal Canadian Artillery, and remain until barrage started. In the absence of the Commanding Officer and Second-in-Command, I detailed myself. Went about 20:30 to St. Mauview and found Jack Evans and Norman Roberts [*representatives of the 61st and 110th Field Regiments, both in 59th Division*] at 8th Canadian Brigade Headquarters. Much damaged, sniper stories, smell of death everywhere. We dug again until midnight and put roof on slit and sleeping bay.

4 July 1944

Slept four hours again till at 04:20. Jack [*Evans*] said we are to watch opening line of barrage – almost impossible in the dark. Went solo with one 38 set between us [*this was an infantry man-pack radio set; artillery equipment was generally much more efficient than that used by the infantry*]. Country too flat to see much, but bursts seemed about right if we had known where they were supposed to be! Up went two Verey lights and down came enemy mortars about the Start Line and some away left. The Colonel said we had finished. The Brigadier said we had advanced 700 yards. OK, so I returned to Battery and saw guns fire the last half hour or so. BBC told us the result at midday – pretty quick I thought. Holmes [*PP's batman*] lost screw filler cap to petrol burner so we are now without. Slept well PM. CO conference 21:00. Saw two lots of enemy aircraft after writing Joy [*PP's wife*] that none yet seen! Two shot down.

A slit trench is the first thing we do on arriving anywhere – it's like taking your hat off entering a house. Last night three men sugared off to get wood and potatoes, leaving one to dig for all. They are the most untidy lot I have ever seen, stuff all over the place, what we'd do if we had to go off somewhere in a hurry I can't imagine, we'd never even start. I shall have them all together at food time and read the riot act.

The rain gets in everywhere, even drips through the hood of the half-track. Thanks be for my waterproof oilskin suit though it sweats inside and swooshes as you walk.

5 July 1944

At last getting latrines sorted out, you have to tell the men again and again, day after day, to try and prevent stinking open pits, no camouflage, and the men looking like tramps. Move this PM is off, so went to baths at Bayeux for Dames and Messieurs, dated 1843. There are nine sort of cubicles and ten baths. Waited over an hour but got really clean, hair and all, for 15 francs. Small pear-shaped bath, brass swan's head taps, cork floating in water attached to plug! Then bought some postcards, had a glass of wine and one of the local Calvados, which tastes like radishes but it is distilled from cider. Hotel Lion d'Or set back from street, very attractive with window boxes full of flowers overlooking the courtyard into which one drives. No drink there, suppose the Press get it all. Plenty of them. Town is untouched by war. Very nice Cathedral with only one small pane of glass broken (didn't go in), compare that with St. Paul's!! Masses of cheese in shops. Most civilian shoes have wooden soles.

The boxed tinned rations, known as Compo. are very good indeed. Breakfast was sausage, biscuits, jam, butter and tea. Lunch was steak & kidney pudding, biscuits, fruit salad, rice pudding and tea. There is also lovely plain chocolate and really good boiled sweets to fill the gaps. Supper will probably be sardines, or salmon or cheese.

I have only spoken to one Frenchman, an old chap who remembers the two previous wars with Germany. Dick [*Captain Plant, 481 Battery*] has got us another cap for the stove, so we are all set again now for our Ovaltine or Bovril which we have in ration box.

6 July 1944

D Troop shelled unintentionally PM. The enemy fire at farms and buildings, road junctions, dust and places they know we'll be in – so we're not. Ten casualties including Sergeant Cooke and Lance Bombadier Read, killed some fifteen yards from me. Probably dust of trucks passing drew fire which was mostly to the right of us. We had only moved in, in columns of dust like Africa, in the morning and digging was well on but a lot of the men were around cookhouse at the time. I told them to disperse and get back to their gun pits and the damage occurred while doing this. Cooke one of the nicest of chaps, not a mark on him until we found a tiny hole in his neck; Read had a gaping hole in his side; the troop behaved well. The difference now from the early days is most apparent, this is the place to learn quickly. A day of conferences; called at 7 Norfolk PM. Went to burials at 21:00 by the station, salvos of our Mediums, thunder and lightning provided effective graveside volleys. Late conference with CO, bed 01:30. Last night he kept me up till midnight talking, good fun though. I remember him as a Subaltern in

3rd Regiment, Royal Horse Artillery, at Aldershot at the 1932 HAC camp. He said he made £500 p.a. racing but only bets on the big races.

One of the gunners at RHQ shot himself through the foot after/during the shelling. Our first self-inflicted wound?

7 July 1944

Very noisy night, apparently AA but some others, bits fell around. This is a very noisy and intense war. The enemy has more artillery than in Africa but a mere drop in the ocean compared with ours. A day of orders and conferences before the Division's first battle tomorrow. Not a hope of getting up to see the ground or getting the rest from 3 – 8PM, as ordered by Ian Freeland [*Lieutenant Colonel and Battalion Commander, see Plate 14*] to 7 Norfolk. Will be very very tired by the time it eases up a bit. Teeing up all day; to 7 Norfolk at 20:00. Move up about 22:30 and dig in other end by 03:00 in corn near Le Landel.

Three of D Troop's wounded moved back today. I hear some are in England already! Got a bit on edge over the coming battle but a quiet meal and sit down helped a lot. The Infantry do not seem to have any patrol information and country is very close, feel we may be in for a costly fight. Much relieved when neither Troop Commander had to march with the Infantry. Basil Johnson [*Captain in 481 Battery*] was going to and I had misgivings but he is Liaison Officer with 3rd Division, on left now. Personally I don't like war and all this beastly noise, but it's got to be done and we may as well get on with it. I pray I may do my duty and that we shall be alright, an anxious time.

Caen, the city that was blocking the advance of the British 2nd Army – and at the same time attracting, as planned, all major German reinforcements to the Normandy front – was a mere 9 miles south of the coast. Operation *Charnwood*, the second major assault on Caen, had been under way since the Canadians attacked Carpiquet Airfield (to which PP refers). The main attack was now made by three divisions of the British I Corps: 3rd Canadian to the west, 59th in the centre and 3rd British in the east. They were assisted by two armoured brigades and there was heavy fire support. An important part of 59th Division's role in Operation *Charnwood* was the attack by 7 Norfolk on the village of Epron, 3 miles north of the outer fringes of Caen. The Battalion was supported by 481 Battery, and PP fought the battle in Battalion Headquarters. See Map 7. This story will be told in Chapter 5.

Caen and Falaise – The Climax of the Battle

Caen was a bataille d'usure*: a grinding attritional clash of arms as disheartening and expensive in life and materiel as the First World War. It was gruelling for the attacking British and Canadians, and also for the defending Germans. But it was not apparent to the soldiers on both sides that Montgomery's strategy was to attract and hold the main German strength in Normandy until the time was ripe for the American 1st Army – when it had overwhelming superiority in its sector – to spring forward and sweep to the east and south.*

Caen the Cockpit

Caen is not a big city, but it is the second largest in Normandy (after Rouen). It has a rich history from the Middle Ages, and possesses a fine castle and ancient buildings, many of which were badly damaged in the fighting. In 1944, the population of the city was about 100,000; and in greater Caen, including the suburbs, about 400,000. The River Orne and the parallel Caen Canal, a mile to the west, flow north-east through the city to reach the English Channel, 9 miles away. There are seven roads radiating from the city (none of course modern *autoroutes*). Greater Caen spreads rather untidily in the form of a cross for about 3 miles from west to east, and about the same distance from north to south.

Montgomery had planned to capture Caen on D-Day, but the fact that this did not happen did not ruffle him because the fierce German resistance there contributed to the eventual success of his strategic plan of attracting German forces to the east in order to relax their pressure in the west. However, the air chiefs thought differently. They were anxious to capture existing and potential airfields around Caen, and they anticipated that this would happen soon after D-Day, in accordance with Montgomery's original plan. The air forces in the field in fact improvised landing grounds within the invasion perimeter that were good enough to provide massive air cover for the fighting troops, and this meant that the airfields at Caen were not in the event as important as had been originally thought.

Nevertheless, the air chiefs, Tedder and Coningham in particular, continued to put pressure on Montgomery, and they enlisted Eisenhower to add the considerable weight of his authority; there is even an unverified story that Churchill also stepped in to support Eisenhower. Caen now took priority. Its capture was in line with Montgomery's strategic plan, although he was not totally happy since he was reluctant as always to incur too many casualties.

Reinforcements continued to arrive in the American and British sectors during June. But while there was no cut-off in the number of fresh troops arriving from the United States, the British army was running out of men and Montgomery knew this very well. He always operated with great care to preserve human life, but Britain's manpower shortage underscored the importance of maintaining the existing strength of the British troops under Montgomery's command. By early July, the last of the British divisions landed. 59th (Staffordshire) was the final one to arrive.

During the first month of the campaign, the British and Canadian armies had only progressed about 6 miles from the coast towards Caen. In Operation *Epsom* on 25–30 June 1944, some progress was made to the west of the city but there was no breakthrough. The next two offensives – Operations *Charnwood* (on 3–8 July) and *Goodwood* (on 18–20 July) – were stronger, but again only partially successful. These two operations also saw a major innovation. For *Charnwood*, in addition to fire from 700 field pieces and ships offshore, heavy bombing support from the Royal Air Force prepared the way for the troops on the ground.

It is not totally clear where in the military hierarchy the decision was made to bring in the bombers, but it was certainly 'at a high political level', which meant Eisenhower's headquarters. At 22:00 on 7 July, 467 heavy aircraft dropped 2,562 tons of bombs, most with delayed action fuses, on northern Caen. At 20:00, before the advance on the ground, 6,000 bombs that exploded on impact were also unloaded in 60 minutes. This massive display of firepower greatly improved the spirits of the attacking troops. But besides this effect on morale, what the bombing accomplished was disappointing. It produced mountains of rubble that impeded the attacking armour and infantry. And after the bombing was over Professor Zuckerman – who had unique experience of the effects of aerial bombardment – concluded that few if any German positions had been hit.

As mentioned in Chapter 4, Operation *Charnwood* witnessed the first appearance of 59th Division on the field of battle. 481 Battery, commanded by PP, played a rôle in one of the small but important engagements of the battle, the capture of Epron, a village 3 miles north of Caen. This turned out to be a tough experience for him, but one full of lessons, in particular the extent of confusion on the battlefield in engagements as intense as those in Normandy.

'A Dirty Battle and a Very Dangerous One'

This quotation comes from the report after the battle by the Commanding Officer of 116th Field Regiment. He should have added that it was also a very successful tactical operation, but all too typical of the unrelenting and heated day-to-day exchanges of fire, attack and counter-attack that characterized the fight for Caen.

On 8 July three divisions were to make the assault. 59th Division was in the centre: two brigades forward with 176th Brigade to the east, supported by 116th Field Regiment. The brigade's objectives were three villages in open cornfields which turned out to be heavily occupied by the Germans. The largest was Epron, the specific objective of 7 Norfolk, commanded by Lieutenant Colonel Freeland, a tough and able commander who would end his career as a Lieutenant General and earn the nickname 'Smiling Death'. The Norfolks were supported by an armoured squadron and by 481 Battery, with PP accompanying battalion headquarters. 59th Division had available six Field and two Medium regiments, and the Field regiments were supplied with 650 rounds per gun. PP was therefore able to call on massive firepower, although there were also many calls for fire support from other units. As well as Epron, the other two villages were La Bijude (½ mile north) and Couvre-Chef (½ mile south-west). *See Maps 6 and 7.*

H-Hour was 04:30 hours on 8 July, and most of the fighting took place on that day although much 'tidying up' was necessary during the course of 9 July. At the beginning, the preparatory gun fire kicked up masses of dust and smoke and this led to groups of men moving blindly during the fighting on the ground. Most radio communications failed, which caused serious problems and obviously handicapped PP in his ability to transmit fire orders. The diary provides continuous evidence of the additional confusion caused by imperfect communications, which among other problems made it almost impossible for subordinate commanders to locate and receive instructions from their Commanding Officers. Among the specific difficulties was the failure of all the 18 sets (infantry backpack radios) in Battalion Headquarters of 7 Norfolk Regiment. In addition, an incorrect Verey signal was sent that La Bijude had been captured, which it had not, so that the Norfolks had to send a rifle company as a reinforcement to complete the job (see below). And the eventual attack on Epron was made because the Brigadier had false information that British tanks were already in the village. Because of the confusion on the ground and the poor communications, the three battalions of 176th Brigade soon became mixed, although local initiatives led to effective cooperation in the battle.

Throughout the fighting there was constant enemy machine-gun and mortar fire and British and German casualties were heavy. 7 Norfolks had to carry out much sticky fighting even before getting to Epron. At 14:00 hours, one of its rifle companies, D Company, distinguished itself and managed to clear La Bijude, despite the loss of half its strength. At 19:00, the battalion moved on to Epron, but although PP called on supporting fire from the artillery, it was already heavily engaged in firing on enemy trenches west of La Bijude. These had to be attacked by infantry from 6 North Staffordshires, supported by flame-throwing 'Crocodiles'. At last, 7 Norfolks, mainly composed of the remaining men of D Company who had returned, plus a company of 7 South Staffordshires, secured Epron and advanced 500yd to the south and pushed out patrols. In the battle, the battalion suffered 153 casualties in killed, wounded and missing; 116th Field Regiment lost 17 men. There were 350 enemy prisoners taken. The engagement marked a measurable step towards the capture of Caen.

PP's account of the battle took the form of a report which his Commanding Officer asked him to write. It is a vivid account of a fierce day of fighting, and is a view (using military clichés) from the 'sharp-end' through the 'fog of war'. It is not intended to be an objective and comprehensive picture of the Epron engagement as a whole. But its perspective carries an unmistakable whiff of powder and it is almost possible to hear the whistle of bullets and shell splinters.

Editorial additions have been italicized. PP's diary resumes on 9 July.

PP official report, 8 July 1944
The Preparation
On 8 July, the Battery was in close support of 7 Royal Norfolk Regiment for their attack on Epron, their first battle. I and one 481 Battery Troop Commander [*Captain Martin Tonge*] joined the Battalion the previous evening. Martin then went off to establish an OP in the FDLs [*Forward Defended Localities*] of 1 Suffolk Regiment [*the right-hand battalion in the 3rd Division, to the east of 59th Division*]. This OP was east of Chateau de la Lande, where he dug all night and was in a reasonable trench for observation from a hedge by H-Hour – and well stonked most of the morning.

Battalion moved up to FUP [*Forming-Up Place*] north-east of Le Landel [*½ mile north of the Chateau*] in open cornfields about 20:00 hours on 7 July, and essential vehicles including anti-tank guns and my half-track moved about midnight to park in a field (much too close together) north-west of Le Landel by 01:15. There we all dug slits, I slept one hour and breakfast arrived about 03:30. The Tank Liaison Officer, Royal Engineer representative, and Anti-Tank Troop Commander were there also, and we were to meet the Commanding Officer of the Norfolks [*Lieutenant Colonel Freeland*] and establish a Command Post before the Battalion was committed. Some AA fire and aircraft during the night. H-Hour was 04:30, at which time the first phase would begin: attack on La Bijude by 6 North Staffords [*also in 176th Brigade*]. When that was taken and 3rd British Division on our left had taken Lebisey, 7 Norfolks were to be launched on Epron across the cornfields east of Le Landel and Chateau de la Lande [*the plan would soon unravel*].

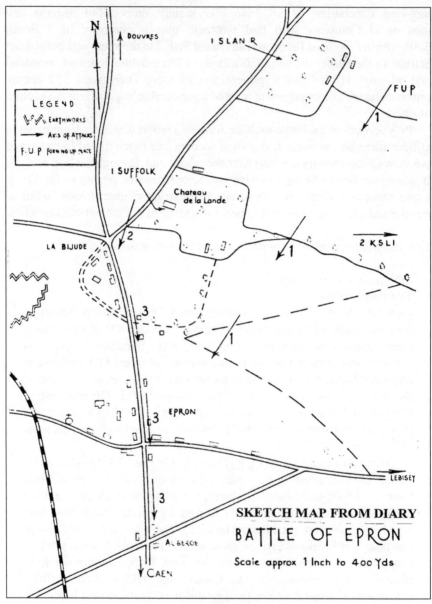

Map 7: Epron. 59th Division was the last of the British divisions to land in Normandy. (The numbers of troops available in Britain for deployment had become very low by this time.) This division included 116th Field Regiment, Royal Artillery, in which PP commanded 481 Battery. This battery supported 7 Royal Norfolk Regiment, which soon established an enviable fighting reputation. On 8 July 1944, 7 Royal Norfolk and 481 Battery fought a vicious but successful battle at Epron, which played a minor role in Operation *Charnwood*, the first phase of the British assault on Caen. This is an original sketch map from the diary.

The First Moves

The worst day of my life.

Just before 04:00, the Tank Liaison Officer, John Wardlaw, said the infantry Commanding Officer wanted to meet him at H-Hour at the north-east corner of the wood behind Le Landel. Royal Engineers were not ready. Infantry Anti-Tank Commander got a lift in my half-track which, with John's scout car, set off for the rendezvous. On arrival about 04:20, I got out of the half-track and went on thirty yards or so to talk to the Tank Liaison Officer, but could see no sign of the infantry Commanding Officer in the half light.

Sharp on time, the fire plan opened up and within five minutes what must have been the enemy DF [*Defensive Fire*] task came down on Le Landel and all along the wall at the back of it where we were. John and I leaped into a one-man slit under the wall beside us and wished it was larger. Things exploded all round, and even with head below ground could feel the blast; we were right in the stonk. After what seemed half-an-hour it stopped and we got out. Both cars seemed OK. I went to mine and found Milner [*PP's driver*] lying by the front wheel untouched. Beside him was the infantry Anti-Tank Commander hit in the leg. Inside the half-track was Gunner Taylor, obviously dead from a piece through the side of his face but sitting up exactly as usual. Bombadier Malam slumped in his seat unconscious but breathing regularly. Gunner Chalk looking rather surprised with both hands covered in blood trying to help, and Gunner Holmes [*PP's batman*] untouched. We discovered later two tiny bits breaking the skin on temple and forearm. Told John to count us out for a bit, tried to bind up Chalk who was nearest; four stretcher bearers arrived and took over. [*PP wrote a letter to Chalk's mother. He was evacuated to England with a 'Blighty' wound and sent PP a cheerful letter from his hospital bed*]

Went to find John Wardlaw and the infantry Commanding Officer but could not, more shells and bombs arrived, but not so intense. Returned to half-track and found they had got them all out into a slit under the wall. Tried radio sets. Could get no reading at all on the 19, although receiving well; the 22 set could not give a sign of life; and the 18 set had a chunk clean through it [*the 19 set was made for Armoured Fighting Vehicles on the move; the 22 set was for short-range divisional communication; the 18 set was infantry backpack equipment*]. More shelling, John turned up and said no sign of infantry Commanding Officer and was going back to vehicle park for news of him [*there were no effective 18 sets in Battalion Headquarters*].

Collected Gunners Holmes and Milner who were magnificent. Decided to go forward to find Martin Tonge's carrier and get a signaller onto the sets. Untangled barbed wire from the tracks. Looked around the

Chateau, odd shelling, but no luck, and the Suffolks' CO [*from 3rd British Division on the left*] could not say where they were. Returned to edge of wood, the casualties evacuated by then. John returned saying they had no news of infantry Commanding Officer back there; he was going into FUP area to try and find him. I said we must get radio going and would come back here at 08:30 to meet him. Despatch rider came by and said CO would be by a lone tree some 400 yards east. Went off again and this time eventually found carrier, east of Chateau behind a bit of wall. Got Hughes [*signaller*] on to my sets, took his 18 set and tried to get infantry CO on it but could get no answer. No one could tell me where he had got to. Hughes got the 22 set going but not the 19.

Went back to find John a bit late, no sign of him at all. Went along towards lone tree, met the Medical Officer of the Norfolks and some assistants, who reported snipers, with odd bullets flying over. Tried crawling, some 'pings' seemed to be in the wire fence just above me. Very tired crawling, shells came over and a party of wounded left the lone tree. Waited for them, they said CO had gone forward with his Command Post, started to crawl back, too hot, so tried running in short bursts. Don't believe there were any snipers at all – just the overs. Returned to Martin's carrier and tried the 18 set again. Heard D Company asking tanks for fire on machine-guns to left flank. Ordered M Target [*fire from the Regiment*], but guns had taken off on U Target [*fire from all guns in the Division*], so that was no good. No answer to offers of assistance to the infantry; couldn't get CO, only D Company.

D Company then started along by us going west, saw Freddy Crocker [*Officer Commanding D Company*] who said the infantry CO was some 300 yards east of us up the line of trees [*D Company was now attacking La Bijude*]. PP's Commanding Officer then arrived with Brigadier, went along together. More shells, got into Boche one-man slit; must have been a small man. It was then arranged that infantry CO go into Epron in a tank; Martin to go in another with a 22 set as well, ready to be humped if required; and I to go with CO in the lee of his tank with the half-track and Martin Tonge's carrier. Went back to fix this, called Martin back, got my 22 set out, improvised one set of remote controls and cable between us. No sign of his tank which was to come to the carrier. Eventually the Battalion Intelligence Officer came by and said the CO had gone on, he knew nothing of Martin's tank and was on his way with Battalion HQ to join D Company west of the Chateau. Decided we'd better follow.

La Bijude

We placed 22 set in half-track and went round onto the road west of Chateau, packed with stationery anti-tank guns and Sherman tanks. Went up towards head of column, and within 200 yards of road junction they said it was not safe to go any further; some tanks brewed up. Inquired for Norfolks' CO and was told he was in the line of trees half right, but snipers were active. Walked over expecting a bullet at every step, but found 6 North Staffordshires there and no Norfolks, so returned. Some shelling, one big dud within ten yards of half-track. Saw some Norfolks and North Staffordshires coming back by the brew-ups, put them in fire positions along track and trees. They said others forward in La Bijude, so took 38 set [*infantry backpack radio*] and went to see. Heavily stonked as I passed crossroads, lay in slight ditch, set wouldn't work so left it. Found mixed Norfolks and North Staffordshires and edge of buildings on right, no officers or NCOs. They did not know where the enemy was. Cross to east of road and found Freddy [*Crocker*] digging in, no sign of CO. Went back for Martin to do FOO with D Company, couldn't find 38 set at all, stonked again, lost map case and assumed set destroyed. Martin went off with another 38 set [*by this time, La Bijude had been taken, mainly by D Company, 7 Norfolks*].

Jim Walker [*Captain, commanding 7 Norfolk Support Company*] came along, saying CO forward in trees and had sent for him and every available man, but he was the only one. Went up with him, well stonked again, found Freddy OK, and my 38 set en route. He saw a fire burning in a building 100 yards away and shot it up for snipers. Odd bullets around all the time, village quite wrecked and houses burning in places. Looked at forward sections in hedges beyond Freddy's Company Headquarters, but no sign of CO anywhere. Left Martin in observation with them and returned to half-track.

Commanding Officer of 116th Field Regiment sent message that Second-in-Command of the Norfolks was coming down main axis in a few minutes and not to miss him. No sign at all in a quarter of an hour, and a soldier nearby said that Lieutenant Colonel Freeland was in an orchard three hundred yards behind us. Went along at once and found an Orders Group about to start. Freeland had no news of the Norfolks' A, B and C Companies and had been ordered to take Epron with the remainder of the Battalion, some tanks and A Company of 7 South Staffordshires (also in 176th Brigade). Protested to no avail, and Brigadier arrived and stressed the importance of this; he said that 3rd British Division were well ahead towards Caen on the left and enemy believed to be pulling out. Orders given, A Company of 7 South Staffordshires on right with Martin; D Company Norfolks on left with two troops of tanks. Commanding Officer put himself and 18 set in my half-track and we went up to the tanks in Freddy's FDLs. No shells for once. Could not support attack, as our guns already booked elsewhere.

Epron

At same time (not co-ordinated by Brigade), 7 South Staffordshires (less their A Company) attacking towards trench system to south-west. Glorious mix-up in La Bijude, tanks opened up with machine-guns and 75s and attack went in. Could see little through trees; nothing came back. Presently a Major in the East Lancashire Regiment [*in 3rd British Division*] came up and said would we stop firing on his men. We in the artillery weren't, so I told the nearest tank officer and the Infantry CO.

D Company went into Epron [*at 20:30 hours*] and on to Auberge like a dose of salts, and A Company 7 South Staffordshires ditto, a bit slower as they were harassed from the south-west. Tubby Ellis [*Second-in-Command of 7 Norfolks*] dealt with the snipers in Epron and by nightfall the Battalion had all its objectives. HQ established at La Bijude, where Freddy had been digging in. Many dead cows made the air foul. And my braces broke early in the day.

PP diary, 9 July 1944

Very refreshed after four hours sleep in a trench only about 4 ft. 6ins. long. Fires all round in La Bijude. Sent for replacements for my truck and gear. Went in Freeland's carrier to Epron and Auberge where on arrival we were shelled by 3rd Division tanks with 75mm HE – not very accurately, luckily. Went on to a little square wood and put Martin Tonge in OP. Shot at on return to Epron by small arms, probably own troops also. What a life, no coordination whatever between flanking formations or even between units. 7 Norfolk casualties not as many as they thought [*but the actual number was 153*]. Shelled at La Bijude PM. Recalled to Battery about 20:00. Basil Johnson [*Captain, 481 Battery*] coming up to be Liaison Officer and Martin returned too. Slept twelve hours after conference with CO.

10 July 1944

Up at noon, washed down and changed all clothes. Searched for Taylor unsuccessfully PM. CO's conference 18:00. Johnny Kell [*116th Field Regiment Battery Commander attached to 6 North Staffordshire Regiment*] and I had a good supper with John Brazier at 243 Battery and played dominoes [*Brazier was the Battery Commander and was killed shortly afterwards*]. My job takes more time and is considerably dirtier than Second-in-Command, and one does not get such a good broad view of the war.

11 July 1944

Found Taylor's grave in a field behind the chateau. Sorted out promotions etc. Truck more or less fixed up yesterday while I slept. Bombardier Devereux got cracking well. Put a cross on Taylor's grave at last light.

12 July 1944

Left at 00:30 and moved to harbour near Sommervieu at 04:00. Fine night, dark and cloudy. Lots of AA, Bofors tracer very pretty all over the place. Slept till 09:00. Padre took me to see Bombardier Malam at 79 General Hospital: very much better today though still deaf. Went to Lion d'Or, Bayeux, to dine with CO, Nobby Clarke [*Second-in-Command*] and John Brazier. Terrific queue. Lost about 2,200 francs at Crap in RHQ mess afterwards.

Operation *Charnwood* had been successful in capturing ground. Most of the city of Caen had been at last taken by the end of 9 July: to the great satisfaction of the attacking troops. But the Germans in the suburbs and in the country up to 6 miles to the south were as viciously aggressive as ever, and the Allied soldiers did not of course appreciate that Montgomery's plan was to continue to attract the enemy in the east so as to impede the flow of reinforcements to the west. *Charnwood* had cost the 3 attacking divisions about 3,500 casualties: 5 per cent of their overall strength and a much higher proportion of the fighting troops. Operation *Jupiter*, an assault by 43rd Division on the western flank, had been relatively much more expensive, with the division suffering 2,000 casualties.

59th Division, having lost 1,000 men, had been blooded. It had done a good job in its first battle. The division was now held in reserve while Operation *Goodwood* was fought, but it was to have a major rôle in the crossing of the River Orne on 6/8 August, an operation that eventually led to the decisive Allied victory at Falaise.

Goodwood was a larger operation than *Charnwood*, and was also preceded by heavy air bombardment plus a far heavier weight of artillery shells than in the legendary concentration before the Battle of the Somme in 1916. However, *Goodwood* was only a partial success and the price was high: 4,000 casualties and 500 tanks (one-third of the total armoured strength). But even the critical Bradley admitted that the operation had succeeded in attracting an enormous amount of German strength, which made the eventual American breakout much easier. Nevertheless, the small amount of ground that was taken increased the ire of Montgomery's opponents in the higher ranks of the Allied forces. In particular, the Air Marshals were disappointed because promised airfields had still not been taken.

The important point was that the apparently inconclusive and bloody fighting at Caen fulfilled Montgomery's strategic objective of holding most of the (by-now fully committed) SS Panzer force. By the third week in July, the sixteen British divisions were facing seven strong Panzer and five infantry divisions. At the same time, the fifteen American divisions were being contained (although not for long) by only two Panzer and six infantry divisions, all extremely under-strength.

During the six weeks between D-Day and the breakout, the butcher's bill mounted. By the end of June – only three weeks into the campaign – the Allied troops had been more than decimated. While the Germans lost 80,800 men, American casualties totalled 37,000, and British and Canadian, 24,700. The greater number of American casualties was due to some extent to the losses at *Omaha*, but to a greater degree to the inadequate basic training of many of the troops arriving directly from the United States. In comparison, most British soldiers had spent a year or more in field training and large-scale military exercises in England, which gave them reasonable military knowledge, particularly of how to use ground in attack and defence.

On 17 July, Rommel became one of the casualties of the fighting. He was strafed in his staff car by low-flying British fighters, was seriously wounded and became *hors de combat*. He never commanded troops again. He was replaced by Field Marshal von Kluge, an experienced strategist, but he was constantly handicapped, because Hitler demanded to approve personally all his decisions.

Between 11 July and 7 August 59th Division, still in reserve, was ready to move at any time. This was reflected in the following brief extracts from PP's diary, which demonstrate that 'in reserve' did not mean 'at rest'.

13 July 1944

This climate is most extraordinary, cold and damp one minute and warm and sunny the next. I am glad that Holmes wasn't hit badly [*on 8 July*] – just a graze on forearm and temple and his tin hat ripped up from brim to crown. He carried on magnificently and that wasn't the end of the day. It was 04:30 and we had another sixteen hours to go. Now I must write to Mrs. Malam; he is unable to yet, but will be OK they say and soon back in England.

14 July 1944

Reconnoitred area Fontenay le Pesnel; digging parties. Took one and a half hours to get there. 14 July celebrations in Bayeux and traffic looks like a Bank Holiday. Bed 21:00, must have a chill or something. Saw Monty driving along Caen road PM. Masses of refugees in ambulances and lorries coming out of Caen. Many were bandaged and in their faces bore signs of the terrible privations they have been through. Odd enemy aircraft active, probably photo reconnaissance. Ours dropped leaflets into occupied France.

15 July 1944

Waiting for orders to move into the line again. Came at 13:45, to move at 14:00! However we did so and after a dusty drive arrived at the new area. Visited 7 Norfolk on the way. All still quiet. Noise starts PM when

1. Armoury House, Headquarters of the Honourable Artillery Company. The main building is on the northern edge of the Artillery Garden (just north of the City of London), and was built in five phases. The central block was originally constructed in 1735, and the roof was raised in 1784. It includes the Long Room which stretches across the first floor with five windows and a balcony, and is today the main dining room. The two wings were added in two storeys in the 1820s and a third storey was added in 1900. The Drill Hall at the back, known as the Albert Room, was completed in 1862 (and recently renovated). Flanking the entrance to the House are two 12-pounder field howitzers made in 1853 and used by the Artillery Division of the Company until 1859. They were probably moved by the detachment using drag ropes and are now displayed on carriages. On the edge of the parade ground are two well-preserved 25-pounder salute guns from the Second World War. In this photograph, the HAC flag is flying; it carries the shield from the Company's armorial bearings. (Copyright Honourable Artillery Company)

2. 25-pounder guarding Armoury House. This is the gun on the right of Plate 1. (Copyright John Philip Jones)

3. 11th (HAC) Regiment, Royal Horse Artillery: group of B Battery officers, 1941. Numbers 2 Captain Sworder (who later commanded B Battery); 4 Major Peter Pettit (B Battery Commander); 5 Lieutenant Robin Smith, who became a highly successful FOO and won two MCs, and PP came across him on campaign in Tunisia and Sicily; 8 Captain Howard Bourne, who died of wounds at the Battle of Knightsbridge in the Western Desert in June 1942. The photograph was taken in the early months of 1941, just before PP was posted away from the regiment. (Copyright the Pettit family)

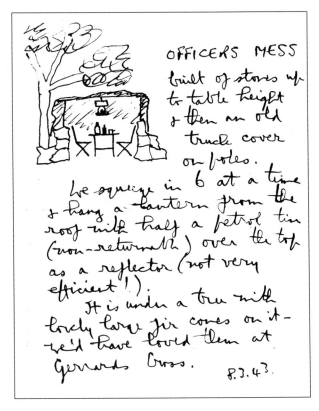

4. Officers' mess trench, Tunisia. PP as artist, dated 8 March 1943, after 17th Field Regiment, Royal Artillery was still in the Bou Arada sector. A fortnight later it moved north to make preparations for the final offensive of the Tunisian campaign. (Copyright the Pettit family)

OFFICERS MESS built of stores up to table height & then an old truck cover on poles.

We squeeze in 6 at a time & hang a lantern from the roof with half a petrol tin (non-returnable) over the top as a reflector (not very efficient!).

It is under a tree with lovely large fir cones on it — we'd have loved them at Gerrards Cross. 8.3.43.

5. Longstop Hill, Tunisia. 'We paid a heavy price for that beastly hill.' (PP diary, 26 April 1943). From the air, Longstop Hill does not appear to be a formidable obstacle. But there is a plateau at the top that is a mass of bumps and ditches: excellent defensive positions for tenacious enemy troops. (Copyright Imperial War Museum NA 3137)

6. The Victory Parade in Tunis. This parade was a festive affair. Highlanders had been forbidden from taking their kilts on active service, but they had different ideas. The British army contingent was led by the Royal Artillery, and PP was the right-hand man in the front rank. (Copyright Imperial War Museum NA 3011)

7. Centuripe, Sicily. Members of the London Irish Rifles looking at the ruins of this small town: evidence of the tough nature of the infantry fighting in Sicily. (Copyright Imperial War Museum NA 5414)

8. Major General Vivian Evelegh, the GOC of 78th Division, is the tall figure on the left. General Montgomery is in the middle, and an unidentified regimental officer on the right. (Copyright Imperial War Museum NA 5404)

9. 481 Battery Headquarters before the Normandy invasion, Ramsgate, Kent, May 1944. Among the seated figures in the fourth row are numbers 6 Lieutenant Sherren; 7 Captain Hobart; 8 Major Pettit; 9 Lieutenant Farr; 10 BSM Wemyss; 12 BQMS Lack. Considering the amount of military action in which 481 Battery was shortly to be engaged, the number of casualties was mercifully small. Two men lost their lives: Gunner Taylor (first row, no. 3) and Gunner Ferneyhough (third row, no. 1). Among the wounded were Gunner Chalk (first row, no. 4), and Bombardier Mellem and Gunner Coddington (who do not appear in this photograph). Gunner Prothero (third row, no. 11) and Gunner Holmes (front row, no. 2) both appear in the diary; Holmes was PP's efficient and popular batman. Bombardier Leese (fourth row, no. 3) was court-martialled in November 1944 and sentenced to loss of seniority. Total strength sixty all ranks. (Copyright the Pettit family)

10. C Troop, 481 Battery before the Normandy invasion, Ramsgate, Kent, April 1944. Among the seated figures in the fourth row are numbers 5 2/Lieutenant Cree; 6 Lieutenant Farr; 7 Captain Tonge; 8 Lieutenant Archer; 9 Lieutenant Luckins. (Lieutenant Farr also appears in the Headquarters group in May 1944.) The diary also mentions Bombadier Devereux (fourth row, no. 12). Total strength fifty-six all ranks. (Copyright the Pettit family)

11. D Troop, 481 Battery before the Normandy invasion, Ramsgate, Kent, April 1944. Among the seated figures in the fourth row are numbers 7 Lieutenant Petherick; 8 Lieutenant Chapman; 9 Lieutenant Johnson; 10 Lieutenant Sherren; 11 Lieutenant Cosgrove. (Lieutenant Sherren also appears in the Headquarters group in May 1944.) Lance Sergeant Cooke (fourth row, no. 5) and Gunner Read (third row, no. 12) were to lose their lives shortly after landing in Normandy. Gunner Milner (third row, no. 4) was wounded on 23 July. Another soldier also mentioned by PP in the diary is Gunner Hughes (second row, no. 1). Total strength sixty-eight all ranks. (Copyright the Pettit family)

COMPO

THE 24-HOUR RATION.

SUGGESTED MENU

Breakfast.	Pocket Meal.	Supper.
Porridge (2 Oatmeal blocks)	4 Biscuits	Minced Beef or Mutton
3 Biscuits	2 Bars of Raisin Chocolate.	(all Meat Blocks)
Tea (half quantity provided)	Boiled Sweets	3 Biscuits
		Tea (half quantity provided)

Also Included : 1 Bar Plain Chocolate, Meat Extract cubes (for making Beef Tea), 2 Packets Chewing Gum, 1 Packet Salt, 4 Tablets Sugar.

METHOD OF PREPARATION.

1. **Porridge :** Crumble oatmeal block finely into mess tin with the aid of jack knife. Add sufficient cold water to make thin paste. Place mess tin on tommy cooker and allow to cook for 4-5 minutes, stirring the whole time and adding more water if porridge becomes too thick.

2. **Minced Beef or Mutton :** Crumble meat blocks finely into mess tin. Add sufficient cold water to make into very thin paste. Place mess tin on tommy cooker and allow to cook for 3-4 minutes, stirring the whole time and adding more water if mixture becomes too thick. When cooked add salt to taste. A meat extract cube or broken biscuit may be added if required.

Please turn over.

3. Tea : Fill mess tin with water to a depth of about 1 in. Bring to boil on tommy cooker. Crumble to a powder half the quantity of tea blocks provided and throw into boiling water and stir once or twice. When it has come to the boil again, remove from cooker and allow to stand for a few minutes so that the leaves can sink to the bottom of the mess tin. Add sugar only if required.

4. Beef Tea : Pour approximately ½ pint of boiling water over half the quantity of meat extract cubes provided and stir.

NOTES.

1. If circumstances make cooking impossible, the oatmeal blocks and meat blocks may be eaten dry in which case :—

    (a) Eat them slowly.

    (b) Chew them well.

    (c) Drink some water at the same time or soon after.

2. The plain chocolate may be made into a palatable drink by breaking into small pieces and cooking in half a pint of water.

3. It is more economical for men to cook in pairs and make the larger part of the mess tin full of tea to give nearly two pints (using all tea blocks in one pack). It is essential to use cookers away from all draughts—using a tin as a shield, or by making a small slit trench.

12. Compo ration. Leaflet accompanying the ration pack for one man's meals in the field for one day. The Compo ration boxes came in cartons of ten, and different individual boxes offered a variety of foods; the cartons could be shared out between men. The diet was appetizing, balanced and nutritious. It was popular with the troops because it was a great improvement over the canned bully beef, M&V, hard tack biscuits and little else that provided the traditional active service diet for the British army. Compo, which was adapted from the American army ration system, began to be issued at the end of the North African fighting, and was in universal use in the campaign in North-West Europe. (Copyright the Pettit family)

TRANSCRIPT OF DIARY PAGE

This transcript differs in detail from the typed version that was prepared after the event, and on which this book is based.

8 July: Words fail me.

9 July: Very refreshed after 4 hours sleep in a trench only about 4 feet round at La Bijude. Went in 100 yards of half a dozen dead cows. Fires all sent for replacements for my truck, crew and gear. On AM at Auberge, were shelled by 3 Div. tanks with 75mm HE – not very accurately luckily. Went on to Freeland's carrier to Epron and Auberge. Shot at on return to Epron by small arms, probably own troops also. What a life, no coordination whatever between units beside each other. 7 Norfolk casualties not as many as they thought but 12 officers hit. Shelled at La Bijude PM. Recalled to battery about 20:00, Basil coming up to be LO and Martin returned too. Slept 12 hours after conference with CO.

10 July: Up at noon, washdown and change all clothes, searched for Taylor unsuccessfully PM. CO's conference at 18:00, seemed to think my story of the battle very funny and wants it written down. Dinner and dominoes at 243 very pleasant change.

11 July: Saw Collum in hospital. Found Taylor's grave. Sorted out promotions etc and various points and actually found time to write to Joy and this! Truck more or less fixed up battle very funny and wants it written down. Devereux got cracking well. Only want back door fastening done by LAD now, net and bonnet muff full of holes. Put a cross on T's grave at last light. CO at conference said I must write down my story of the battle it was so funny! Didn't think so.

13. A page from the original diary. Like most well-educated British men and women, PP had stylish handwriting, but its stylishness was often at the expense of legibility. What made the diary pages especially difficult to read was the small size of PP's notebooks. The dimensions were 6in by 4in: a comfortable size for the breast pockets of an army battledress jacket. This made it convenient to make an entry on most days. This original page for 8–11 July 1944 is accompanied by a transcript. (Copyright the Pettit family)

14. Lieutenant Colonel Ian Freeland, CO of 7 Royal Norfolk Regiment, commanded the successful but costly crossing of the River Orne on 6–9 August 1944. 481 Battery was in direct support, and PP was with battalion headquarters. It was after this operation that he was awarded the Distinguished Service Order. In this photograph Freeland is himself receiving the DSO from General Montgomery. (Copyright Imperial War Museum B12197)

15. Scene of the area around the village of Falaise, where the German armies in Normandy were virtually surrounded by 23 August 1944 and suffered terrible losses. This is a group of German prisoners – a small fraction of the total – who fell into Allied hands. There is no indication in the photograph of the incredible devastation on the ground. (Copyright Imperial War Museum B9624)

16. A Sherman tank. During the course of the Second World War, more than half of the tanks used by the British army came from the United States. They were mostly Shermans, the major armoured workhorse of the Allied armies in North-West Europe. It was fast, mechanically reliable and comfortable for its crew. But its main gun was less powerful than that in most German tanks. The Sherman was gasoline-powered, and had a frightening tendency to catch fire if hit near the fuel tank or the interior ammunition racks. (Copyright Imperial War Museum B7517)

17. A flail tank. A British Churchill tank built to destroy mines by flailing the ground in front. This was one of Hobart's highly effective 'Funnies'. (Copyright Imperial War Museum B7501)

18. A 25-pounder gun. A battery of 25-pounders crossing the River Orne in Normandy, after the fighting. The gun and its limber are being drawn by a QUAD tractor. (Copyright Imperial War Museum B9166)

19. The Reichswald, scene of the first major operation by 21st Anglo-Canadian Army Group on German soil. This took place in February 1945, and prepared the way for the crossing of the Rhine. The photograph shows 2 Seaforth Highlanders mounted on Universal Carriers, moving along one of the small roads in the Forest. (Copyright Imperial War Museum B14458)

20. Commandos moving through the ruins of Wesel, a town on the Rhine near the German frontier. (Copyright Imperial War Museum BU2317)

21. The Rhine Crossing. This operation, on 24 March 1945, was the largest airborne assault in history. But most British troops were ferried across the Rhine. In this photograph, the smashed bridge is at Wesel, and soldiers of 1 Cheshire Regiment are being transported on Buffaloes, which were newly introduced amphibious vehicles. (Copyright Imperial War Museum BU2335)

22. The Guards Armoured Division formally greeted by the city of Brussels. This reception took place on 28 July 1945, and the senior officers of the Guards Armoured Division were presented to the Burgomaster of Brussels. In this photograph, PP is the second figure from the right. He was now a Lieutenant Colonel and Commanding Officer of the 55th Field Regiment, Royal Artillery (West Somerset Yeomanry). Note that he is wearing 'Nell Gwyn's Left Eye' on the left shoulder of his battledress. (Copyright the Pettit family)

23. Peter Pettit in peace and war: pencil drawing of PP in battledress. (Copyright the Pettit family)

24. Peter Pettit in peace and war: PP on his return to his solicitor's practice in London. (Copyright the Pettit family)

MAJ. P. PETTIT

25. PP's medals. These are on display in the Medal Room at Armoury House. They are the Distinguished Service Order (DSO); 1939–1945 Star; Africa Star with 1st Army Clasp; Italy Star; North-West Europe Star; Defence Medal; Second World War General Service Medal; Territorial Decoration with two Clasps. The Territorial Decoration (TD) was awarded for twenty years' commissioned service; the Territorial Efficiency Medal (TEM) was given for twelve years in the ranks. In both cases, wartime service counted double time, and clasps represented additional years of service. Both the TD and TEM usually have green and yellow ribbons. However, King Edward VII granted the HAC the unique distinction of using the colours of the Royal Household: a ribbon of dark blue and red, edged with thin yellow stripes. (Copyright Honourable Artillery Company/Richard Argent)

26. This painting by J.Wanklyn, also in Armoury House, shows an HAC 25-pounder being fired during one of the Regiment's annual training camps decades after the Second World War. Presented to the HAC by Major G.D.M. de Margary TD, in celebration of the fifty years of service with the Regiment of the 25-pounder field gun. (Copyright Honourable Artillery Company/Richard Argent)

Scots attack on left. Terrific drumming of hundreds of guns, no room at all in this area. I have never seen so many mediums so near together.

16 July 1944
Firing during night and tanks pass through, woke me up. Up at Zero Hour 05:30. We are reserve brigade, and only Basil Johnson [*Captain in 481 Battery*] committed, in a Sherman tank supporting RAC. He did well. Yellowhammers singing 'a little bit of bread and no cheese' in English just as at home. Hanging about all day. 177th Brigade did well, 197th Brigade not so well. Joined 7 Norfolk PM, conference 24:00 hours after big firework display by AA and during fire support for another show. Digging in puts us among the mice, beetles, ants etc.

PP letter to his father, 16 July 1944
Food as usual is good and plentiful, we actually have white bread now in 2 oz. rations. There is little or no drink and nothing to do in their spare time so most of the soldiers want to get on with the war and go home. This is nothing like Africa as far as the air goes. The sky is usually full of ours and we comparatively rarely see a few enemy fighters dodging the AA.

PP diary, 17 July 1944
Bed 02:15 for about four hours flat out. Then to reconnoitre but mist blankets everything. Hanging about again. CO made several plans, none of which carried out.

18 July 1944
Still in reserve but during the day turned out 7 Norfolk to relieve 1/7 Warwickshires tonight. Reconnaisance with Lieutenant Colonel Freeland. Area very devastated. Three of us standing together in a field, open trees in front, a hedge on right opening into next field. The top half of a man lying on top of a hedge. A bullet cracked past on right, another on left – we moved! Very close country, no suitable OPs at all.

19 July 1944
Left 00:30 and went up in half-track to HQ area. The boys got on digging while I collected wire. Sent Martin [*Tonge*] with Freddie Crocker [*7 Norfolk*] to Landet and got up to Warwickshire CO, Finlinson, at side of dusty track with 38 set myself. Had already laid on SOS [*the most urgent Defensive Fire*] task before we left, but Warwickshires' move into Landet upset this and had to move it 600 yards west. No sleep. Went round devastated area with CO. Every building, tree and bush was hit, and all the cattle, muck and rubbish everywhere. Dead Boche in buildings and

places. Very tired. Managed six hours with a blanket and a couple of greatcoats.

20 July 1944
Walked round all AM. Hot, exhausted. Quiet AM and afternoon. Rain after tea clears air. Holmes dug me a fine dugout, slept well and dry under a roof of table tops and six inches of earth.

21 July 1944
Raining when I woke and until 13:00. Very wet and muddy everywhere. Lakes appeared in dugout and roof of car, and in slit trenches and gunpits. Holmes has found a trilby hat that keeps the rain from going down his neck. I laugh every time I see him, a grand chap. News of a revolt in Germany interesting [*he refers to the bomb plot against Hitler and the attempted* coup d'état *by members of the German General Staff*]. I have said for some months that anything may happen. Boche have probably b- - -d off from our front but the policy is that we do not advance yet. Conference at RHQ, unimportant, muddy drive. Whisky there with Johnny Kell [*OC 244 Battery*]. Grub with him and Boche 3-star Hennessey which the *Times* correspondent brought them from Cherbourg. Back to another meal and a rum ration!

22 July 1944
Small arms fire and shells in the night. Rain again. Mortared PM and Gunner Milner hit through chest, a hole front and back, hardly any blood; Holmes blown over but unhurt. Put on field dressings and got Milner away very quickly. I am now the only one unscathed of the original crew of my half-track. Chicken 'killed in action' very good for dinner, with broad beans and new potatoes. Patrolling goes on apace, 7 Norfolk reputed to be the only thrustful ones.

24 July 1944
In afternoon went to see Milner in 3 Casualty Clearing Station. Hole through left lung but may not need operation.

25 July 1944
Divisional Commander visited AM. Arranged handover to 243 Battery PM and went up damaged tower at la Seneviere which we take over from them. Very fine Camembert we got yesterday. I now sleep on valise in a hole about three feet deep; it has branches, corrugated iron and doors on top except at feet end where I get in. That end is in the mess tent. The other half of the tent holds a table which I am writing on and have just eaten off and we have borrowed six nice little chairs.

26 July 1944

At 03:30 this AM shells in regimental area, one dud put dirt pattering on our tent, found crater of another thirty yards away. Two killed in 243 by direct hit on their slit. Fine and hot PM. Digging parties away in Cheux area for a new position, very crowded, full of trees and shell holes. Later came orders for dumping ammo. Later still our move cancelled altogether. Slept very well indeed.

27 July 1944

Saw a kettle boiled on cordite, fed in slowly from the blue bag down a chute! Clever, called it a Normandy cooker. Area full of leaflets in German, probably dropped by RAF and blown back by freshening wind. Div. Concert Party going strong, small parties go PM. Grub with 7 Norfolk, good cider. Tubby Ellis [*Major, 7 Norfolk*] and Norman Hardy [*Adjutant, 7 Norfolk*] came back to our tent for drinks and each fired a gun, much to the delight of Gunners. The Jeep is a very useful and constantly-used weapon though I go into battle with the half-track usually. It is very unhandy and awkward but it does carry my communications about and there are too many for a Jeep.

28 July 1944

I needed another wireless operator. The Signal Sergeant recommended Ferneyhough as the best available so I said OK. He then said that Ferneyhough had asked not to be given this job because he was certain that he would be killed and that he, the Sergeant, was quite sure that Ferneyhough was not funking it but seemed to have a premonition. I said Ferneyhough would have to do it as there was no else up to it. I think by this time that my Battery HQ had acquired a bit of a reputation for casualties.

29 July 1944

Looked at Bayeux Cathedral again and reproduction of the Bayeux Tapestry they exhibit now in aid of refugees. Bought cheese and butter [*while PP was away from the Battery it was unexpectedly called into action. When PP returned to RHQ he learned that Battery HQ had moved forward, under the temporary command of Captain Dick Plant*]. Got Jeep and kit ready but seems silly to try and take over in the middle of someone else's battle, so left it till early next morning. Ferneyhough badly wounded (died later) and half-track battered, a large gash in the armour of driver's door, both front wheels punctured and radiator tap broken. Dick said they had been mortared frequently.

30 July 1944

The Padre is simply magnificent, he spares no effort and is a positive hound at finding out where our men get to when they are hit – difficult and lengthy job as they go to Advance Dressing Station, Casualty Clearing Station, and then hospital. I saw a cuckoo last night and a horde of Lancasters this AM – not birds of a feather though they both drop eggs in other people's nests as a habit.

31 July 1944

We are to relieve 6 North Staffordshires' Gunners (243 Battery). Dudley [*Lieutenant the Honourable Dudley Ryder*] in OP, and I at Battalion in Norfolks' old positions. Bombardier Leese now in my crew, sent them off and went to conference at 18:00. MMGs getting into position by the track, another noisy night! I went to demonstration by Major Tubby Ellis's company of Norfolks and tanks, of advance through thick country. The tent is hotter than the heat outside. Dust is thick everywhere. Food is damned good and heaps of it.

1 August 1944

Thick mist AM, visibility 100 yards. Cleared by midday and hot. Saw two red squirrels looking rather out of place amid the broken trees and hedges. Fired odd M [*Regimental*] Targets as result of Infantry requests on patrol information, the only thing to do in this thick country. Battalion began feeling forward at 21:00. Stayed up ready to assist by fire. A Company on right OK, others held up by mines and MG fire.

2 August 1944

Bed 02:30, very tired. Orders Group about 08:00 still tired. Odd MGs and anti-personnel mines in hedges make progress difficult. Field telephone line mangled by tanks, anyway OP at le Rond Buisson not very good. 242 Battery of 61st Field Regiment relieved us PM.

3 August 1944

Breakfast in bed and up at 09:00. Enemy withdrawing. 197th Brigade moving up on Point 210. Battery moved about 14:00 hours to Etregy area. Dug PM. Very hot and dusty. Nice tea and wasps at RHQ. Basil [*Captain Johnson*] with Johnny Kell [*OC 244 Battery*] at 5 East Lancashires. No orders, so bed 23:00. Heavy artillery duel soon after for about two hours, heard three consecutive duds from enemy, none near. Things seem to be moving a bit, by the news. All the men are very keen to hear what is happening.

4 August 1944

Move forward behind Point 210. No noise forward, enemy seems to have gone some way. Own patrols down to River Odon. Hot, wore denim trousers and shirt sleeves. Joined Norfolks about 16:00, they moved near gun area 17:30. The one narrow road crammed with Brigade and Recce Regiment moving down it. They moved through Villers Bocage 21:00 and on south-east to Point 185 without opposition. Arrived at dusk, laid on Defensive Fire etc. and had forty winks before Orders Group at 00:45 for advance to the River Orne tomorrow.

5 August 1944

Three hours sleep. Up 05:00 but no early start as new tanks not arrived. Left 09:30. Martin [*Tonge*] had to wait for OP tank. Nothing known of southern flank. Infantry on tanks, reconnaissance squadrons in front and some lorries with road material! Quiet advance to La Caine through ordinary countryside undesolated but not a human being is left. Waited there a bit while Recce Regiment would not get down to the river. On to Neumer, our recce prolonged by shelling, mortar fire and 88s. The latter obviously aimed at tanks slightly in front of us, but all missed and burst in trees with a resounding crack a little to our left front – then you heard the thing coming! Put Martin in OP, arranged SOS and DF tasks. Very tired indeed. Our southern flank open, no one knows anything, odd Boche came in. Finish digging in shale and relaxed in blankets 23:00.

While 59th Division was in reserve and getting ready to move towards its next battle, the crossing of the River Orne, the rest of Montgomery's forces had been fighting Operation *Goodwood*. This had been planned to coincide with Operation *Cobra*, the American breakout from St Lô. But there were not enough British-based heavy bombers to mount both attacks simultaneously. Operation *Cobra* was therefore delayed and there was a further holdup because of the need to clear the start line, which was the road running west from St Lô. The battle began on 25 July, after a one-day postponement caused by the complex arrangements for air support. Eventually, 2,500 bombers cleared a path for the men on the ground, but the bombing was in places too close to the troops and caused 600 American casualties. In addition to the air bombing, the army artillery fired 140,000 rounds. By now the Americans had twenty-two divisions in their sector, and fifteen were committed to *Cobra*.

Before the battle began, the eight German formations opposing the Americans had been reduced to a total of 30,000 men, the equivalent of two full-strength divisions. The Germans fought bravely, but their defensive front was too thin. The breakout to smash the Normandy deadlock had come at last. The American thrust was directed south-east out of the *bocage*, and six divisions of Patton's 3rd Army, an army not yet formerly activated, tore down the western coast of the Normandy peninsula, aiming for Avranches from which they would turn the corner and debouch into Brittany.

On 1 August, the Americans formed Bradley's 12th Army Group, comprising the American 1st and 3rd Armies. They mustered initially twenty-one divisions compared with Montgomery's sixteen. The total Allied strength was now 1.5 million men. Bradley gave a good deal of thought about how he would control an army group without interfering with operational directives of the army commanders who reported to him. He soon got the balance right. The formation of 12th Army Group was the first step to remove the American armies from Montgomery's control. This was eventually completed in September 1944.

In preparation for Operation *Cobra*, Montgomery had shifted the right of the British line to be nearer the American left, to increase its security. The American divisions were by this time sweeping south and east and would soon move into the broad plains of France beyond the wide neck of the Normandy peninsula.

Montgomery now embarked on another offensive in Normandy from the country south of Caen. He had the same objective – holding the weight of the Panzers – that had worked so well since the beginning of the campaign. The new offensive was Operation *Bluecoat*, launched on 25 July, a prolonged slogging match through difficult terrain in the countryside south of Caen. The British formations were to attack south-east to press the Germans in what was to become the Falaise pocket. During the course of the action, the 59th Division was given another sticky job, and PP was again involved. This was the crossing of the River Orne, near the Forest of Grimbosq, about 8 miles south of Caen. This crossing was intended to provide a route for British formations to move to the east to support the Canadians and Poles, who were due on 7 August to begin Operation *Totalize*, the assault on Falaise from the north (described later).

'A Devastating Fire was Put Down at Will'

This quotation comes from a succinct and dramatic report on the crossing of the Orne by Lieutenant Colonel Freeland, Commanding Officer of 7 Norfolks. The crossing of the Orne and establishing a bridgehead on the opposite bank was the job of 176th Infantry Brigade, supported by 116th Field Regiment. PP accompanied 7 Norfolks during the battle.

The River Orne flows downstream (i.e. north towards Caen), between steep banks. The Forest of Grimbosq is 2 miles east of the planned crossing point, and stretches north-west to south-east. *See Maps 6 and 8*. The plan was that, during the night of 6/7 August, the attacking troops would wade across the river: 7 South Staffordshires on the left, and 6 North Staffordshires on the right. Immediately afterwards, 7 Norfolks would pass through these two battalions to established defensive positions within a mile of the forest.

But as is normal in battle, unexpected problems arose. In the darkness of 6/7 August, the Norfolks lost their way on their march to the river and had to find a crossing place when they got there. They received a warm reception from German *Nebelwerfer* fire, but there were no casualties. By dawn on 7 August, all companies were dug in. But unfortunately A Company was ½ mile too far south, and was soon surrounded by twice the number of German troops, and this made it impossible for the rest of the Battalion to provide direct support. There was a fierce fight and sixteen men were killed. After the Company had exhausted all its ammunition, the rest of the men were taken prisoner. This was a terrible start to the battle.

At 18:30 on 7 August, a Panzer Grenadier Regiment Battle Group, supported by tanks, launched a heavy counter-attack on D Company, to the north of the Norfolks' position. This was contained by them, and there was much jubilation by the soldiers in the ranks. A second German attack followed at dawn on 8 August, also on the northern sector. Three companies of 7 South Staffordshires were forced back across the river, but D Company of the Norfolks, commanded by Captain Jamieson who was twice wounded, conducted a heroic defensive battle. The Orne crossing was now secure and the Battalion had done its job splendidly and was relieved at 8 August. It had suffered the heavy loss of 232, killed, wounded and prisoners; 84 were from A Company, most of them 'in the bag'.

Over the course of 24 hours, each gun in 481 Battery fired 1,000 rounds. Working at Freeland's headquarters, PP had on call the massive fire of 6 Field Regiments and 1 Medium: 170 guns. The effect of this can be readily guessed, hence the title I have given to this episode. PP's report, written shortly after the battle, paints a vivid picture of the dangers and bravery of the infantry and his own intense and productive contribution to this successful battle. It was the high point of PP's military career. (*See Map 8.*)

6 August 1944
Slept eight hours very well. Planning for crossing of River Orne. Battalion HQ mortared in afternoon due to dust of tanks; when they crawled, no shells. Position obscure, and enemy still west of river to south being dealt with. Enemy obviously also east of river, but Bill Addison [*Adjutant, 116th Field Regiment*] walked across and up to railway running parallel on east side, unhindered! Got Basil [*Captain Johnson*] up to have a look at the ground. Plan eventually was to cross north of us and get Grimbosq with 7 South Staffordshires; 6 North Staffordshire to enlarge; 7 Norfolks to exploit to the forest. Basil carried 22 set as artillery representative. I was with essential vehicles column. Odd naps over radio, otherwise no sleep. Fire from enemy mortars and guns.

PP official report, 6/7/8 August 1944
7 Norfolk were in Neumer, over 2,000 yards south of the crossing place, and were to do as much as possible to divert the enemy's attention before moving north in their turn for the crossing. H-Hour was about 20:00 but they did not cross until after midnight. The crossing place for infantry was about 1,000 yards north of the bridge site [*Bailey bridge erected for vehicles*] and this probably diverted the enemy's attention as it was the obvious place. It was anticipated that the bridge would be completed by 07:00 on 7 August, when the essential vehicles of battalions would cross first. In our case, these comprised anti-tank platoons, carriers for Commanding Officers, Company Commanders, 481 Battery [*Basil*], stretcher Jeeps and my half-track. These moved to an orchard about 2,000 yards west of the bridge, just before dark.

The Crossing
The Battalion crossed without a casualty and set off on compass bearings to their objectives. These were reached and occupied without much opposition, but A Company on the right went too far south and three wounded survivors said they had been surrounded and captured. The other companies were disposed on the ground: D in the area buildings and orchards just south of Grimbosq; B 250 yards to the south, with Battalion HQ in a small orchard by a farm on the road leading up from the bridge site; C immediately south of B.

About 07:00 on 7 August, the Norfolks' essential vehicles moved off without warning us; we just managed to tail onto the column. They made good progress down to within 300 yards of the bridge when there was a hold-up and some mortar fire. The morning mist was very helpful on this forward slope though it was well wooded most of the way. It now began to lift. Eventually the column crossed the Bailey bridge and halted, the tail within 50 yards of it at the foot of the sunken road leading up the other side.

There was some shelling or mortaring a couple of hundred yards up the road and some small arms fire. Carriers were turning round and individuals from the head of the column came back down the road. Infantry CO's carrier came back with all hit except his driver, and I took them to the RAP [*Regimental Aid Post*] over the bridge beyond which the road was jammed with traffic. I halted the carriers, Adjutant returned on foot and then we put all vehicles into the side of the road and pushed men up the banks on either side into fire positions. Apparently head of column was shot up at road junction some 500 yards up the road and several carriers brewed up. Enemy in houses nearby and odd riflemen in the trees. Nothing to be seen from tops of banks. It transpired that the

North Staffordshires' FDLs were along the bank on the right of the road but no one seemed to know how far.

I found a carrier burning merrily up the road, tried to put it out with an extinguisher, but the fire had too strong a hold and a box of grenades was well alight. Got a chap to unhook the 6-pounder gun and run it down the road a bit out of the way. Found some North Staffordshires on the bank above, their Intelligence Sergeant winkled out some snipers from the opposite bank. No one really seemed to know where our own troops were and certainly not where the enemy were. The Boche were trying to hit the bridge all this time with heavy shells and mortars, most of which went over. Churchill tanks and MO's vehicle managed to find a way across the river either side of the bridge and the armoured bulldozers prepared an exit for them onto the road. Eventually they passed through the column and went on to deal with the enemy by the road junction.

Things quietened down after a bit and the column moved on. About four infantry carriers had been hit but the Boche put the guns on some others. We felt in full view of the enemy all the way from the road junction, some shells went over and when the column halted in the open we all wondered what would come. However we moved on again and all arrived safely in Battalion area. Basil had two small slits by Command Post dugout with his set in between and working well, so half-track was put about 100 yards away behind the wall of the farm buildings where the RAP was. Brigade 'O' Group took up the afternoon. It was very hot and difficult to keep awake. Everyone had a good meal at 15:30.

First Counter-Attack

At 18:30 Battalion Commander had ordered a Battalion Orders Group. It was just starting when heavy mortar and shell fire broke it up. The CO sent everyone away again when the first counter-attack began.

I had dived into Basil's slit and he into the Command Post. The battle was on and for the next three-and-a-half hours I worked the set and became almost hoarse while Basil acted as Liaison Officer and poked a cheerful face round the corner of the dugout at frequent intervals. Tanks were heard to the east and south moving north, and Spandaus chattered at intervals. We put fire down continually round the Battalion locality. A few bullets came around but at 22:00 the attackers had had enough and withdrew. They then put down some mortar and shell fire on the Battalion area. The 22 set [*short-range divisional radio*] gave up after a closer one than usual, and it would not go although there was no sign of damage. It was obviously better to fight with the artillery set in the infantry Command Post dugout rather than outside. My 22 set (which was working temporarily) was put into the dugout where it would not work at all. Infantry then laid a line from Command Post to the half-track and we opened up 18 [*infantry*] set to duplicate the communications for the night. Basil slept. I dozed over the radio. Nothing much happened.

During the attack the Boche had returned to the road junction area and dominated the road from the bridge with tanks and infantry so that no transport could reach the Battalion and no casualties could be evacuated. After dark the Battalion Intelligence Officer [*Lieutenant Hammond*] was called to Brigade HQ, on the high ground west of the river. He went off in a Jeep, after a snack and a whisky with me, but he and his party were not heard of again after commencing the journey [*Hammond was later posted as missing*].

During the early hours of 8 August tanks were heard moving in the forest. But no attack by moonlight developed. Just before dawn the half-track was moved to a spot immediately in rear of the Command Post between it and the hedge, as it was felt this would be more satisfactory for close cooperation. A slit behind it and adjoining one entrance to the Command Post was deepened, and a shallow trench dug under the vehicle. The remote control for our 19 set [*used for Armoured Fighting Vehicles*] wouldn't work in the Command Post (our end seemed bewitched) so Basil went in there again and I remained on the set outside.

Second Counter-Attack

About 08:00 the position was again shelled and mortared, and another attack came in with infantry and tanks through the village of Grimbosq. This lasted until well into the afternoon and I was hoarse with frantic radio calls to satisfy the almost continuous demands for fire by the CO. Six Field regiments and one Medium regiment were on call through our own CO, and their fire was put down everywhere around the village and to the east. In the middle of the battle the whole area was smoked very thoroughly. The infantry cursed and eventually we managed to stop it, but not before one or two men had been hit by canisters and some buildings had been set on fire, including the RAP. Most of the slates on the roof, which were hot, fell onto the place where the half-track had been! The roof of the RAP fell in and the MO and his staff put up a grand show moving the majority of casualties elsewhere. One shell case landed beside the half-track.

In the end the infantry thought the screen had been of value as it hid the Churchill tanks moving up, but it was not asked for and completely stopped all small arms fire. No one could see to shoot. The smell was foul. I wondered if gas warfare had started. When they were not actually attacking physically the enemy fired shells and mortar bombs at the Battalion area with accuracy, and their bullets whined all around the

Command Post so that at the time it felt they were aimed. This possibly was so because after the battle three Spandaus were found within 150 yards, just behind the RAP buildings. Bombadier Leese spent most of the day trying to get the 22 set to work and finally achieved this after many hours' work and some improvisation.

At one stage the Infantry Commanding Officer asked for a linear target on call about two or three hundred yards north of Battalion HQ, in D Company's area. It didn't look so good. Battalion HQ was on its toes, every man had his allotted place and grenades were handed round – even to Basil. My gunners took up their weapons but we forgot about our grenades in the half-track. I gave this target the codeword 'Blue Pencil' because I had marked it on the map in blue and it sounded appropriate. [*This was an echo of a BBC radio show during the war which made a joke about military censorship by substituting the phrase 'blue pencil' for the words that were deleted, e.g. 'my blue pencil sergeant'*] On hearing this, Johnny Kell [*Commanding 244 Battery, attached to 6 North Staffordshires*], destroyed all maps and codes and his infantry did the same! It never occurred to us, but thoughts of action on capture and the possible escape route west flashed through one's mind. However D Company, who had put up a magnificent fight all day, held firm and 'Blue Pencil' was not needed. By about 16:00 I was dozing over the set between transmissions but some cold tea and sweets put me on top again.

D Company's decisive action was a considerable feat of arms. It was specifically recounted by Lieutenant Colonel Freeland in his post-battle report, which is inserted before PP's diary entry for 9 August.

The Consolidation
It was fairly quiet in the evening but unwise to stray far from a hole as the Boche kept shelling and mortaring at intervals, including *Nebelwerfers*, most of which went over luckily. They also had a good 'hate' on the road leading down to the bridge and something brewed up well with firework effects. Meantime a track had been made along the railway and up through the orchards and about 20:00 breakfast and the haversack lunch arrived. It was very welcome after thirty hours since the last meal. There were rations in the half-track but one couldn't very well eat them in full view of the infantry, who had none; the crew managed something underneath the vehicle. We could probably have fed the Command Post and most of those near it, but the Battalion Commander would not accept the rations as he couldn't feed part of his Battalion and not the rest.

It turned out that Basil's carrier and my Jeep had come up the previous evening and had been within 200 yards of us for twenty-four hours without our knowledge. The Jeep looked like a sieve, it was so full of holes but the driver alright. 7 South Staffordshires, most of whom had been withdrawn across the river during the day, arrived under command of 7 Norfolks and were put in the village. I made a fire plan but this was not needed in the end. All was quiet, the enemy had gone and was going a long way, perhaps further than we had thought. Martin [*Tonge*] came up with batteries and mail, and recce parties arrived from relieving units and took over the following morning. [*Plate 18 shows 25-pounders of relieving columns crossing the Orne*]

It felt good to be alive. The sky, the trees, the air, the grass took a new value, and the quiet was richness itself. The Regiment had fired 1,000 rounds per gun in twenty-four hours. The Infantry were very tired indeed but in great heart and absolutely on top of the world; they didn't give a fig for Hitler and all his works. It was a pleasure to have been with them in such an action.

Extract from Lieutenant Colonel Freeland's post-battle report
The Boche had noted Sergeant Courtman's section of anti-tank guns from their action during the attack of evening 7 August, and now quickly put both out of action. Sergeant Courtman went on firing the last remaining gun by himself, the remainder of the crew being casualties, until he himself was killed by a shell fired by a Tiger tank. The forward platoon of D Company (Lieutenant Bushell) was partially overrun and a very confused situation arose [*Lieutenant Bushell lost his life*]. Of the troop of Churchills supporting D Company, two were quickly knocked out, so the remaining anti-tank defence was reduced to one 6-pounder and the remaining Churchill. The enemy infantry worked round through Grimbosq and attacked D Company from two sides, and it was while trying to attract the remaining tank commander's attention by climbing up onto the tank, that Captain Jamieson was wounded in the right eye and left forearm. Shortly after this the CSM was wounded, but luckily Captain Jamieson was able to carry on commanding the company after a short interval. He reorganised the remainder of D Company round the reserve platoon and Company HQ, and throughout the morning beat off all enemy attacks, inflicting heavy losses on the enemy. The Boche tanks were forced to withdraw from D Company's position as artillery was put down on them. They never came out of the Forest again that day for they were hunted continually by the artillery.

PP diary, 9 August 1944
Before he left, David Jamieson, who commanded D Company (which

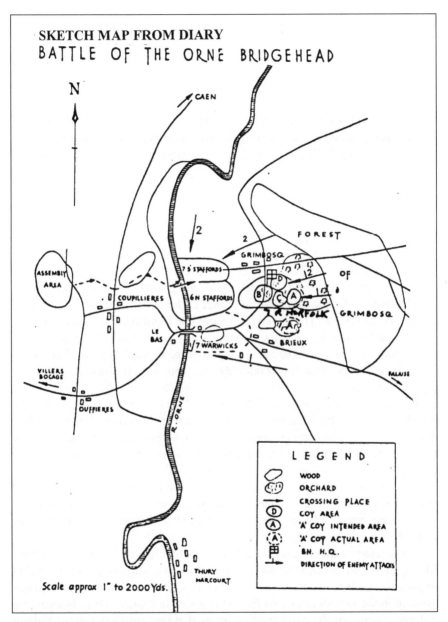

SKETCH MAP FROM DIARY
BATTLE OF THE ORNE BRIDGEHEAD

N

CAEN

FOREST

GRIMBOSQ

2

OF

ASSEMBLY
AREA

7 S STAFFORDS

COUPILLIERES

6 N STAFFORDS

GRIMBOSQ

NORFOLK

LE
BAS

BRIEUX

7 WARWICKS

VILLERS
BOCAGE

FALAISE

OUFFIERES

R. ORNE

THURY
HARCOURT

Scale approx 1" to 2000 Yds.

LEGEND

WOOD
ORCHARD
CROSSING PLACE
COY AREA
'A' COY INTENDED AREA
'A' COY ACTUAL AREA
BN. H.Q.
DIRECTION OF ENEMY ATTACKS

Map 8: The Orne bridgehead. The Anglo-Canadian forces fought their way south of Caen against heavy German resistance, in preparation for the American break-out to the west. On the night of 6/7 August 1944, 7 Norfolk and 481 Battery had the job of crossing the River Orne, to protect the western flank of the major Anglo-Canadian thrust south of Caen in the direction of Falaise. The Orne crossing was successful but incurred heavy losses to both attackers and defenders. 481 Battery greatly distinguished itself. This is an original sketch map from the diary.

had borne the brunt of the enemy attacks) and was twice wounded, walked across the orchard to thank me for the artillery support. Left about 11:00. Called at Brigade en route (which was very different from journey out). All were very pleased and Brigadier stopped *en passant* and said so. Streak [*Corbett, CO of 116th Field Regiment*] wanted to hear all about it, and I fell asleep on grass while he was talking to another. So he let me go. Back to Battery 13:00. Battery Commanders' Conference 18:00. Gin all round and bed at dark after duck with 244 Battery. Very sorry to hear John Brazier [*OC 243 Battery*] killed. My prayers answered and all the lads came out of it OK. No letters to send to next-of-kin.

10 August 1944
Up 11:30 for CO's conference 12:00. Awards to be put in. Visit 7 Norfolk PM. Casualties 13 officers and 200 other ranks, but that includes whole of missing A Company [*the actual total was 232, killed, wounded and missing*]. Rumours of Brigade breaking up, and we to support 56th Brigade. These were confirmed. Put Basil [*Johnson*] up for a medal, and three for Mentions in Dispatches: Martin [*Tonge*], Gunner Holmes and Gunner Milner. Derek Farr [*Lieutenant*] on recce this morning in our own FDLs brought five rabbits, so had CO to dine. Jolly good meal but he was very late and arrived to send us out in support of the Royal Dragoons. Several 7 Norfolk came after dinner but only saw them for a few minutes.

PP had spent some time with Lieutenant Colonel Freeland discussing the possible awards of the Victoria Cross. More than one member of 7 Norfolk had displayed the highest heroism during the defensive battle on the eastern side of the Orne. However it was finally decided that only Captain Jamieson's name should be put forward, and he received this magnificent decoration. PP's diary also includes a citation for a Distinguished Service Order (DSO) for PP himself (Plate 25). This is a medal generally given to Lieutenant Colonels and above. It was an extra-special recognition of the services of Peter Pettit, who was of course a Major.

These diary extracts end on a high note. However, at about this time Montgomery had reached the conclusion that 59th Division had to be disbanded to provide reinforcements to other formations. 59th Division was the junior division in the British army and the last to arrive in France. There is a striking difference between the number of divisions that the British put in the field in France and Flanders during the First World War and the number under Montgomery's command. The Second World War demanded large numbers of men for the campaigns in the Far East and the Mediterranean, and so did the RAF's bombing campaign on Germany. In addition, the demands for men in the Royal Navy and the Merchant Navy were even greater during the Second

World War than in the First. Churchill considered that the Battle of the Atlantic was the most vital conflict of all. The British were always short of men.

In all battles the main losses are naturally suffered by the fighting troops, which in the Second World War accounted for 58 per cent of total strength, compared with 74 per cent during the First World War. Because of the greater mobility of the British army in the Second World War, each infantry division had more than 3,500 vehicles, which demanded large numbers of drivers and mechanics. Many divisions became ineffective because of losses in the front line, despite the large numbers of non-fighting soldiers still in the ranks.

The decision that 59th Division was to be broken up was announced in a special Order of the Day by Major General Lyne, dated 19 August 1944. The gunner regiments in the Division were then put together into an Army Group Royal Artillery (AGRA), which meant that PP continued to serve in 116th Field Regiment. However, his military career was to take him in new directions during 1944, and these are described in Chapters 6 and 7.

Bradley's Trap

The encirclement of the German forces was now under way. The British and Canadians operated aggressively in the country south of Caen: the British attacking from the north-east and the Canadians, with a Polish Armoured Division, advancing on Falaise from the north. The mainly Canadian assault, Operation *Totalize*, was a remarkable affair. See Maps 6 and 9. It was conceived by Lieutenant General Simonds, a Canadian army officer who had been born in Britain and who was considered by the end of the war to have been the best corps commander in 21st Army Group. *Totalize* began with a night attack by columns of Canadian and Polish tanks, guided by the ingenious use of searchlights. There was no preliminary artillery bombardment, but heavy air bombardment to seal the flanks. Then the infantry was moved forward, carried on 'jury-rigged' armoured vehicles constructed from the chassis of self-propelled guns, with ten men in each vehicle. This was the first use of what later became known as Armoured Personnel Carriers (APCs), an innovation that revolutionized the mobility of infantry during the 1960s. (*See Map 9.*)

The attack made excellent progress for two days, then suffered savage enemy counter-attacks which slowed things up. But while *Totalize* was under way, the Americans were moving fast. They were sweeping east, then turning north and finally north-west to trap the enemy. The idea of trapping the Germans in a pocket was made on 8 August by Bradley, who was by then commanding a rapidly growing American force. Bradley's concept represented tactical opportunism of a high order. He still reported to Montgomery and Eisenhower, and these Generals immediately saw the exciting possibilities of the encirclement of the Germans, and they gave their approval without delay. In the execution of the plan, the British and Canadians had difficulties (as mentioned)

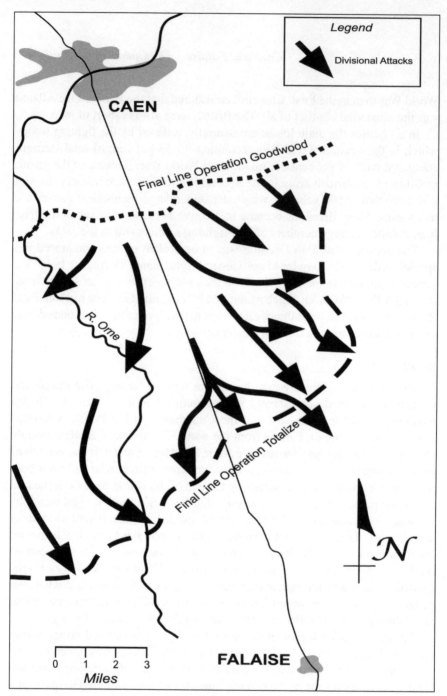

Map 9: *Goodwood* **and** *Totalize*. The final Anglo-Canadian attacks, against undiminished German resistance, were Operations *Goodwood* (18–20 July 1944) and *Totalize* (7–9 August). These held down the German forces although forward progress was very slow. Meanwhile, the American break-out on 8 August, Operation *Cobra*, was dramatically successful. The Americans swept in an easterly direction, to the south of Falaise and then looped round to meet the Canadians, a move that enveloped the German defenders. Very few German troops escaped the gap at the mouth of the Falaise pocket after 23 August.

because they were meeting stiff German resistance. The Germans were also making an expensive and unsuccessful counter-attack on the American 1st Army at Mortain.

The mouth of the pocket was not totally closed when the battle came to an end on 23 August. Bradley's stated reason was that he would not take the risk of two armies fighting forward and meeting from opposite directions, because of the likelihood of chaos and casualties from 'friendly' fire. However, some analysts have argued that he was reluctant to expose inexperienced American troops to ferocious German resistance. The retreating Germans were however pressed into a shrinking pocket by the Americans from the south, the British from the west, and most of all by the Canadians and the Poles from the north. The Germans were finally channelled into a passage a few miles wide, where they were pounded from the air, but 40,000 German troops, minus their equipment and supplies, skillfully evaded the trap. The Americans rather unfairly held Montgomery responsible for their escape.

Nevertheless, the Bradley plan was a considerable success. His estimate of German losses was 10,000 to 15,000 killed, 50,000 prisoners and the wreck of two armies' equipment (Plate 15). The Falaise pocket was a scene of unparalleled devastation.

After he had retired, Bradley wrote two books. The second of these, *A General's Life*, published in 1983, was bitterly antagonistic towards Montgomery. Bradley nevertheless acknowledged that Montgomery's strategy for Normandy was effective:

> Monty's self-assigned *Overlord* mission was to hold the Caen hub and draw the Germans on him while my armies broke out, wheeled east and also cleaned out Brittany. This had gone more or less according to plan. While Monty's forces had failed to exploit the D-Day landings and capture Caen and deliver territory for Allied airfields, his presence and limited maneuvers such as *Goodwood* had indeed drawn a great weight of German forces to him, thus making our breakout achievable.

At the end of the Second World War, three American soldiers (four if the airman Arnold is included) were elevated to the unprecedented rank of five-star General. The army generals were Marshall, MacArthur and Eisenhower, the last such appointments except for one final addition long after the war. This was Bradley, whose reputation in Tunisia, Sicily and North-West Europe – perhaps most of all for his Falaise victory – led to an outstanding peacetime career. He became eventually Chief-of-Staff of the Army, and Chairman of the Joint Chiefs during the Korean War. His critical attitude to his near-equals in the military hierarchy remained as unrestrained as ever, and MacArthur received the same treatment from him as Montgomery had received in Europe. But Bradley ended his long life as a respected military guru, and the last of the legendary Second World War generation of military leaders.

Chapter 6

Brussels and Antwerp –
Montgomery's Concentrated Thrust

Following the catastrophic German defeat at Falaise, the two victorious American armies rampaged over France, with the enemy on the run. Before long they were joined by new formations, and in September all the American armies were cut loose from Montgomery's battlefield control and from now on reported, through their own Army Groups, directly to Eisenhower. To Montgomery, the occupation of territory was less important than finding a way of annihilating the German army. His strategy, which he followed to the end of the war, was for the 21st Anglo-Canadian Army Group to advance in a powerful but narrow thrust north-east. Brussels and Antwerp were captured in early September, and Montgomery's forces were then directed towards northern Germany, the country's centre of industry and commerce.

Keeping the Germans on the Run

The campaign to liberate Western Europe reached its triumphant conclusion in eleven months: a historic achievement in view of the fighting prowess of the German army. The first two months – the struggle in Normandy and the encirclement at Falaise – witnessed close cooperation between the two national armies. However, for the remaining nine months of the campaign, their strategies diverged and the armies moved further apart on the map. The Americans were surging east over France. With Free French divisions under command, they pursued the Germans east to the Seine, then to Paris (with a French division leading the way into the city) and with little delay onward to Alsace-Lorraine. Victory seemed near. But the retreating Germans had not been brought to battle; their tactical withdrawal was not a case of scuttling away. Meanwhile, the British and Canadians were advancing north-east towards the Low Countries.

It is fruitless to ask whether a continued policy of cooperation might have shortened the campaign and reduced the loss of life. Eisenhower deserves credit for the victory. But his specific talent – his ability to get the most out of powerful and effective mavericks, especially Patton and Montgomery – drove him to dilute his resources in response to the number of calls on them. There was Patton, with the instincts and energy of an old-fashioned cavalry leader, who wished to win the war without outside help; Montgomery, who was calculating and obsessively single-minded; and there were the Free French, who had a passionate desire to liberate their country. Eisenhower's inability to establish priorities led him to spread his resources too thinly. This was to mean problems later in 1944.

While the Falaise trap was closing and Montgomery was beginning to make his plans for his thrust north-east, British activity in Normandy was confined to the western flank of the Falaise battle. At this time 59th Division learned that it would shortly be disbanded. PP was still leading the active life of a Battery Commander in the field. 481Battery was east of the River Orne 2 miles south of Grimbosq – the site of their heroic battle at the loop of the river – and 30 miles north-west of Falaise. The Battery had by now parted from their close comrades, 7 Norfolk Regiment. For a short time they supported a Regular armoured regiment, the 1st (Royal) Dragoons; then returned to the infantry. In this case it was to 2 Essex Regiment, a Regular battalion (a unit that did not greatly impress PP). Here is a reminder of the main dramatis personae in 116th Field Regiment: 'Streak' (Lieutenant Colonel Corbett, Commanding Officer); Nobby (Major Clarke, Second-in-Command); Johnny (Major Kell, OC 244 Battery); Tom (Major Whitehead, OC 243 Battery); and PP's comrades in 481 Battery: Basil (Captain Johnson); Martin (Captain Tonge); Dick (Captain Plant); Derek (Lieutenant Farr); John (Lieutenant Sherren); Dudley (Lieutenant Ryder); Bert (Lieutenant Chapman).

11 August 1944

Awakened 01:30 and given RV for 06:00 hours with RHQ at HQ Royals. Order call 05:00 but awoke 05:40 myself! Just made it but nothing much doing and returned to breakfast. Then took half-track, including Gunner Prothero as third operator, to Royals' orchard and did little all AM. Only one squadron east of river and all patrols held up less centre one. Martin [*Tonge*] at the Royals' squadron HQ. Quiet PM. Eventually had a drink or two with them, discovered Mandelson (late of B Battery HAC) was in one of the squadrons. Released at dark, went to old gun area which was to be Wagon Line and found no one. Dark and dusty drive to new WL. Heard signal truck mined and burnt out with driver trapped, bad. His body no bigger than a child.

12 August 1944

Called to RHQ soon after 10:00 hours before finished cleaning up. We are to go and support 2 Essex Regiment in our new brigade, no information except location. Joined them, they seem to have very young officers and not digging very energetically. Most of them in a wood in a ravine. Martin relieved FOO there. Moral support the chief consideration.

His view about 20 yards! Fired a few Mike [*Regimental*] targets for them when small groups of Boches came through woods. Some casualties and the rest to stream area. Holmes [*commanding A Company*] in bad state. Glosters trying to take Thury Harcourt, guns very busy all the time. Went to Brigade 20:00, when Dick [*Plant*] came in Jeep. Johnny [*Kell*], wounded in neck and ribs but full of beans. CO said CRA thought Grimbosq a very good show. Air full of dead cows and bluebottles, apples and tanks – stinks – and dust attracts shells. Slept in half-track, reasonably; near radio and too tired to dig.

13 August 1944

Enemy seems to have withdrawn, mist early. Conference 15:00 RHQ. All in good form and eager for news. Back to find Essex moving on, replacing South Wales Borderers. Recce OP with Basil [*Johnson*] and Martin, then back to RHQ to fix DF tasks and get supplies. Also had foot dressed, bite scratched open during night, same place that got septic at Algiers. Moved after dark, very uncomfortable. Did not dig, enemy reported withdrawn some way but we are not yet in Thury Harcourt. Slept well beside half-track at edge of wood.

14 August 1944

2 Essex to move forward to Point 168 [*a map feature*]; shelled 11:00 by one or two guns, accurate but little damage. Wood track very bad for carriers, tracks come off. Martin in OP to cover advance. Remainder of Bn. went through thick woods. Essex now ordered to *Grater* feature and Caumont to NW. Somewhere in all this I was told (I think by a Frenchman) that there was a dead English officer in a farm building. I went to investigate and found him lying as if asleep on the hay where they had put him. Not a mark on him. It was Clifford Lucy (late of B Battery HAC and the *Times* staff) [*the story was as follows*]. I had sent Basil to B Company during the advance and called Martin up here. Clifford was sent back, and he was soon killed. It appeared his carrier was mined and the sergeant stretcher-bearer said no sign of life. Very bad luck, probably the only casualty in the whole brigade today. Took Clifford's stuff and asked infantry to arrange to send back when transport up. Thury Harcourt still not clear, line of communication almost impossible until it is. No RAP forward yet. I am sure it ought to be, and with 7 Norfolks it would be. Allied heavy bombers in hundreds over quite low PM, huge dust cloud and smoke. Heard next day that part of load dropped on Canadians and Air Marshal Coningham! 243 Battery collected Clifford. Met Mounstephen (late 11th HAC Regiment, RHA) as Essex liaison officer at Brigade HQ. Moved again at dusk into a most impossible orchard at

Esson. Small place, very narrow entrance and in village. Naturally we were shelled, dug a bit and then had five or six hours' sleep under car. Small groups of mines all over the exits from village. Quite a few children. Boches seems to have withdrawn too fast to take every human being, as they did earlier.

15 August 1944

Put Basil out on *Grater* feature early. Magnificent OP, fine view S, SW and SE. Visited next hill as well, in heather and bracken, luscious. Idle and tiring doing nothing. No one has any information about flank divisions or brigades. Recce Regiment very slow in getting information in front. Got Martin back to Battery PM, and Basil later. Battalion at one hour's notice from 20:00 hours but by 22:00 no orders. All went down to sleep expecting to be hooked out and on at some awful hour. Possible new area already occupied by 61st Field Regiment. No sign of enemy. Slept very well, nine hours.

16 August 1944

After breakfast, orders to return to Battery – which is now three miles ahead of us! The Brigade, if not the Division, seems to have been pinched out of the front. Nice to get back to own home and have tent and relax. Visit 7 Norfolk with CO in afternoon; they are in very good form. Read Lieutenant Colonel Freeland's account of Epron, very good indeed. He promised me a copy of the Grimbosq one. Moved 20:00 to a valley three or four miles south-east. Bed 22:30, no digging as no enemy reported in front. BBC says Flers is the centre of resistance. We are between Flers and Falaise.

17 August 1944

Feel very sleepy after ten hours in bed. Dull, drizzle, prepare to move about 10:00. Sent Basil as rep. with 61st Field Regiment. 177th Brigade [*supported by 61st Field Regiment*], going towards Putanges where they expect to meet the Yanks. Mike targets from Basil. Fine and sunny after lunch. Had a few drinks in our tent after dinner, including one and a half bottles of champagne marked 'Reserved for the German Army'. Moved about 20:30 to orchard and field area off main east-west road from Point d'Ouilly to Falaise. Basil still with CO 61st Field Regiment. Martin sent off to Essex near Traprel as we moved. Vehicles badly need maintenance.

18 August 1944

Rejoined Essex 09:00. Saw 4th Armoured Brigade moving south down Traprel road and hear Yanks are in Putanges, within range of our guns.

Many civilians on roads with cattle and farm carts piled high with their belongings. Saw a fox on a lead. Essex ordered forward about 19:30. Went with CO to Brigade and move cancelled. Very interesting listening to two members of the French Resistance; they were eventually taken on by the Essex and given kit and uniforms, much to their delight. Slept long and well.

19 August 1944
Back to Battery by lunch. Division said to be pulling out for a week's rest. Nobby [*Clarke*] off on harbour recce, so I did forward recce. (We shan't go there.) Battery moved 14:30, solely because 2nd Army Commander's tactical headquarters is in front of us and cannot bear guns firing over them. Battle obviously over. You would have thought CRA would be big enough to say OK, then cease fire. Lovely AM, and thundery PM. Showers after tea. Basil back about 20:00. Johnny [*Kell*], came in for a drink, and then to see CO 21:30 about move to rest area. Had a few drinks and much fun.

20 August 1944
Nothing doing. A quarter of guns and vehicles down for a day's maintenance, and remainder sorting out kit and packing. CO said Division breaking up. We are to be 25-pounder regiment in AGRA [*Army Group, Royal Artillery*]. Lots of civvies about wanting to get back to Thury Harcourt area. News very good, armour over Seine, perhaps enemy retiring to Rhine?

21 August 1944
Rained hard in night and then all day. Moved 12:30 to area north-west Thury Harcourt for rest.

22 August 1944
Brilliantly hot sunny day. Monty spoke to Field Officers of Division at 10:00. Very interesting about the big plan and how it worked out as he wanted it. Said nothing left seriously to oppose us in France. And 59th Division, not being a peace-time formation, was selected to be bust up. I addressed Battery on subject at 12:00. Dick [*Plant*] away all afternoon getting new guns.

23 August 1944
Heavy rain during night. Divisional Commander spoke to regiment in the afternoon. Waiting over an hour on the grass in the sun. Bitten all over. CO dined with us. Norfolks dropped in and lowered our drink stock

to danger point. Crap game resulted (after I had gone to bed) in Derek [*Farr*] winning £57 from Nobby.

25 August 1944
Drove to Caen, plenty of people there and the twin steeples still OK. Martin given some butter and Camembert – in exchange for sardines, strictly forbidden but done within fifty yards of Military Police HQ. Back through Villers Bocage, very badly damaged and hardly a house fit to live in. Aunay-sur-Odon, the worst I have seen yet – a heap of ruins and only the gaunt front of church standing over there. Dick, despite headache, very successful at canteen and got 21 bottles of whisky. Paris liberated.

26 August 1944
Inspected troops AM. Basil very difficult and had given his troop the day off, not so much as 'by your leave': trucks filthy in places and work not done. Martin's troop very good. Many Dakotas over at intervals: part of supply service to advanced US forces. Monty said he could ferry 2,000 tons a day forward to them: or more probably food for Paris. Had most delicious mushrooms for tea.

I heard Monty on the news the other night and saw him the very next day, most interesting he was. He arrived in corduroy bags [*trousers*], an old shooting jacket and the old double-badge beret. Took off the jacket, a leather jerkin and a green spotted scarf, leaving a plain grey polo sweater with the ribbon of the KCB alone on it [*Knight Commander of the Order of the Bath, which made him Sir Bernard Montgomery*]. A real successor to C.B. Cochran [*the well-known London theatrical impresario who specialized in musical comedies*]. He showed us what he'd planned, how it had worked out and how he countered the German moves.

27 August 1944
Church service AM, met Tom Whitehead, new Commander of 243 Battery. Went to Grimbosq after lunch, the forest shattered where we had fired. Saw two Panthers killed by 6-pounders, and scene of Sergeant Courtman's gallant action and his grave [*described in Lieutenant Colonel Freeland's post-battle report, which is interpolated in PP's diary entries*]. One Panther blown to bits and turret plate right the other side of village. Other brewed up: both at under 100 yards' range. No piles of dead Boches left, but hear a Frenchman found two big graveyards in the Forest and many unburied. Saw about twenty ourselves and quite a bit of equipment. Whole area very battered, and you can't walk for broken branches. Tea with remains of Norfolks [*the casualties suffered by*

7 Norfolks at Epron and the crossing of the Orne had cost the battalion half its strength. It was withdrawn from the line and gradually fattened with reinforcements. But on its return to action the losses sadly continued. On 10 December, PP heard that substantial numbers, including many men he knew, had been killed and wounded].

PP, letter to his Father, 27 August 1944

At the moment we are living in a strip of orchard between cornfields, about 600 feet up, with lovely views over hill and valley, for five, ten, twenty miles in various directions except north and east. You would say a perfect sight! We are in a tent and very bothered by flies and wasps. The trees are cider apples and every farm has its press and huge 400 gallon casks hidden away somewhere. We've tasted quite a number of different brews.

After 59th Division had been disbanded – something carried out with the minimum amount of publicity – its three field artillery regiments remained intact and were named the 59th Army Group Royal Artillery (described later). This group was kept in reserve to provide support ad hoc for infantry actions. After Normandy, PP remained until December with 116th Field Regiment, whose ORBAT (Order of Battle) remained unchanged.

116th Field Regiment lived comfortably in its orchard until 8 September. It then moved to another location, Acquigny, just west of the Seine, an area now securely in Allied hands. The Regiment stayed there while its trucks were being used to reinforce the advance to relieve the British troops at Arnhem (as explained later). During this relatively peaceful period, PP visited Normandy and Paris and left graphic descriptions of the desolation left by the recent battles in Normandy and Falaise. Meanwhile, the Regiment was very busily occupied with 'internal economy': administration, maintenance, training, church parades, improvised (and very energetic) sports and putting the men through trade tests. All ranks also did their best to cement the *entente cordiale*. PP lived well and enjoyed the local farm produce, since the French had suffered much less shortage of food than the British. He enjoyed regular baths, and perhaps more importantly regular bottles of champagne.

3 September 1944

Paris bears little sign of war though every now and again one sees a damaged building – not often. It must be the least damaged capital city in Europe. Even the Tuileries Gardens are kept up as usual. On the way back we saw a railway yard knocked sideways by bombs, engines all over the place and the whole thing unusable, very accurate work indeed.

8 September 1944

The swallows are flying close to the ground all round the tent, in and out between the apple trees. There were masses of them earlier on during a very heavy shower. I think they are gathering together before migrating south – I would like to go with them into the sunshine.

17 September 1944

Church Parade on football field and remainder of AM planning week's work. There was a Memorial Service in the local church for fallen French and we sent a delegation. Martin [*Tonge*] put a huge wreath on the War Memorial. At 18:00 there was a Fête of welcome on the village green to the English troops. Lots of folk dances and songs by small girls beautifully dressed – Basil [*Johnson*] said there were several he would like to meet in ten years' time.

21 September 1944

Went to Rouen with Dick [*Plant*] for pay. Had three good Benedictines, what looked like doubles at four shillings. Lunch at Café Mexicana and looked round shops. Nothing much except for the one pretty girl I have seen in France so far. Our turn to run dance at Salle des Fêtes at Louviers tonight. Went there, spent the time drinking white wine in the bar.

23 September 1944

Drill Order AM, very pleasant. We were faster than the other batteries, and the Regiment was faster than the other two yesterday and the day before, so I reckon we are the best battery in the AGRA. Saw troop of enemy ten-barrelled mortars [Nebelwerfer] on a self-propelled chassis, knocked out by the roadside [*these mortars normally had six barrels*]. Some still loaded, also carrier and cable layer, all half-tracks.

30 September 1944

Warning order to move Monday, advance party tomorrow. Caught up some sleep after lunch and a bath. Bed early.

While 116th Field Regiment was occupied in this way, the British and Canadian armies, which included a Polish division, now pushed north-east. In doing so, they besieged the Channel ports of Le Havre, Boulogne and Calais (liberated on 12 September, 22 September and 30 September respectively), and Dunkirk (which held out until the end of the war). Capturing these ports eased some of the problems of supplying the advancing armies besides – a matter of great importance – capturing the launch-pads from which the V1 flying bombs had been raining on London since 13 June. It was October before the V2 rockets began to be fired, and they were dispatched from places in the Netherlands which had not yet been captured by the British army. Montgomery's soldiers had by then won dramatic victories by overcoming slight opposition to capture Brussels on 3 September and Antwerp on 4 September (although the port was not cleared until the end of November because the Germans still dominated the exit into the North Sea from the island of Walcheren, which they still held). (*Map 10.*)

By 15 September, less than a month after the beginning of the pursuit, Belgium and Luxembourg had been taken and the Americans had reached France's eastern provinces. The Americans had by now been joined by the eight divisions that had landed in the south of France on 15 August and which had advanced with little opposition up the valley of the Rhône. (This invasion, Operation *Dragoon*, had been bitterly opposed by Churchill and Brooke because it sucked resources from the Italian front, which was carrying out a vital task in keeping German divisions occupied.) By mid-December, the Americans had pushed forward everywhere as far as the German frontier, while the British and Canadians had taken parts of southern Holland.

On 10 September 1944, Eisenhower had taken direct operational command of the Allied forces in the field, which by then totalled more than 2 million men, one-third of them British and Canadian, and the rest American, with smaller numbers of Free French and Poles. Eisenhower controlled three army groups: Montgomery's 21st British and Canadian Group in the north; Bradley's 12th Group, comprising the 1st and 9th US Armies in the centre; and Devers's 6th Group, made up of the 3rd and 7th US Armies and the French 1st Army in Lorraine. These mighty forces were continuing their aggressive action, but were increasingly hamstrung by a shortage of supplies, which had to be brought forward by road along routes which became longer as the advance continued. The successful attacks on the French rail system before D-Day had left much of that network still out of action. Each army comprised multiple divisions, and an American division needed supplies totalling 700 tons – the loads of 233 3-ton trucks – *per day*, so that the extent of the logistical problem and the need for more ports can readily be seen. In contrast, a German division needed less than a third of the daily supplies of an American division, and the German lines of communication were becoming shorter as the Allied lines were advancing.

The Other Side of the Hill

The puzzling question is why the German army, which had such formidable military skills and extraordinary powers of improvisation, could have accepted the loss of such vast swathes of territory, including two capital cities, Paris and Brussels, and the major port of Antwerp. Why did the German generals not form a defensive line on a natural barrier well short of the German frontier, instead of on the lines they eventually constructed along the great rivers in the north, the Rhine, the Maas and the Scheldt? These lines were in place well before the onset of winter, and were to provide a formidable block to the advancing Allied forces.

The reason why the Germans were unable to make a stand in France and Belgium was a crippling shortage of resources. For a start their losses in Normandy and the Falaise pocket totalled at least 400,000 men plus vast quantities of materiel. Half the losses in men were accounted for by prisoners: a larger number than the Russians had taken at Stalingrad and those that the Anglo-American army had captured in Tunis.

The problems were compounded by events that shook the 'grip' of the German generals. The overall German commander at the time of D-Day was von Rundstedt, one of Germany's most experienced and talented generals. But he had by then concluded that Germany would lose the war, and because he offered this opinion too freely he was sacked in early July. On 17 July, Rommel, the operational commander of Northern France including the vast and vulnerable coastal sector, was gravely wounded and never returned to duty. Hitler suspected that he had been involved in the unsuccessful bomb plot of 20 July, and he was shortly afterwards forced to commit suicide. Von Kluge, another talented professional who had replaced von Rundstedt, was also implicated in the plot and he also killed himself after he had been recalled to Germany where he would have been met by the Gestapo.

After the plot, Hitler became paranoid about the loyalty of the Army General Staff, and demanded to approve all strategic and even tactical decisions. This emasculated the commanders – who possessed the professional competence expected of German General Staff officers – and Hitler's interference virtually guaranteed the defeat of Germany in the field. After von Kluge disappeared from the scene, command in the west was passed to a very different type of general, the able, ruthless and pro-Nazi Model (who also committed suicide in April 1945, when he had come to the end of the road, having realized that a German victory was impossible).

In the summer of 1944, the most desperate demand on German resources was from the eastern front. Here the Russian armies were on the offensive and were knocking on the doors of East Prussia, Poland, Czechoslovakia, Hungary and Yugoslavia. The Germans were attempting to contain the advance of 163 full-strength Russian divisions supported by 32,000 guns, 6,500 tanks and 4,700 aircraft. The Russians outnumbered the German defenders by two-to-one in infantry, and to a vastly greater extent in guns, tanks and aircraft. The Germans had to fight for their lives, and they continued to do so to the end.

If the Russian front was not enough, twenty-six German divisions were fighting a bitter defensive campaign in Italy. And the endless and ruthless bombing of Germany by the British and American air forces demanded enormous numbers of flak guns and fighter squadrons to defend the Fatherland.

This campaign had surprisingly little effect on the production of armaments, since manufacturing could with difficulty be shifted to other places. However, the bombing turned many German cities and towns into rubble and it caused vast casualties among the civilian population, who miraculously maintained their morale, chalking on the ruins of their houses 'Our walls may be broken but our hearts are not'.

Anglo-American Discord

Shortly before Eisenhower became the overall field commander of all the troops on the ground, he made a long-maturing strategic decision. He resolved to continue the attacks over a broad front and not a narrow one. In contrast, Montgomery remained totally convinced that his existing strategy of a powerful narrow thrust would win the war in 1944. He visualized a single advance by a phalanx of forty divisions (two-thirds American and one-third from the 21st Army Group) aimed at the north German plain and onward to Berlin.

However, Eisenhower was convinced of the wisdom of his own broad-front plan for two reasons, one military and the other political. The military reason was that he believed in reinforcing success. Patton's 3rd Army and Montgomery's 21st Army Group had shown themselves to be particularly aggressive and achieved notable victories, which persuaded Eisenhower that they should continue to be supported. In addition, promising attacks in other sectors would be followed up as opportunities offered. The political reason – a strictly non-military consideration – was that 1944 was a presidential election year, and public opinion in the United States was likely to demand that the American armies in Europe should be run independently, and emphatically not under the command of Montgomery, as they had been since D-Day.

Montgomery opposed Eisenhower's plan passionately. He believed that a mighty assault on the lines of the one he planned would be unstoppable (although he might have been more cautious if he had foreseen the way in which Hitler managed to fashion an army strong enough in December 1944 to make a very serious attack through the Ardennes aimed at Antwerp). To spare American feelings, Montgomery offered to serve under Bradley, but this was an idea that Eisenhower did not welcome since he was insistent that he was himself going to run the whole show.

Montgomery was so persistently vociferous that Eisenhower finally lost patience and decided to sack him and replace him with Alexander. The effect of this on public opinion in Britain would have been disastrous, but Montgomery's Chief-of-Staff, the able and loyal – and politically sensitive – de Guingand, contrived a way for Montgomery to climb down, when it was made clear that Eisenhower meant what he said. The broad-front strategy became the Allied policy, although the dispute between Eisenhower and Montgomery was to continue vigorously for years after the war in the memoirs of many participants (including the German generals, who tended to support Montgomery).

British eyes were still fixed on the north German plain and attacking Germany by that route. Montgomery now conceived an imaginative plan to provide a jump-start for such an attack. The operation, codenamed *Market Garden*, aimed at occupying a narrow salient through south-eastern Holland to open a Rhine crossing at Arnhem. The troops had to carry out two tasks. First, they had to seize by *coup de main* a number of bridges over the rivers running east to west, the most important being those at Eindhoven, Nijmegen and Arnhem. The second task was to push a relieving force for 70 miles to reach the last bridge: which became alas 'the bridge too far'. The first bridges were taken with great gallantry by ground assault by two American airborne divisions (both of which PP would shortly encounter). There was a British air drop at Arnhem, and the north of the bridge was captured after some delay by a single battalion, although it was not strong enough to hold it. (The Battalion Commander was Lieutenant Colonel Frost, whom PP had come across in Tunisia.)

The relieving force from the south meanwhile also had problems. Before the operation began, British military intelligence did not detect two German Panzer divisions that were refitting in the Arnhem area. The 1st British Airborne Division of 10,000 men, with no artillery support except for tiny portable field guns and 3in mortars, was too weak for the Arnhem operation; and it landed too far from the objective. The signals also failed. Most seriously, it was foolhardy to rely on relief from elements of XXX Corps, in particular a single formation, the Guards Armoured Division, which advanced towards Arnhem nose-to-tail down a single road. Much of this was raised on dykes and vulnerable to small-scale but punishing attacks from the flanks. Although 43rd Division provided a supporting assault across the lowlands on the left, delays were inevitable. Since 1 August, XXX Corps had been commanded by Lieutenant General Horrocks. He was by temperament ebullient and optimistic, and very experienced. He had just returned to active service after recovering from wounds suffered in North Africa.

Market Garden was launched on 17 September, with the promise that the British troops at the Arnhem bridge would be relieved within a couple of days. The single heroic battalion that managed to get to the bridge held the north end until this small force was wiped out on 24 September. Of the 10,000 British soldiers who landed at Arnhem, only 2,500 came out; 1,000 had been killed and 6,500 became prisoners, a large number of them wounded. Perhaps Montgomery had been infected with the view that the German army was on the run. But with his considerable experience of his opponents' military skills, he should have known better. (*See Map 11.*)

PP was shortly going to deploy his guns in the Anglo-American salient that remained in Allied hands after the end of the *Market Garden* operation. This was still where XXX Corps were fighting defensively.

59th AGRA and the Move North and East

In the British army in the Second World War, an Army Group Royal Artillery (AGRA) was a formation made up of a number of gunner regiments at the disposal of a higher military organization, usually a corps. It augmented the artillery regiments which were an integral part of a divisional organization and under the orders of a divisional commander. The AGRA was headed by a brigadier, with the title Commander Army Group Royal Artillery (CAGRA). Most AGRAs were composed of Medium Regiments, deploying heavy guns. But 59th AGRA was made up of 59th Division's three original Field Artillery units. They were soon gainfully employed.

On 1 October 1944, 116th Field Regiment prepared to move north, ordered to concentrate 30 miles west of Brussels. It was soon directed east into southern Holland, under the command of XXX Corps. When it got there, it rather unexpectedly found itself fighting in harness with American units of airborne infantry. In the confused fighting, it also worked in close cooperation with other British gunner regiments.

2 October 1944

Fast column left 07:15 and slow at 08:15, with self in command. Hardly any sign of war north of Seine. Long talk with farmer who was one of 240 prisoners so far repatriated from Germany. Nice red wine and a large pan of hot creamy milk before bed.

3 October 1944

Left at 09:00 after more hot milk, with eggs and butter given us. Through the Somme battlefields to Albert and past quite a few cemeteries, all amazingly neat after four years' occupation. Cambrai, where a baker woman gave us a very welcome mug of vegetable soup. A very cold, wet drive. On to Valenciennes, where everyone turned out and shouted and waved. Into Belgium. Magnificent roads, smooth as glass, much better houses than those we had seen in France. Renaix, very nice town, excellent textile factory where men and officers slept. Orders 20:30 to move to Bourg Leopold area AM; I to do recce.

4 October 1944

Left at 07:45 after a very good sleep. Beastly cold in Jeep. Via Ninove to Brussels, and stopped for wonderful glass of coffee. Clear fast run to Louvain, but very much traffic after that. No room in Bourg Leopold, so AGRA went on to pine woods. Fixed batteries in and then found mobile baths, and arranged for Regiment in morning. Damp mist and evening

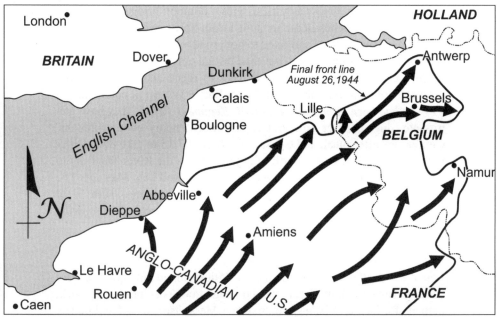

Map 10: The advance to Belgium. The German army had suffered such losses in Normandy and the Falaise pocket that they were unable to slow the rapid thrust of the 21st Anglo-Canadian Army Group to the north-east, and the divergent American advance to Paris and then further into France. The 21st Army Group front line had reached far into Belgium by 26 August, although some of the hinterland behind the front was still being cleared. (Brussels was liberated on 3 September; and Antwerp on 4 September. The major port of Antwerp was not opened until the end of November, when the last of the German resistance in the mouth of the Scheldt had been crushed.) The launch sites for the V1 flying bombs on the Channel coast of France and Belgium were sealed off and later taken one by one. The advance to Belgium had been dramatic, but the subsequent moves north and east into Holland and Belgium proved much more difficult, because of enemy resistance and the arrival of winter.

horrid. Regiment only arrived at dusk, but all in then, and hot meal ready. Camp said to have been bombed last May, with 4,000 Boche casualties. Brigade Major said recce parties leave 07:30 for AGRA HQ twelve miles south of Nijmegen; Regiment move in two days [*there was soon considerable confusion*].

5 October 1944
Left at 07:45, much traffic. Had earlier been told everyone was to leave not two days later, but at 09:30. No one on top knew of this. On arrival I set about finding cover for all – odd spaces in barns etc. Recce after lunch with Derek [*Farr*]. Saw a Jerry plane shot down on way to Graves and Nijmegen. A big bridge over the Maas near Graves, but bridge at

Nijmegen is huge. One-way traffic, with a pontoon bridge for a return. Apparently ten Boches in rubber suits swam down river one night with high explosives in floats and fixed to both road and railway bridges. One span of railway bridge down, but road bridge only damaged.

Met Commanding Officer and went to recce take-over from my brother Paul's old regiment, 55th Field. Barrie Wilson in command [*in 1939 he had been attached to 11th HAC Regiment, RHA*]. They have gun pits etc. dug. Quieter now, but expect more enemy counter-attacks. Conference after meal, and CO says we leave 07:15 to take over. Bitter north-east wind. The area north of Nijmegen (on the River Waal) up to Arnhem (on the Neder Rijn) is known as the Island [*see Map 11*]. The Germans were north of the Island, holding Arnhem. 116th Field Regiment was initially south of the Island, although during the following weeks it moved on and off it.

6 October 1944

Left at 07:00 after a good night in barn. 55th Field did not know we were coming. Their 439 Battery command post and troop positions full of muck; perhaps for lack of a battery commander. Mess disorganised and no tea. Saw Barry Girling and Jackie Bland after noon, Gilbert Wells hit on head a day or so ago. Pat Blamey called just before RHQ rang up for me. All four ex-B Battery, HAC, now in 90th Field. At about 16:00 found we support 508th (US) Regimental Combat Team [*RCT, equivalent of a British brigade. This was in the celebrated 82nd Airborne Division commanded by the 37-year-old Major General James Gavin*]. Laid on Martin [*Tonge*] and went to find further information. We liaised with American artillery (75mm parachute guns), and Colonel Mendez commanding the RCT of tough-looking paratroops. Dark now, back to grub late and fix Defensive Fire tasks. Saw a couple of planes shot down in flames.

7 October 1944

6th Field Regiment arrived 11:00. Took Battery Commander to Martin. Handed over and said goodbye to Colonel Mendez. Radio said we were to leave it to 6th Field and do something else! I returned to Battery command post. Derek went to recce new area near Zetten. 6th Field took over command post. Saw Nobby [*Clarke*], and toured area looking for our next assignment, to provide fire support to 327th RCT (US glider infantry) [*this was in the equally celebrated 101st Airborne Division, the 'Screaming Eagles', commanded by Major General Maxwell Taylor*]. This western edge of bridgehead is a salient, and can be shot into from three sides. Our zero line north-west, and machine gun fire to north, where there are some enemy tanks this side of River Lek. Bed in mill.

Masses of civvies around. FDLs deserted. Saw a huge Lancaster force today; Holmes [*PP's batman*] stopped counting at 360.

8 October 1944
Basil [*Johnson*] went as rep but infantry have a company in the line and he manned an OP. I went to American Command Post as rep. Excellent commanding officer, Major Inman from Colorado.

9 October 1944
Up 02:30, to fire on enemy coming out of a strip of wood: they went back. A little more later. Boche bangs around a good bit off and on. Lots of stuff over about 17:00 and two attacks followed. Artillery and mortar fire break them up. Nothing heard of Basil after the initial shelling and mortaring. He returned OK, but his OP in a loft was hit twice. He and his chaps beat a strategic retreat to the cellar.

10 October 1944
Martin arrived about 06:00 hours; Basil went back to refit. We established a better OP in hayloft; left Martin there. Returned PM to see our new Defensive Fire group on the ground. All except 6th Field Regiment who seemed south of area, so corrected them. Took about three hours due to other targets. Saw one Boche and one hare! Attack expected after tea, but did not come. Dull but mild. The whole country is as flat as a table, market gardens and fruit, some corn, trees along the roads and around houses. Houses full of holes. Bang-bang-bang, rattling the windows. Streak [*Corbett*] is very annoying at times, I am sure he tends to give away OPs by visiting them.

11 October 1944
Up 04:00-ish, to fire on suspected working parties. Slept again till 09:00. The daily newspaper service was OK in France, but it doesn't extend to Holland yet. It is amazing how these Dutch hang on amongst the fighting, almost in the front line. The huge apples and pears are luscious; we found some good jam and pickled onions by the Command Post which is a wrecked factory. When I went to Basil's old OP again, it had been ransacked from top to bottom; I am afraid by British troops.

12 October 1944
Basil relieved Martin early AM. The battalion we are supporting are to move into another battalion area tonight; two companies already in line. Fine and breezy early. These American chaps, being airborne, have only three companies though larger than ours. Plenty of anti-tank, automatic

and semi-automatic weapons. They are completely re-equipped after each operation: new outfits, weapons and all. Lovely radio and line equipment, lighter and handier than ours. Battalion HQ and attached officers are Galbraith (Idaho), Adams (Cleveland, Ohio), Niland (Tonawanda, New York), Goldfarb (Akron, Ohio), Lemon (South Carolina), and Richardson (Oklahoma). Damn good lot [*the American Regiment subsequently sent a very positive report about the cooperation of 116th Field Regiment*]. Sent Basil on before dark to take over OP right up in FDLs.

13 October 1944

New command post in a fully furnished modern school house, although the school is wrecked. We move again tonight owing to divisional re-shuttle. Spent day finding out about it and showing 6th Field Regiment in. Sent Basil home and Martin up to Tom [*Whitehead, Commanding 243 Battery*], to take over OP on north of front. Slept in comfy chair three hours.

14 October 1944

00:30 in pitch dark, long slow drive. Wet. Gave three a lift in my half-track, but found we could not get over wooden bridge, so we went another way round. The other three went on in a Jeep. Arrived about 05:00 to find a hell of a jam. The Jeep ditched 150 yards down another track. Took over from Tom, got Jeep out and trucks parked by first light. Good CP in cellar. My lads went in loft. During a late shave several shells whistled over, and then a round of gun fire produced smoke and dust under window. Called to radio by CO. Went to see Martin's OP; after two and a half hours' shelling they are in good heart. More shelling PM. Martin's party all sleep in own FDLs. Martin did very well and fired lots; infantry delighted. Two German companies apparently supported by tanks firing from their lines. Slept eleven hours very very well; chucked a stray dog off bed in middle of night. Glad to see a conspicuous white house over the lower Rhine in German territory burning merrily.

15 October 1944

As we are in full few of enemy, Inman [*American CO*] decided to move CP half a mile north tonight. Our third move in four nights. Recced PM. Got line fixed in before dark, and Dick [*Plant*] up as relief party. Just about then grub was up and as usual I became busy. CO wanted fire. Dick went on to establish communication in new place, then CP moved. I stayed till Dick ready. American E Company started calling for fire, and I fired seven rounds per gun. Lemon [*American officer*] observed and said he would pull our fire into own troops if need be. It was only fifty yards in front. About a company of enemy had appeared 100 yards wide, and we saw them off [*the remainder of Battalion HQ was now going to move forward*]. Radio in Jeep would not work, so by the time Dick got through and Galbraith [*American officer*] was ready, I had remotes and telephone line to fix. We set off in inky darkness and rain. About half way I put the half-track into a steep ditch on a corner. Summoned three QUADs [*towing vehicles*], but they could not do the job. We had to clear the road for a troop of Shermans, so we gave up and went forward in the QUADs. Found Dick had a nice room. Two hours' sleep from 06:00 hours. Various further attempts to pull out the half-track, but this was eventually done by a Sherman tank.

Martin and I got to Nijmegen PM, and had a beer in officers' canteen. Orange and red sky, heavy cloud and rain made a threatening scene on the way home. Dudley [*Ryder*] and three men went for forty-eight hours' leave to Brussels.

17 October 1944

Wrote letters and rested. High wind and heavy rain. There is some popping going on, I think ours mostly; we've had several shindigs between 16:00 and 18:00 since we hit this sector. It is an odd time to attack because it is difficult to hold strange ground properly at night against an enemy who knows it. Crump, crump, something pretty heavy landing somewhere. And there go our guns shooting at something. Quite noisy, because four of my guns shoot almost over this house. Sound travels far and loud at night.

Considering that almost everything from guns to butter has been coming to us across the Normandy beaches all these months, I am not surprised that we've not had gin or whisky for a month or so and beer for nearly two. Ammunition and food rightly take precedence. Holmes [*PP's batman*] seems to have aged a bit. He's worth millions of these young bastards who have tummy or knee trouble as soon as they are detailed for duty in a forward area.

18 October 1944

A brilliant sunny morning but very heavy rain this afternoon. I jibbed at walking round the battery in it and in the mud, but I suppose I ought to. Those who have to sleep by the guns under a tarpaulin get very damp but we try and work in shifts and get the others into buildings. The front line houses will not be worth living in for a bit; they get shot up often and some burn. I am due to relieve Dick, so it will be three days before I shall be back in my double bed again. Got up to Battalion in last light with Basil, found that because of a missed meteorological correction to a fire order, we had hit one of our own men earlier in the day. The maps are inaccurate for orchards etc., they are reasonably accurate for roads. American infantry still going strong but counting the days until they are relieved.

19 October 1944

Visited OP behind pond. Basil said he had found Bombadier Leese asleep in blankets about 05:00 when he was supposed to be on set and telephone. That settles it, I'll bust him. American 363rd Division being relieved tonight. Extensive fire support arranged.

20 October 1944

Up 03:30 to fire on noises reported by American F Company. Six heavy explosions behind enemy FDLs, believed to be demolitions. Our tanks came up AM to fire at churches in Wageningen, which they riddled with 75s. Suggestions that enemy may breach dykes and try to flood the Island, but we are miles from the sea, and I doubt that this is possible until the spring when the Rhine fills with melting snow. We are about 30 feet above sea level. Americans report sirens recently from enemy lines. I heard something like a slow, high projectile this afternoon, but they said that the sirens wailed like ours. All talking of rocket guns. Dudley did not see a thing all day at OP. We think enemy have withdrawn, particularly after demolitions last night. The spotless Dutch house is no longer spotless.

21 October 1944

Patrol last night found enemy weapon pits abandoned. Combat patrol at noon went about two-and-a-half miles west well beyond Ophausden village, which was reported a wreck. Prisoners say it's heavily mined and booby-trapped. We'll have to move guns up to get in range again. Enemy withdrawal is a nuisance because with only two divisions on the Island, we don't really want to advance west and lengthen our front. Johnny [*Kell*] came up to relieve me after dark. Fine mild day but cold night. Bed about 01:00.

22 October 1944

Collected the Americans Inman and Niland after lunch, went to swimming baths in Nijmegen. Tea and biscuits at 50th Division Officers' Canteen. I then brought them back and we had a good evening, easily disposed of our new drink issue.

23 October 1944

Regiment moved too early for me. Then rejoined Battery at Afferden south of the Vaal; good farms and electric light. Area never occupied by Boches or us. Locals carry on farming. Slept long and well. Gunner Coddington wounded by Schuh mine.

At this time, 116th Field Regiment had withdrawn from the front line, although the Batteries still participated to some extent in the fighting. They were living in good civilian billets. The weather was wet and cold and was getting worse, and the troops were not as occupied with 'internal economy' as they had been in France in September. Since the military action was limited from now until early December, I have truncated most of the diary entries.

24 October 1944
Looked round battery; they all seem to have the right idea now and are in good heart. Coddington lost his right foot and has a bit of shrapnel in one eye. US signaller who trod on the mine was killed. CO approves a 48-hour pass for Antwerp for Johnny and me. Johnny postpones owing to a shortage of troop commanders; also a round from 6th Field Regiment fell in his CP and hit six men, so he must restore confidence. Tossed up, and Basil [*Johnson*] won, and comes with me. Getting chilly at nights. Boils are very popular over here. I can't imagine what it is, because there is masses of fruit for the taking.

25 October 1944
PM went to CO via Nijmegen, about thirty miles and the only way by road. FOO patrolling is off, but every second day we send out one officer with infantry escort to forward OP to shoot Boches. Saw Tom [*Whitehead*] in new CP for centre section; fixed Dick [*Plant*] and Martin [*Tonge*] there. Drove back in dusk. Three searchlights on river now, illuminating the railway bridge and the boom. Trip to Antwerp postponed by 24 hours. There is some banging going on tonight, and not all the right way either.

26 October 1944
The electric light fails every evening soon after dark. A pity because the house radio is electric so we don't get the news.

27 October 1944
Left 08:30. Sandwiches *en route*. Antwerp about 14:30. Heard some loud bangs which they said were flying bombs. Drank in many different cafés for five hours and had hardly any effect on us. No dinner. The drill in one café seemed to be to drink and buy a hostess one, possibly more; a few words with Madame and then to a salon behind a mirrored door where the rest of the deal was made and so upstairs! We drank quite a lot

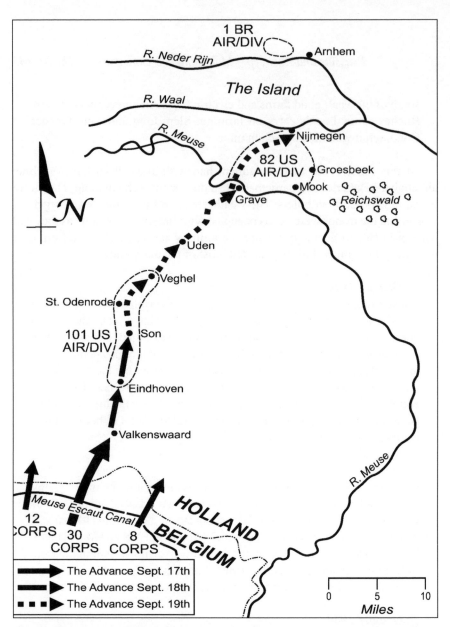

Map 11: The route to Arnhem. Operation *Market Garden* was a plan to seize the three large river bridges in south-eastern Holland by airborne assault: something that might have opened the door for an invasion of Germany. However, success was only possible if a strong armoured thrust moved quickly enough to relieve the lightly armed airborne troops. But this column, driving along a single road, was vulnerable to enemy attacks on its flanks. These attacks delayed the advance for a number of crucial days, with the result that the column did not manage to reach the bridge at Arnhem over the Neder Rijn before the battalion holding the north end of the bridge was overwhelmed by much larger enemy forces. After this failure and the loss of the 1st British Airborne Division, Allied troops moved into the low-lying region known as the Island, between the Neder Rijn and the Waal, much of which became no-man's-land. PP was in this sector for two months from 6 October 1944, although military activity was not intense because the ground was constantly liable to flooding.

of beer watching the sport, if sport it is with such hags! We automatically walked on the concrete pavement and nearly got run over as it was a cycle path.

28 October 1944
Lovely hostel, tall rooms, panelled, paintings, salon, radio, band with lunch, excellent cooking, sofas and bar with inexpensive drinks. Walked miles around town, lovely fruit in shops: grapes, pears, apples, peaches. *Thé dansant* went with a bang, a big one which broke some windows and a skylight and put all the lights out. Drinks on the house. Had dinner (rather late) and went out again and stuck to beer. As a result I was up several times in the night. The enemy use flying bombs to keep us awake. Once the sound seemed to roll all round town for some seconds. These were V2 rockets, not V1 flying bombs. [*Although the V1s and V2s were aimed mainly at London, a number were also directed at Antwerp after it had been occupied by the British army*]

29 October 1944
Saw the Scheldt and docks and quays AM, all more or less ready for use when Walcheren cleared of Germans and the route to the sea is open. Large rabbit market in one street and a sort of Petticoat Lane nearby, crowded. Departed. 120 miles in four hours. Regiment still at Afferden, but infantry had withdrawn.

30 October 1944
Field General Court Marshal PM for Bombadier Leese. Court in tent, cold biting wind. We waited a bit but were told not today. Nice warm CP with stove. All quiet, slept well.

31 October 1944
Walked round forward company area AM. All quiet. Patrol two to three miles ahead all day. Saw nil. Report of tank near FDLs, but special patrol found nothing. I now look forward to reading the *Times* every day again. After the war, I'd like to take *Esquire* monthly and *Time* weekly from the States, plus a French weekly and *Punch* and *Country Life* or *Field*. So many of us assume that because the American language and English language are so much alike, the people are also. In fact they are not.

1 November 1944
Walked around rear company area PM. Put Martin [*Tonge*] up for a medal; and two Other Ranks for Mentions in Despatches.

2 November 1944

Could see lots of flak and big flashes in the direction of the Ruhr. More bangs this evening, it's noisier here than in the line. Utterly exhausted by 22:00. Saw about 1,000 bomber raid go over at midday.

3 November 1944

More shells in our area after dark. Some casualties. Water pump packs up!

4 November 1944

Talked to troops about War Memorial, they seem very anxious to do something to benefit those not so fortunate and their dependents rather than all gunners, e.g. grants and hospital wards rather than a Gunner Club. No one likes the idea of statuary. Battery released from duty for two nights. Some comic shells have landed around this area; they go into the ground and then along under the surface like a mole for about ten yards and burst underground making a huge hole, flinging dirt all round; not very dangerous.

5 November 1944

Church parade. It is howling now, cold and dull.

6 November 1944

Regiment moving back to the Island tomorrow. It will be much more convenient for OPs and line communications. Someone swears he heard a flying bomb in the night, said it seemed to burst in enemy territory! Streak gave me a bit of DSO ribbon. I am very pleased and flattered to be able to wear it. [*The Island was in low ground and susceptible to flooding. The enemy made every effort to rupture dykes and divert canals to cause the water in the River Waal to rise and flood the Island, and the Allied troops protected themselves as best they could. But it was touch and go. Operation Noah was the codename for the plan to evacuate*]

7 November 1944

Visited Martin's OP. Fun after dark, plotting bearings to enemy self-propelled guns and trying to catch them before they move.

8 November 1944

I'm to take over all 327th Glider Infantry RCT. But we'll all be relieved by Canadians soon, I guess.

9 November 1944

Moved to 327th HQ in Zetten; shelling in area at 17:00 and 21:00.

Interesting talk on Washington State from one of the American officers, Captain Dennis.

10 November 1944
Field General Court Marshal on Leese. Guilty. Roads covered in mud and verges deep in mud. Island roads are full of holes where the rain and unaccustomed traffic are making them steadily worse. Our US friends not going until 26 November.

11 November 1944
Forgot it was Armistice Day until 13:00. Decided I am very lucky to be alive, sitting in the warm and dry, compared with at least four of my friends who have fallen in this damned war. Glad to hear on the news that the British and Canadian armies are having their quietest time since D-Day. Reading Guedalla's 'The Duke' (life of Wellington). I find it difficult to keep feet warm. Winter in this low, flat, exposed country is a harder proposition than in England.

Two Spitfires strafed the road by the railway a few days ago and blew up a petrol lorry. Advertisements for Vim, Rinso etc. in the small shops make it look like a British village [*Vim and Rinso were brands from Unilever, the Anglo-Dutch conglomerate. When the Germans invaded Holland in 1940, the two parts of the company were split. The Dutch division manufactured and sold the brands on the Continent, while the English division did the same for the identical brands in Britain*]. The children are learning some choice expressions from the soldiers as they are told to get off and out of the trucks!

Haven't seen an open fire yet, they are all upright stoves standing out in front of fireplaces. This house is huge but very efficient and was, I am told, a boarding house for girls who went to school up the road. Someone is making a loud noise with MGs; Boches about a couple of miles away I expect. Someone is snoring outside my door.

12 November 1944
The American drive towards Aachen is for Cologne, and is intended to finish the war. Another attack due for Venlo. We stay here at present. At 13:00 Regiment ordered to move south of the Waal, apparently because water has reached flood height. Our 327th RCT pass through a covering position and go right back beyond Grave. This is Operation *Noah*. Now we can barely clear our FDLs with Supercharge [*maximum strength explosive propellant for shells*], but the Canadian guns can do the mission for us. Very wet and muddy, several vehicles hopelessly ditched.

13 November 1944
Rain all day. Martin [*Tonge*] returned from Antwerp. A flying bomb demolished the building over the road from the café he was in. He said the windows came in at them, all went black, he picked himself up off the floor and felt his way to the door.

14 November 1944
Fine at last. CO says he will bring one Battery back this PM, but later decides not to. Glad Johnny [*Kell*] relieves me tomorrow. Getting very international: Canadians, Yanks, and us all on the same radio net, and Poles seem to butt in too. River up to 11.57 metres at 18:00, Operation *Noah* all ready for evacuation of Island. Might be a very sticky operation if enemy shell area and bridge. Got very cold and went to bed with feet like icebergs.

15 November 1944
Look at Battery area AM and Johnny relieved me. Padre and doc. come to our mess now and make us half-a-dozen plus Derek [*Farr*] and John [*Sherren*] who come in for meals. River's down a bit now and the Regiment returned to the Island. Shelled all around us about 23:00.

16 November 1944
The four Yanks came for the evening with two bottles of whisky, which helped out our five Port, one-and-half gin, half whisky, five beer, two Bordeaux. A quiet, amusing evening. A very nice modern house owned by Catholic priest. This area is very Catholic. Germans are still trying to cut us off by flooding. Several new ferry sites are signposted, in case we have to evacuate without a bridge.

17 November 1944
One of my troops has now received about six enemy shells on the position; look for alternative gun position. Padre's radio very welcome. The Boches have a radio station at Arnhem which comes up on our wavelength and cuts out our programmes.

18 November 1944
Walked round AM and found two alternative positions. Very muddy ditches after eighteen hours of rain. Gun pits and dugouts flooded and being bailed out. The men all have an extra pair of socks and they need them to keep on changing wet ones. We have asked for gumboots. Despite the weather all are very cheerful and full of beans. Milder today. Now on biscuits, no field bakery. Plenty of potatoes: a shell dug some

up nearby a few nights ago. Leese's FGCM sentence: loses seniority up to 10 November. What does a non-Regular care about that? Ridiculous sentence, he expected to be reduced to the ranks.

[*It was thought that some British troops at Arnhem had managed to hide from the Germans just north of the Neder Rijn*] The British on the Island mounted Operation *Pegasus* to recover them. No success: nobody turned up, since Operation *Market Garden* was now too far in the past.

19 November 1944

Recce to regimental areas all day. Tired, muddy and smelly, having been in two muck heaps all over my ankles. We found a bomber which had crashed beside a house. Being near the front line, it was not looted – torn to shreds – as those further back are by eager civilians and soldiers. Saw V2 go up away to north-east: long train of white smoke went up in the sky at angle of about seventy degrees and disappeared. I hear they come down as fast as a meteor in the sky with a thin tail of red fire.

20 November 1944

Took Basil [*Johnson*] a ribbon for his Military Cross, and his batman could sew it on. Adds a bit of tone to the place. Artificial moonlight [*from powerful searchlights*] every night, until the moon gives its real light later.

22 November 1944

Rained all day. Battery dug forty-eight gun pits and the diggers deserved their rum ration. Arranged with RE for dummies and stores to be put in tonight [*dummy soldiers were meant to mislead the enemy about the strength of the British positions*]. Bert [*Chapman*] put a registering gun in at last light. Evacuation of civilians goes on.

23 November 1944

Saw dummies AM: very effective. Maintenance party of RE wander about and keep fires going.

24 November 1944

Walked round AM. Medium gun in ditch by RAP, nearly vanished! Dummies behind our Mess and 200 yards from a troop of gunners: not very clever. Canadian battalion want to come into our area for a night or two on way out. 51st Division on way up. We look like moving in a few days. Johnny [*Kell*] rang up and asked if I would like to go with him to Brussels. Would I! Got CO's permission and fixed leave for 07:30 next morning. Loud gun almost outside our post, it made some huge bangs last night. We all went to American HQ for a drink and chow; sat round telling stories. One of the Yanks told of the girl who said 'I'll give you half an hour to take your hand off my leg', which brought the house down.

25 November 1944
Left 07:45, very wet at first, delayed on road by huge column of tank transporters, so did not arrive in Brussels until 13:00. First class accommodation at the Metropole. Johnny started an amazing good evening by playing piano in the band at a café, and from then we never looked back. The dinner we were taken to was delicious: tomatoes stuffed with shrimps, poulet with salad and salted *frites*, then a gateau. Lovely hotel bath.

26 November 1944
Completed business and drove home after lunch. Glorious sunny day. Arrived just after 19:00. Saw a V2 going up in the moonlight, a yellowish light reminiscent of a shooting star in reverse.

27 November 1944
Recce area in sandpits south-east of Nijmegen by railway north-west of Mook.

28 November 1944
Moved AM at intervals to sandy hillside north-west of Mook. Easy digging. Very wet drive to Nijmegen to find Wagon Line. John [*Sherren*] and I luckily got the only room in a bungalow. Holmes and company in the cellar. John will be in Command Post tonight. Derek [*Farr*] returns from Antwerp in the morning, and John and he will share duty in Command Post. We have some gumboots now. I am wearing an American jacket at the moment. Very good for the tummy and the small of the back and wrists gather up closely, but besides these things it is no warmer than my battledress. Surprising how so few men catch colds, even though they paddle around in wet gun pits and damp, all day and half the night.

29 November 1944
Misty morning and then lovely and sunny. Derek and party back from Antwerp. Said they heard sixteen V2s and a lot of casualties from glass. Our first rounds fired into Germany, with TOT [*time on target*] 10:47. CO showed me letter from Monty that Regiment is to be dispersed. Infantry reinforcements so badly needed! Modest rum ration: I must go to bed while I am warm from it.

30 November 1944

To go to Brussels to get orders. Took Johnny [*Kell*] and left 09:40, arrived 14:00. Regiment to billet near Courtrai as soon as possible. Bombardiers and below under thirty-two to go to infantry. Remainder and tradesmen to go as reinforcements; officers the same we expect. Dined and slept at Metropole again.

2 December 1944

Very wet and muddy ride back to Nijmegen. Electric light has failed. My feet are like ice. There is a rum ration beside me which will soon get down to my feet.

3 December 1944

Told troops AM. No orders to move yet, and AGRA say that we must stay, as they can't do without us. One of the sergeants won £25 at Crap off Canadian REs, and today a 150mm. shell came through his tarpaulin onto and through a bombardier's empty bed (all the others were occupied), into the ground under it – and didn't explode. Dyke south of Arnhem has been blown by the Germans and the Island is flooding slowly.

4 December 1944

We move on 6 or 7 December, meanwhile fire our twelve rounds per gun per day maximum.

7 December 1944

Went off early to find accommodation for Regiment and RASC. Main body left at 11:30. We were allocated one of the outer ring of old fortresses around Antwerp. Regiment arrived after dark in pouring rain. I was tired and glad of an excellent meal and easy chair.

8 December 1944

Regiment left 08:00 to next location, Harlebeke. Hear that I am posted to 43rd Division, who are in Germany somewhere [*the hard decision had been taken, at a high level, to break up 116th Field Regiment to provide infantry reinforcements. The officers and a small number of other ranks would be transferred to other gunner regiments*]. Nobby [*Clarke*] posted with me. I go as Battery Commander. Today was absolutely bitter, streets slippery and snowing hard. Lovely road signs around now, on a succession of boards and trees and telephone poles at about 100 yard intervals: 'V1, V2, VD, Hitler's Secret Weapons'.

10 December 1944

To Brussels and saw a Lieutenant Colonel at the Military Secretary's office who rang the Royal Artillery and learned that I would be high up for promotion in my new Regiment. Perhaps! Very wet drive home, got lost in driving rain and sleet.

12 December 1944

Posting order arrives for me to go to 112th Field Regiment in 43rd Division.

Hard Winter Weather, a Thin Allied Line, and a Serious Surprise from the Enemy

PP's move almost coincided with an unexpected setback to the Allied armies. This was partly the result of the way in which Eisenhower's earlier decision to spread his strength had led to weaknesses in the Allied line.

Not surprisingly there was a general feeling that the front had now congealed and the troops were settling in for the winter. The Allied line was a very long one – from the English Channel to Switzerland – and was in places thinly held. Where the American and British fronts met was near the supposedly impassable Ardennes forest, a front held by four under-strength American divisions that were recovering from battle. This was precisely the route taken by the German armoured columns during von Manstein's dazzling *Sichelschnitt* offensive in 1940 that drove the British to evacuate their army from the Continent. 'Those who forget the past are compelled to re-live it.'

The Ardennes was the place chosen by Hitler in the autumn of 1944 for a counterstroke aimed at impeding and perhaps totally frustrating the progress of the Allied armies, by recapturing the port of Antwerp. The Germans managed to put together a new army of twelve *élite* divisions, although not all at full strength. These were eight Panzer, two Panzer Grenadier and two parachute divisions, and they were all assembled in total secrecy. They were helped by the overcast, foggy and snowy winter weather, which kept on the ground the Allied aircraft that would probably have spotted from aerial reconnaissance what the Germans were up to. The Germans also kept total radio silence, which meant that nothing was detected by *Sigint* from *Ultra* at Bletchley Park.

The German assault began on 16 December and made immediate progress. Bradley was not unduly disturbed, but Eisenhower took the matter more seriously and moved two armoured divisions from neighbouring formations to provide support. The magnificent 101st Airborne Division (including 327th RCT which PP had supported at Nijmegen) was also moved by truck for 100 miles to the important road junction at Bastogne, which was isolated but held. They made history by their defence of this little town.

The German advance – the 'Bulge' – was soon 60 miles deep, although the Germans were stalled in many places by a shortage of fuel. The alarm caused by the depth of the German penetration was increased by widespread rumours of English-speaking German soldiers in American uniforms spreading panic and misleading information. Most of them were caught and duly shot. The response of Eisenhower and his subordinates Montgomery and Patton throughout the battle was totally professional. Montgomery, who was now reinforced by the temporary transfer of the American 1st and 9th Armies, provided a solid barrier on the northern flank. Patton facing east, carried out the remarkable feat of pivoting his 3rd Army to attack north into the 'Bulge'. Then the weather cleared, which greatly favoured the Allied defence, because of the dominance of Allied air power.

The American armies were unquestionably shaken but they soon recovered their fighting ability. Antwerp was never in danger. But the butcher's bill for the Americans was 19,000 fatal casualties; the Germans also took 15,000 prisoners. On 1 January 1945, the German air force made a suicidal all-out assault and both sides lost large numbers of aircraft. But the Allies could afford the losses; the Germans could not. By mid-January the Ardennes gap was closed, and the Germans had lost 100,000 men, killed, wounded and captured. The German army had to a large degree shot its bolt. It would still be capable of heroic defence, but attacking was beyond its ability.

Chapter 7

The Reichswald, the Rhine and Into Germany

The German Ardennes offensive was repulsed with considerable losses on both sides. But afterwards the Germans continued to fight with their customary grit and professionalism, although with weakened resources. The German army benefited from shortening supply lines; and the soldiers were defending their Fatherland. The German army was incapable of a fresh offensive, but during the last months of the war the Allies were forced into a hard-contested fighting advance. 21st Anglo-Canadian Army Group continued its concentrated thrust. It crossed the Rhine onto the north German plain, capturing Wilhelmshaven, Bremen, Cuxhaven, Hamburg, Kiel and Lübeck: reaching these ports before the Russian armies advancing from the east.

Holding the Northern Edge of the 'Bulge'

PP's posting on 12 December 1944 was to 112th Field Regiment, which he joined on 15 December. The Regiment was part of the celebrated 43rd (Wessex) Division. This Division had seen much action during the campaign and during its course suffered almost as many casualties as its original strength. It was commanded by Major General Thomas, who had begun his regimental soldiering in the Royal Artillery. He was well-known for his aggressiveness, and his hard driving made him unpopular although the officers and men did their jobs very well. 116th Field Regiment had been (as mentioned earlier) part of the Army Group Royal Artillery attached to XXX Corps. 43rd Division was also in this Corps.

112th Field Regiment was commanded by a Territorial, Lieutenant Colonel Graham Gadsden (who did not at first impress PP). PP's old comrade Nobby (Major Clarke) soon became Second-in-Command. There were only two batteries: 220, commanded by Major Steele-Perkins; and 217, commanded by PP, with six other officers: three captains and three subalterns. 112th Regiment was 100 miles east of Brussels, at Maastricht in southern Holland. 43rd Division had just moved back after a successful offensive over the border in Germany, where it had taken the small but important town of Geilenkirchen. (*See Map 12.*) On his way to 112th Regiment, PP passed through Brussels and found six HAC friends in the Officers' Club. He reached the Regiment that evening and had dinner at RHQ: six courses and no shortage of drink!

15 December 1944
Went round Battery, good-looking, alert lot. Mostly with unit for four years. Officers fairly new, they have lost six in the Battery. We seem to have a huge lot of stuff, including six extra lorries, four cows, a horse and a cart. Went to 7 Hampshires (our Battalion) in evening and saw Ginger Rogers in *Lady in the Dark* in Technicolor.

16 December 1944
Harbour party went after breakfast. Battery moved 13:30 to Beek. Parked along roadside, men in houses and barns. CO gave me his appreciation of Battery in detail after tea; he is a man who goes down to details and has been in the Regiment the whole war and CO for over two years. Too long really. It seems we are here for forty-eight hours.

17 December 1944
Maintenance and baths. Voluntary evening Service. I've inherited a Jeep, which is a great blessing. We have a fine collection of easy chairs and settees which travel in an old German lorry. I like the chaps; will have to get to know the officers a bit. I am writing in the kitchen-parlour of a small double cottage; it is warmer than the Mess. The family, still in the house, are well off artisan-type people with three young children.

There is a certain amount of banging and fireworks going on tonight. It looks like the odd enemy plane or two having a crack at something. I have been out to see a flickering white light not far away which the chap in the house says is a plane shot down. The last two nights we have had thick white frosts. The kilns and ovens of brick and tile works make good dug-outs with a roof or two over them. Holmes [*PP's batman, who moved to the new Regiment with him*] is always first in the meal line, and got himself a new hat and jacket as soon as he arrived.

On 18 December, two days after the beginning of the German Ardennes offensive, the news about this got to PP. He thought that the attack on the Americans was very like Rommel's strike against the Americans at Kasserine. PP wondered whether the Germans had committed the 6th Panzer Army and decided to fight it out this side of the Rhine. (The Germans in fact attacked with *two* Panzer armies.) Meanwhile, the staff of 43rd Division was making plans for the continuation of the offensive into Germany. These were immediately cancelled and the Division prepared to redeploy. 112th Field Regiment would soon be playing a part in holding the northern flank of the German salient.

19 December 1944
Moved 12:30. Long slow column over Juliana Canal, and then to the Maas. Better after that. The sign-posting of the divisional route was very good. We stay at our new location, now all under cover; maybe a day or two. Our destination is Goirle, just south of Tilburg. But just in case we might be wanted in the south, we will probably linger until the German attack against the Yanks is really held.

This outfit [*Battery, not Regiment*] did not seem to have much of a Mess, so I am trying to get one going. Why people can't live as decently and comfortably as they possibly can I cannot imagine. The difference between a north country battery [*as in 116th Regiment*] and a southern one [*as in 112th Regiment*], is really amazing. Holmes is almost the only northerner, but gets on well with them all. A sterling fellow, though a bit careless. A number of the soldiers here come from middle-class homes.

Holmes told me today about working his passage home from the States pre-war. Signed on a cattle boat as a trimmer, got sore hands in a day and traded his job as a cattleman, so he spent the rest of the seven-and-a-half weeks' trip feeding and watering cows and giving them new straw.

20 December 1944
Slept well but cold. Regiment put at an hour's notice from 10:00 to move south towards enemy attack. No more news by lunchtime. Very foggy and dull, inclined to drizzle. PTM [*Prepare to Move*] forthwith at 15:50. Led off quickly to RV north of Russon. CO there. Split the billets in the village of Lowaige with 220 Battery. Orders 22:00. Tomorrow we support A Squadron, 43rd Recce Regiment. Bed 01:30 [*21 December*] after giving orders. Over a dozen flying bombs passed over. Battery HQ fed before move (except for my driver and me). Lorry used by the cooks overturned. Scrounged grub off one of my gun troops.

21 December 1944
Left 07:00. Found three good OPs on high ground and slag heap. Country full of Yanks, who are very suspicious of us, but talked our way around their questions. Three bridges in use. Ken [*Lieutenant Wade*] put Battery in action at Alleur. Madame at Chateau had lost her husband on the first day of the war, and two sons subsequently. Had aided many Allied airmen.

Enemy has made deep thrust on narrow front. The northern flank we hold is firm, and plenty of troops are available for counter-attack. Good long night at last.

22 December 1944
Conference at RHQ at 09:00, but got lost on bad roads. Discussion of leave roster to UK. Visited local US General Hospital PM. They want us to show prisoners that we are armed because they are getting arrogant. Two British nurses on strength. Flying bombs on and off all day. Gunfire heard after tea and unconfirmed report of enemy near the Meuse.

23 December 1944
The momentum of enemy advance seems to have slowed up and Yanks have retaken some places. First mail for ten days, all re-directed.

24 December 1944
Flying bombs still going off at intervals. Enemy getting on well towards Namur. Good old 101st Airborne Division holding out well at Bastogne, and supplied by air. Leave roster: I am third in line among the officers. Cold Christmas Eve. I shall retire to my warm blankets as soon as possible.

Everyone is on the *qui vive* now. I was stopped by a sentry the other day – it was mutual. After producing identity and explaining what I wanted I went in with the sentry sitting on the bonnet, did what I went there for and returned to the gate where he dropped off. Today, I had in my Command Post a couple of almost certain spies whose papers were suspicious; on being searched they had on them photos which they couldn't have had if they had been genuine civilians. So we handed them over to the right people.

25 December 1944
White frosty morning, cold and sunny day, mist in the Meuse valley. Recced south-west a bit. Church Service with Recce Regiment Padre at back of café at 12:00.

PP letter to his father, 26 December 1944
I live in a gamekeeper's cottage. He wears breeches and a glorious hat, like a French general with silver braid. Various windows broken by the flying bombs which shake the house. One flew overhead this evening, quite out of control. It went round in varying circles, tilted to the horizontal, then went off into the brilliant moonlit night.

The men enjoyed their tinned turkey, pork and beef. Having served them we had ours. As we began, the CO arrived at the end of his Christmas round of the Regiment: rather an undertaking in present circumstances. He was in good form, aided by champagne and brandy.

The enemy's Christmas attack is a bold and well-timed effort, but it must have cost him a lot of men and tanks, and the Yanks are no longer likely to withdraw. Some of my friends are in it; I know they will fight very well and will not give up.

PP diary, 26 December 1944
Similar day. Over 200 Allied heavy bombers streamed over us PM. Warning order PTM at 07:00, so bed early.

27 December 1944
Moved 16:30, to Maastricht near where we were before. This time into action, but DF rôle, no OPs. Small pits already dug by 51st Division. Everyone under cover, very cold and misty.

28 December 1944
Slight snow in night, slippery roads today. Baths for all at Galeen Colliery. Hear about officers in 116th Field Regiment: thirteen subalterns for infantry; Derek Farr coming to me – good [*this move was cancelled because he had to go into hospital*]. Orders at 21:15, we are in Army Reserve in three rôles. Last night my feet were ice blocks. Long stream of heavy planes is going over now and has been for some time.

The Unstoppable Advance
During the frigid weather of January 1945, it became increasingly clear that the German Ardennes offensive had been decisively defeated and would not be repeated. The staff of 21st Army Group therefore returned to its plans to resume the offensive; the immediate objective was the Reichswald. This was to prove an inflection point in the campaign in the west. From now on, despite the fact that the German army was never routed, the progress of the Anglo-Canadian and American armies was continuous and uninterrupted until the final German surrender in May 1945.

To explain the Reichswald operation, Map 12 needs to be looked at in some detail. Arnhem on the Neder Rhein in the north, was still in German hands. Nijmegen on the Maas, 20 miles to the south, was held by the Allied armies. The low-lying land in between, called the Island, was dominated by British troops, although (as explained in Chapter 6) the danger of the Germans flooding it meant that the ground was not permanently occupied. Maastricht, 80 miles south of Nijmegen, is at the southern end of the small projection of Dutch territory called the Maastricht Appendix. A couple of miles south of Maastricht, the Ardennes forest begins. The German frontier runs from north to south, and takes a large loop below Arnhem before continuing south again.

The Rhine flows north from Switzerland and eventually swings west through southern Holland (where it is called the Neder Rijn) towards its exit into the North Sea. The Maas (Meuse in French) is to the west and roughly parallel to the Rhine. Past Nijmegen it continues in a western direction until it reaches the delta from which both the Rhine and Maas debouch into the sea. Before the end of 1944 the German frontier had been breached in parts by the Allied forces, notably by the British at Geilenkirchen east of Maastricht, and by the Americans at Aachen close to the Maastricht Appendix, where a brutal battle was still going on.

The Reichswald is a deep forest nestled in the loop of the German frontier just south of Arnhem. Its importance was due to what lies beyond the forest to the east: the Rhine and the Ruhr, the industrial heart of Germany. The British objective was to advance to the Ruhr from the north, while the Americans aimed to advance from Aachen in the south. The forest itself is irregularly shaped, about 9 miles long and 5 miles wide, and stretches north-west to south-east. It was bisected by the Siegfried Line, erected by the Germans during the 1930s, and although this had been neglected for years it still contained some formidable concrete barriers. The forest is dense and crossed by a number of unmetalled 'rides' that cannot take mechanical transport. It was all-in-all a tough obstacle for the attacking troops. The assault was under the overall command of the Canadian 1st Army, but mostly carried out by Horrocks's XXX Corps.

While the planning for the Reichswald battle was in progress, PP's diary was devoted to the routine of winter campaigning, and I have selected only brief extracts. The main thing he did was to reconnoitre battery positions, many of which were not actually occupied. However, the pace of activity increased in late January 1945, when the weather thawed. On 26 January, 112th Field Regiment was transferred to the 52nd (Lowland) Division, which had been brought in from England to join 21st Army Group. This Division was to play an important part in the Reichswald battle. It was the right-hand division of an attacking force totalling 200,000 men, the largest Allied assault since Normandy. The advance was preceded by a formidable artillery barrage, witnessed by PP on 8 February. The British and Canadian troops suffered heavy casualties, but the battle was a total success and included the capture of Cleve and Goch. During this time PP was living in civilian billets. In Holland, these were still occupied by Dutch families. When he moved across the frontier to Germany, the billets were often although not always deserted.

PP's sojourn with 112th Regiment was shortly to come to an end. He was fortunate enough to be granted a brief period of leave, and he left for England on 13 February, after having been out of the country for eight months. On his return at the end of February, he had orders to report as Second-in-Command to 55th Field Regiment. This was to be his military home until the end of the war, and his service there was to be extremely successful.

29 December 1944
Recce battalion area with 7 Hampshires, muddy tracks are frozen and

impassable to wheels. Misty, could not recce OPs properly. [*PP was still billeted with the Dutch gamekeeper's family*] Sat by fire in billet, and Emily (aged 15) played piano with loud pedal hard down.

30 December 1944
Recce another area; slight snow after tea.

31 December 1944
Icy roads, boys skating. Heavy air activity, bombers. My Dutch family very delightful. Rum and whisky, piano and supper, good wishes all round. Bed at 02:00 [*1 January 1945*].

1 January 1945
Recce another gun area. Great excitement when a German fighter was shot down in flames and hit the deck going full out, about 400 yards away on the edge of the village. We filled in the deep hole made by the engine.

2 January 1945
Recce two further areas. Blankets and sights must be kept dry. To HQRA for tea. Back to change and a late tea. Taken two hours later to Recce Regiment cocktail party. Everyone well away.

3 January 1945
Recce gun areas in US sector. Aachen, a big town, an awful sight with all those acres of rubble. Few civvies left. Went nearly to Eupen, the Ardennes country with pine woods and undulating fields. Germans pulling back out of the tip of their salient. Visited a captured German prison camp. Prisoners worked in a mine, said to have been Russians. Wooden huts with double-tier bunks, concrete floors, whitewash. Still snowy and icy in the Ardennes, about 850 feet up.

4 January 1945
Warmer, turned to slush and top of ground thawing, although underneath still like a rock. Hope to start initial training [*for battle*] next week.

6 January 1945
Lunch with Lieutenant Colonel Freeland [*former CO of 7 Norfolk*], now commanding 1/5 Queen's Regiment.

7 to 10 January 1945
Nobby [*Clarke*] and I went to Brussels, partly on leave and partly to fix regimental leave centres. We did a bit of shopping and visited

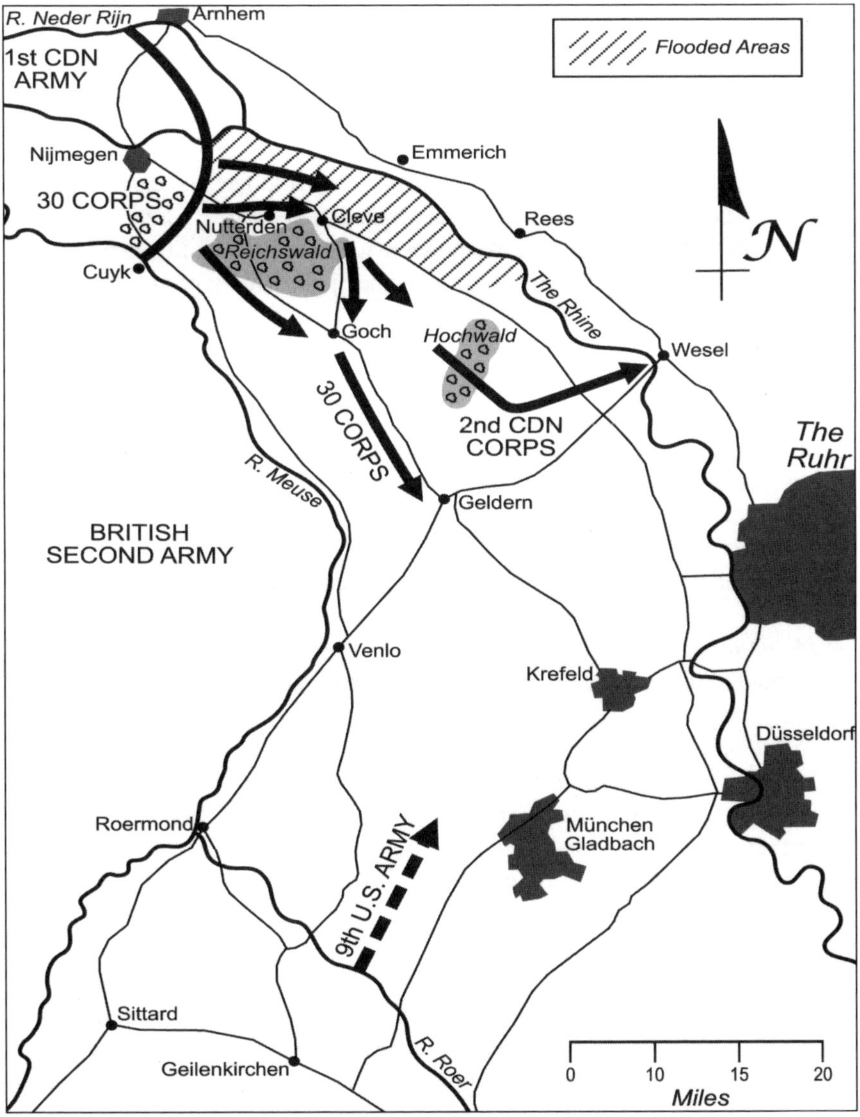

R. Neder Rijn Arnhem

1st CDN ARMY

////// Flooded Areas

Nijmegen

Emmerich

30 CORPS

Nutterden Cleve

Rees

Reichswald

Cuyk

The Rhine

Goch *Hochwald*

Wesel

N

30 CORPS

2nd CDN CORPS

R. Meuse

Geldern

The Ruhr

BRITISH SECOND ARMY

Venlo

Krefeld

Düsseldorf

9th U.S. ARMY

Roermond

München Gladbach

Sittard

Geilenkirchen

R. Roer

0   10   15   20

Miles

Map 12: The Reichswald, approaching the Rhine. In the harsh winter weather of February 1945, XXX British Corps and 11 Canadian Corps embarked on a difficult but successful assault on the Reichswald, and incurred heavy casualties. This dense wood was heavily strengthened by concrete fortifications built inside it. It was occupied by strong German pockets in the wood itself and in the surrounding areas. PP, commanding a battery of 112th Field Regiment, Royal Artillery participated in the preliminary artillery preparation for the battle on 8 February. He was in-between appointments. He departed on leave on 13 February and returned at the end of the month to become Second-in-Command of 55th Field Regiment, Royal Artillery (West Somerset Yeomanry). After the British and Canadian troops had cleared the Reichswald, they began to prepare for the set-piece crossing of the Rhine.

innumerable cafés and bars. Meals at Palace Hotel good. Luscious bath every day. The clear cold of the Brussels area vastly preferable to the icy, damp, misty cold of Holland.

11 January 1945

Recce a gun area for 79th Field Regiment. Very cold feet and ears. Issued with a snow suit, hooded in canvas which is delightfully warm-feeling, plenty of pockets too. Jeep broke down twice. Nearly had a fit when I saw two men with moons and stars painted on their jerkins like any circus clown.

13 January 1945

Regiment moved into Germany again, to Teveren. 7 Hampshires in the same town. Recced regimental area, OK for two batteries. Started living in RHQ, very good Mess. These German houses, if at all recently built, have the most terrific reinforced concrete cellars.

14 January 1945

Dined and wined with 7 Hampshires at other end of town. Excellent claret.

16 January 1945

Armoured division began pushing up the east bank of the Maas.

18 January 1945

Thawing rapidly. 7th Armoured Division has got on alright. 52nd Division started this morning. We start in two days, probably put off a further day. Our position only 2,500 yards behind FDLs [*with the improving weather, the British army was again beginning to take the initiative*].

21 January 1945

Recce another area. Infantry attack seemed to be held up by mines. Saw two Flail tanks stopped. Our road blocked by burnt-out vehicle. Hear that Johnny Kell is with 5th Regiment RHA.

22 January 1945

Flails left odd grenades and mines on the road, but RE soon cleared them. 7 Hampshires did very well and captured Putt and Waldenrath, with over 200 prisoners. Eric Rankin [*Captain, 217 Battery*] slightly wounded in cheek. This operation is called *Blackcock*. 'Max' Miller [*Lieutenant, 217 Battery*] shot a chicken, which we had for dinner. The MO remarked that he supposed it was the original Black Cock! The RHQ Mess Bombardier was a head waiter at Bognor.

23 January 1945
Tried to find Eric [*Rankin*], and learned he was evacuated to 39th General Hospital. Saw gun with breech split by cartridge being fired. Lucky it didn't fly and kill detachment. Suggest saboteur put TNT in cartridge instead of cordite. This part of Germany must be very Catholic, houses full of religious pictures and crucifixes.

25 January 1945
Find it very difficult every morning, leaving warm bed for cold room, filthy bare floor. Very cold night, 27 degrees of frost. Call on 81st General Hospital and found Lance Bombadier Bonser very cheerful, very comfy after operation last night [*he was a NCO in 217 Battery who had been wounded with a hole in his thigh*]. Eric Rankin in Brussels. Operation *Blackcock* very successful: 800 prisoners and few casualties.

26 January 1945
Recce a new area and put 217 Battery in during afternoon. Area very badly shot up. We come under command of 52nd Division and pull back out of the line.

28 January 1945
All very quiet and we expect to be here another four to seven days. CRA arrived at teatime and said I am posted to the Guards Armoured Division as Second-in-Command [*later learning that this would be to 55th Field Regiment*].

31 January 1945
Batteries moved to their concentration areas. Fast thaw today. Nobby [*Clarke*] put out signs [*to direct vehicles*]. What a dog's breakfast, no information, no time, and a long way to go for information, and no RHQ people.

2 February 1945
Went to Brussels to 21st Army Group RA headquarters about getting more men. Not much success. Found Eric [*Rankin*] had been moved again. Called at officers' leave place. Madame said our chaps were 'très gentil' and I bought a lot of Pommery to take on leave.

3 February 1945
On way back to Battery, met John Sherren [*Lieutenant, formerly 481 Battery*]. Just in from Britain, having escaped infantry. Said Derek [*Farr*] in hospital, a nervous breakdown.

7 February 1945

A filthy move. Road very narrow and winding, and in parts they laid pale fencing in front as we moved slowly along. Through Nijmegen into forest area west of Groesbeck. Battery in tents and dugouts in pine forest. Guns in clearing, tracks awful. We therefore had to come back through outskirts of Nijmegen. Met two members of HAC: B and A Batteries respectively.

8 February 1945

[*The bombardment for the Reichswald Battle was about to start*] About 1,200 guns opened up at 05:00 and went on every four minutes until 09:00. I was reminded of the colossal bombardment across the Straits of Messina. Went to 55th Field Regiment and saw Barrie Wilson [*Lieutenant Colonel, CO*], who said I could have leave and join afterwards. Welcomed me and I feel I will enjoy it there with him. Guns firing all AM, news scarce as usual. Big attack, five divisions. Saw prisoners PM, mostly young lads.

Our battery transport is frightful, they don't repair what they ought to and miss the faults, and imagine others. Had BSM and Vehicle Maintenance Sergeant up before CO for inefficiency, and he warned them that next time he would break them. 43rd Division and Guards Armoured Division in reserve.

9 February 1945

The attacking divisions seem to be getting on alright [*Plate 19*]. Regiment came out of action first thing. Recce parties went up to forward area, to support 4 Somerset Light Infantry. Battery commanders and one OP to join Battalion 15:00, but I do not see them moving before the 10th. At 19:00, warning order to move about 04:30 [*10 February*], which caused great consternation. Later amended to 06:00.

10 February 1945

About 06:30, no move until further orders. At 08:30 put on one hour's notice. At this stage of the war all this lack of sleep before battle is inexcusable. Any fool could have foreseen there would be a delay on the one usable road. Johnson [*Captain, 217 Battery*] a bit quiet, writing on a table in the corner. Asked what he was doing, he said he was saying goodbye to his wife as he felt certain that he would not survive the Reichswald Battle. He didn't, I heard later.

11 February 1945

No move yet. Two hours' notice. With any luck I go on leave on 13 February. Finished by 19:30 and dined with Hampshires.

12 February 1945
Rained nearly all day. Lunch with Hampshires. Sorted kit PM. One road forward under one to two feet of water. Regiment almost bogged down. Most of Cleve is ours. Over 3,200 prisoners up to now.

13 February 1945
Holmes cooked breakfast, and eight of us left late, about 07:20 in three-ton truck. Very warm and fine, but the vehicle wasn't pulling very well.

In this way PP left for England for his leave, having arranged for his batman, Gunner Holmes, to transfer with him to 55th Field Regiment. On his return, he left Victoria Station at 23:00 on 23 February, and crossed the Channel on the evening of 24 February. On 26 February he borrowed a Jeep and started to look for 55th Field Regiment. He found Cleve and Goch flattened and full of bomb holes. There were many British units around, and after driving through seas of mud, he found the Regiment in a farm. He then returned to 112th Field Regiment to make departure arrangements and obtain a tank suit (an extremely well-insulated one-piece garment), plus a good ration of spirits. Traffic was very thick when he returned to his new Regiment and the Guards Armoured Division.

'Nell Gwyn's Left Eye'
Every division in 21st Army Group had its own sign for visual identification. It was displayed as a cloth patch sewn at the top of the arm of the uniform, and as an emblem stencilled onto the vehicles in the division. One of the best-known divisional signs was the 'Ever-Open Eye' used by the Guards Armoured Division. In 1915, a Guards division had been formed from a dozen Guards infantry battalions, and this division was the first to use the 'Ever-Open Eye'. After 1918 the Division, and the sign, went into abeyance. It was revived in the Second World War.

The design is a dark-blue shield with a red border (these two colours being the ones associated with the Brigade of Guards), and the eye is straight in the middle. The soldiers called it 'Nell Gwyn's Left Eye'. Nell Gwyn was a well-known courtesan who was originally an orange seller in a London theatre. It is not explained how she managed to look in two directions at once, but it was thought that with her left eye she viewed the world as a whole, while her right eye was fixed on her best-known lover, King Charles II. The King had been exiled and came to the throne in 1660. The three senior regiments of Foot Guards were raised during the time of the Commonwealth in the 1650s, and were made the King's personal troops on his return to England, when they were joined by two horse regiments that became known as the Household Cavalry. History has always had a rich meaning for the British armed services. But during the Second World War the Guards regiments expanded their role in a totally new direction.

After the British army had escaped from Dunkirk in 1940 without its equipment and supplies, it was obvious that the British military leaders had to concentrate on providing the weapons and other equipment for the soldiers who were now responsible for the defence of Britain and, it was hoped, would eventually resume the offensive. This had to be the first priority. At the top of the list were tanks, since the German Blitzkrieg had demonstrated that armour was the decisive weapon in ground warfare. The tank had been invented by British ingenuity during the First World War, but the British army had neglected to develop it in the 1920s and 1930s, mainly for lack of adequate funds for the armed services, and because so much of the money that was available went to developing new fighter and bomber aircraft.

Since the relatively small number of tanks that the army possessed in 1940 and 1941 were fighting in North Africa, Brooke, who commanded the Home Army, decided to raise two new armoured divisions whose original rôle was home defence. The reorganization quickly took place and training began, but the troops had to wait for many months before their tanks arrived.

One of these two divisions was intended to be a *corps d'élite* composed of infantry battalions of Household troops. They came from five marching regiments each composed of a number of battalions, plus two regiments of Household Cavalry. They were and are rather a closed community, usually referred to as the Brigade of Guards (or the Brigade). The ethos of the regiments, based on discipline and pride – reinforced by the social cachet of their officers – makes for a high degree of military efficiency. During the Second World War the Brigade was made up of Regulars, Regular Reserves and Special Reserves (i.e. those who had never been Regulars). There were no Territorials, and the 'hostilities only' recruits, officers and men, were selected and trained according to Regular army standards. When the Guards Armoured Division was formed, the men were already well led, strongly disciplined, and excellently trained as infantry, but they now had to learn the special skills of armoured soldiers: tank driving and maintenance, gunnery and efficient radio communication in a mobile battle. Courses and cadres were immediately set up, and all ranks of the Division acquired and constantly practised the necessary skills during the period of more than two years before they went to war.

The Division was raised by Major General Leese, a well-known Coldstreamer. But in the autumn of 1942 he was posted to North Africa to take over a corps in the 8th Army, with whom he fought in Africa and Italy. In early 1944 he replaced Montgomery as head of the 8th Army when Montgomery returned to Britain to take overall command of the army assault on Normandy. After the end of the war in Europe, Leese was sent to Burma as ground force commander, under Mountbatten, the overall director of sea, land and air forces in the region. In Burma, Leese took the extraordinary step of relieving Slim from command of the celebrated 14th Army, because Leese thought that he was tired. Mountbatten's role in this plot is not totally clear. The officers and men of the 14th Army were outraged at the threat to remove Slim, who was both a popular and an extremely successful general who had defeated the Japanese. London disowned Leese's decision. The result was that the general who returned home from Burma was not Slim. It was Leese, whose army career came to an end. Slim replaced him.

In 1942, Major General Adair, a Grenadier, succeeded Leese in command of the Guards Armoured Division, and led it throughout the campaign in north-west Europe. The division made a name for itself despite the inadequacy of its Sherman tanks (as described in Chapter 4). But Adair was never one of Montgomery's favourites, and he received no further promotion when the Division was disbanded at the end of the war in Europe.

In 1941, the British did not fully understand how an armoured division should best be organized and deployed in battle; there was over-reliance on the weight of armour. However, the war in North Africa made it clear that an armoured division had to have a strong infantry component to occupy the ground that the tanks had overrun. The Guards Armoured Division, which was originally organized on the basis of three brigades, two armoured and one infantry, was reshaped before it went into battle.

After months of field exercises in Britain, the divisional organization evolved in a more balanced fashion. When it landed in Normandy, the formation was made up of one armoured reconnaissance battalion; one armoured brigade (of three armoured battalions and one motorized infantry battalion); and one infantry brigade (of three battalions). The 'teeth' of the division were four armoured battalions (with this name, although that used in the Royal Armoured Corps was armoured regiments); four infantry battalions; four gunner regiments; plus an independent machine-gun company. The artillery comprised two Field regiments (of which the 55th was the senior), plus one anti-tank regiment, and one anti-aircraft. There was also the normal complement of engineers, signals, Service Corps, Medical Corps, Ordnance Corps and Royal Electrical and Mechanical Engineers (specialists in repairing tanks). Each armoured battalion had sixty tanks which, as described earlier, were not as well protected or as heavily armed as those in the German army.

In addition to the Guards Armoured Division, the Household troops also formed the 6th Guards Tank Brigade. This had the heavier Churchill tanks, although even these were not up to the standard of the German ones. During the campaign this brigade captured a German Panther, which was named 'Cuckoo' and used against its previous owners. It was said to be the best tank that 6th Guards Tank Brigade used during the last months of the war.

Montgomery's 21st Army Group contained two armies (as described in earlier chapters). The larger was the 2nd British Army, which at its full strength in the autumn of 1944 contained 1,000 tanks in 4 armoured divisions and the 6th Guards Tank Brigade; 10 infantry divisions; plus the 2 British airborne divisions that were part of the Allied Airborne Army (one of these was lost at Arnhem). The smaller was the 1st Canadian Army that contained five divisions, the 4th Canadian Armoured, the 1st Polish Armoured and three Canadian infantry divisions. A British corps was added as an occasional reinforcement to the Canadians.

The Guards Armoured Division landed in Normandy in late June 1944 and was almost immediately sent into battle to the west of Caen, where it began to suffer casualties. On 18–20 July, in Operation *Goodwood*, it was one of three armoured divisions and large numbers of infantry who attacked the Germans in the southern outskirts of Caen, through the rubble left by the heavy air bombardment. Of the 750 British tanks that advanced, 200 were knocked out by enemy fire. Then, in the Canadian advance southward to Falaise, the Guards Armoured Division made costly and unsuccessful attacks. However it made more progress in the British attack that was part of the wide movement to close the neck of the Falaise pocket. This led directly to the victory in Normandy.

After its bruising experience in these early battles, the Guards Armoured Division was at last freed to carry out the traditional rôle of tanks, to get on the move. It soon charged north-east and was the first element of the British army to liberate Brussels. The Division covered more than 90 miles in 14 hours.

The Division was next given a key role in Operation *Market Garden*. It was ordered to push north in a highly vulnerable Indian file up the elevated road to relieve the American airborne divisions at the first river crossings, and then to come to the aid of the British airborne division at Arnhem. As explained earlier, enemy attacks on the flanks delayed the advance, and the beleaguered British at Arnhem remained isolated and were virtually wiped out. The Guards Armoured Division was only 8 miles short of the Arnhem bridge. This was a dreadful blow to the morale of all the Allied troops, but they had by now become hardened to the misfortunes of war.

The Division's next task was also a difficult one, the assault on the Reichswald. It was shortly after the successful conclusion of this battle and while the British army was getting to the west bank of the Rhine, that PP joined the 55th Field Regiment. It was a Territorial unit, formerly the West Somerset Yeomanry, a regiment raised in 1794 as yeomanry on horses, but gunners since 1920. (112th Field Regiment was spun off it in 1939.) He was welcomed by 55th Field Regiment, partly because his younger brother Paul had commanded one of the batteries for a year in England and was remembered with respect and affection. PP's Commanding Officer, Lieutenant Colonel Barrie Wilson, was a Regular whom PP had known before the war. He had been attached as a young officer to 11th (HAC) Regiment, RHA, and had been known for his elegant appearance (in PP's words) 'with legs designed to fit into the smartest riding boots most of us had ever seen'. 55th Field Regiment had three batteries: 373 (commanded by Major Carew-Hunt, who was killed and succeeded by Major Peploe); 374 (commanded by Major Taylor); and 439 (commanded by Major Yorke). Holmes said 'they're a much nicer lot' than his last Regiment, and this sentiment was seconded by various Other Ranks who transferred (or who wished to do so).

During the remaining weeks of the war, PP's main job was to find gun positions for the Regiment and to place batteries on the ground, often under enemy small arms fire.

28 February 1945
Finished looking round batteries. Met CRA, 'Chink' Phipps, who formerly commanded 13th (HAC) Regiment, RHA. Battle goes well, we carry out fire plans for two other divisions and are getting left out of the hunt. We'll have to move, probably tomorrow. I sleep in a barn, Holmes cleared a patch among the straw for my bed etc. So far we have eggs for breakfast daily, some of the hens which escaped are kind enough to lay as a mark of their appreciation. There is still a Boche in the farm and also some Russians, conscripted labour. Shell holes and gun pits and the usual refuse of war.

1 March 1945
Advancing slowly, heavy fighting on Corps front.

2 March 1945
With CO in Divisional Operations Room. General Horrocks came in, and waiting for the Divisional Commander gave us the picture. Said we would be all along the Rhine in three days. O Group 19:00, Division starts at 06:00 [*3 March*]. My recce party well up with leading brigade. Later, start put back to 10:30 [*3 March*]. Later still, postponed. Showers of sleet, hail and even snow. I have my own Humber staff car. Holmes and our kit travel in it, and it has a lean-to tent which unrolls from the roof at the back and gives room for a bed and the tailboard acts as a table. Haven't enjoyed such comfort since Sicily.

3 March 1945
Another broken night and hanging about all day. Orders to start next day.

4 March 1945
Got up at 05:30, then further talk of postponement. Returned to bed. 10:30 put at two hours' notice. All the delay has been caused by blown

bridges and culverts, extensive cratering of roads, and the rain. After lunch, HQRA said they would move at 15:00. More delays. Traffic very thick. Impossible to get CO's Jeep up column.

5 March 1945

Met CO about midnight [*4/5 March*] and recced Regiment area, luckily no mines. Put batteries in. Mostly in at 05:00 or slightly after. Utterly exhausted; waited for a meal which was very welcome, bed 06:30 and slept flat out until 09:30. Guns had plotted a few targets, but survey not very quick. Picked up a lot of peas and beans, all frozen, which should be useful. Fields very soft and difficult not to get bogged. Visited a less muddy farm and CO decided to move RHQ in the late afternoon. A vast improvement because we got rooms in occupied house and found central heating working well. Heaps of coal and chickens: these people aren't terribly short! We ask for rooms, which we cleared. A bit of weeping by females. It is an odd feeling actually living in a German farm with all the Jerries there.

6 March 1945

Recce new area, no mines luckily. Forest to east, not yet clear, but Irish Guards going through it after lunch. Examined the farmer who said he'd been a gunner in the last war and was in the Volksturm now (got his arm band). His son had to be in the Hitler Jugend; they had had to buy the Nazi banner we found upstairs. He knew the way we treated their prisoners in the last war, and did not expect to be shot or ill-treated. Sat up till about 02:00 [*7 March*] talking and drinking whisky with CO, and slept like a log.

7 March 1945

Visited HQRA in morning. CRA ordered recce parties to move forward and I sent them off. CRA and Staff Captain to tea. A lovely piece of sandy country with pine woods and rich-looking fields. Our office lorry is called Somerset House. Lovely spring day, rather cold at dusk. What vandals we are in Germany: chuck all the contents of house out of windows, ruin quite usable sheets and furniture, china and chairs. Walked around batteries with CO. We are here about two or three days, and then likely to pull out and go to Mook-Gennep for ten to fourteen days, in preparation for obvious *Drang nacht Osten.*

8 March 1945

Walked round regimental area. RSM fixed up a bath tub PM, heated water in a copper. Followed CO and had a lovely bath in barn. Just before tea recce parties called for move forward into Bonninghardt area. Put Command Posts and Gun Positions in – luckily no mines. Arranged to share RHQ with the Regimental Aid Post of 5 Coldstream. They are assembling for their attack, but this was put off till tomorrow. Met their CO, Lieutenant Colonel Roddy Hill, whom I had come across before the war and also in Tunisia; also Nevill Whitmee [*ex-B Battery, HAC*]. Regiment arrived just after dark. Barrie [*Wilson*] and I have a room together again. Floors in house all give way; we keep on putting our feet through.

9 March 1945

On return to the Batteries, found they had received some fire again and lost two dead and four wounded (two of whom returned to duty). Not all guns in pits and I feel that urgent need to dig deep isn't altogether appreciated. Nor is the need to apply a dressing to a wound at once. Heaps of sheep and lambs around here. Many killed or injured first by our fire and then by the enemy's. Last night was rather disturbed, a hell of a din going on, mostly friendly. The Germans are getting a bit split up now. A number lie low doing nothing and surrender as soon as they get a decent chance. Others fight like hell. In France they all fought, very few deserted.

10 March 1945

Walked around AM. A Medium regiment and another battery coming in behind us. During the night enemy withdrew from their bridgehead this side of the Rhine, and blew up the bridges at Wesel.

11 March 1945

Went off with CO to look at gun areas for next battle. All very peaceful and quiet today. Got some eggs for Mess, civilians seem to have been evacuated at very short notice, leaving hens and some cattle. After battles our chaps have damned well broken into locked houses and turned them upside down in search of valuables. It's just what we are fighting against. Fine day, gooseberry bushes showing green in the gardens and buds in the hedges. Saw the Rhine; it doesn't seem very wide. We are in a very comfortable house at present. The rest of the Regiment is not so lucky: dugouts in the sand and stoves and tarpaulins. It isn't really cold. The radio in this Mess drowns the noise, distracts the mind from the war. Radio Arnhem [*German*] plays good dance music.

12 March 1945

Left 09:00. Traffic very thick and the forty miles took till after 11:30. Pine woods already full of miscellaneous Canadian units. Was told they would be shifted out to make room for us. Plenty of room for batteries. Quick trip to Nijmegen. On return find that Regiment moves 08:00 [*13 March*].

13 March 1945
Left ahead of Regiment. Found a small house a quarter of a mile down the road as a Command Post, plus three huts for A Echelon and LAD. Regiment arrived meanwhile, so we had to park RHQ on one side while all this was arranged, and had lunch there. Fixed up forty-eight hour leave accompanying Barrie to Brussels. This was postponed by message at dinner to meet CRA in morning twenty miles away for recce. Yet another area I suppose. Why can't staff officers decide on things and stick to their decision? Untrained to think further ahead than next week or more broadly than their moustaches.

14 March 1945
Left 09:00. Lovely spring day and quite warm. Our recce the other day wasted. Got some details of our part in the forthcoming battle, but nothing of the big plot. Did recce and returned. People already in area, and difficult to find buildings to hide whole Regiment. I have really done nothing at all dangerous and hardly been near an enemy bang. This is much more like Africa and Sicily; I was rarely in the middle of the fighting there. Anyway, for the next few days the only things that can do me any harm will be the drink, American drivers and very long range rockets [*the Regiment was having a quiet life, and the 48-hour leave in Brussels was extended to five days, and turned into a spectacular series of parties*].

15/16 March 1945
Went to Brussels, arriving 13:30. 120 miles. Spent the afternoon looking up Barrie's friends. [*The 55th Field Regiment had been one of the first to arrive in Brussels and went into action surrounded by girls and champagne. The Regiment made many friends and Barrie and PP were about to renew these friendships*] Met some nice people, drank any amount of bubbly and danced with various girlfriends at night club. After dinner, although the car was locked we found car window smashed and cigarettes, gloves, kit bag, towels etc. gone. Also small haversack in which I keep writing case and all my letters, photos, pen etc. (Luckily found the haversack under the car later.) Returned to night club, and while dancing after midnight, military police raided the place with Belgian police. They took all our names. One girl, Lucy, a huge wench of about twenty, had to be home by 00:30 [*16 March*] and was very worried. Rather a bore. Our host and his brother have a big town house and a butler, also a very nice Jaguar car.

17 March 1945

Got up late. Beer, then breakfast of a dozen oysters and white wine. Then lunch and then made a few calls on army business. Tea at Officers' Club. Barrie got some bubbly at the Guards Division Club. Went to Tirlemont to visit other friends of Barrie. Lovely house and furniture. Umpteen wines, gorgeous grub. Bubbly again on return. Slept very well.

18 March 1945

Got up about 10:30. Immediately after breakfast walked into town and took aperitifs by station. Lunch with four wines. Afterwards, champagne and sweet cakes and so it went on all evening. Supper and dancing. Back before midnight for a final beer. I have not been so royally entertained this side of the Channel. At the meals, served by old family retainers on super china with two or three wine glasses, the diners use the same knife and fork all the way through.

19 March 1945

Breakfast about 10:30. Walked over fields and saw three mallards on a little stream. Two helpings of soup, brains, pork and soufflé for lunch. Left at 15:00 amid invitations to return. Good run back: four hours to cover 107 miles. Celebrated Barrie's DSO in the Mess with bubbly and brandy. Luckily we don't move tomorrow.

20 March 1945

Lots of air activity, lovely clear skies and sun. My car and Jeep being renovated.

21 March 1945

CO went to Corps Conference. Met him there and also Eric Riseley [*late HAC Infantry*], now commanding Light AA Regiment of 51st Highland Division. Went on to see Regiment area. Ammunition already dumped and very well camouflaged. We move tomorrow night and the big battle, crossing the Rhine, starts on the afternoon of 23 March. This week we have a bottle of bubbly each in the NAAFI ration, also beer and whisky, and there is some cognac.

22 March 1945

Officers briefed in the afternoon. Report that enemy has very little left and that, the crust once broken, he won't be able to stand again except in isolated places. The going is good for our armoured break-through. No limit to our objectives. Code name *Plunder*. Went ahead about 18:00. Thick smokescreen all over area from Cleve to south. Drank quantities of tea. Cleared up a bit and reasonable at midnight.

23 March 1945

Regiment arrived soon after midnight [*22/23 March*] and spread around area. Fine moonlight night. Bed 03:00 utterly worn out; better by 08:00. Another grand day, birds singing, daffodils, pansies and violets.

At noon the whole area came to life, batteries started digging pits, and 439 Battery opened the scoring by firing smoke at an observation tower over the river. [*The plan for the massive attack is now described*] Counter-battery programme starts at 17:00. Each of sixty or more hostile batteries that have been located will get about sixty tons. Then each of 120 enemy posts will catch it, while Tactical Air Force bomb every town and village the far side, then bomb the two Panzer divisions which are the only enemy reserves. 1st Commando Brigade cross the river near Wesel and edge up to the town ready to go in as bombing stops [*Plate 20*]. They get extra pay! At 21:00, 51st Highland Division cross at Rees in Buffaloes [*armoured tracked vehicles that could be propelled on the water to cross rivers*] [*Plate 21*].

At 10:00 [*24 March*], 6th British Airborne Division and 17th US Airborne Division drop on high ground above Wesel and on crossings over Issel River.

[*PP's description of the actual operation now follows*] Artillery fire rather spread out and didn't seem to reach the intensity one expected before H-Hour. Field, Medium, Heavy, Super Heavy, Anti-Aircraft, Anti-Tank, and four captured German 88s all joined in. Bed early to make up for last night. Soon slept though noise seemed greater and whole house shook, stopping the wall clock.

24 March 1945

Another grand day. Dakotas came over at 10:00. Counted over 300 of them containing paratroops. We could only see haze and smoke. Soon many came back, and I only saw two on fire. One hit the deck nearby after four 'chutes came out. They were quickly followed by Dakotas towing gliders in what seemed a never-ending stream. Then heavy British bombers as tugs for more gliders. Several tell-tale pillars of smoke round about the flat country. For a solid hour aircraft went overhead. Saw at least three gliders come off tow over us and circled to find a landing place, with their tugs fussing around like hens. One four-engined tug came along with its tow rope streaming out behind but with no glider attached. Must have lost it earlier on – he did not want to miss the fun for that.

Saw another stream of planes to the south-east, presumably the Yanks: all the tugs were Dakotas, and many towing Waco [*American-made*] gliders. Even more Yanks came along after 11:00. Two groups of

Liberator bombers came over very low, bomb doors open, one came back so low that it had to climb over the trees in the village. There were hundreds of fighters stooging about high up. And the AOPs were in the sky so as not to miss anything. This terrific spectacle took place in relative silence: the guns were not firing owing to danger to the aircraft. Very few odd German shells came in reply. Walked up to the dyke road by the Rhine in the afternoon and saw Buffaloes of 15th Scottish Division crossing steadily. Attack goes well. 15th Division has already contacted both British and US Airborne troops. Didn't see enemy aircraft all day. Several enemy air attacks on crossing areas after nightfall. Heaps of AA.

Crossing the Rhine at Wesel was a spectacular operation and brought very few casualties. However Bradley, the senior American field commander – of a force that was now larger than Montgomery's – was extremely critical of this substantially British assault. He believed that the enormous effort needed to mount the Rhine crossing was unnecessary. The American 1st Army had, through a rapid *coup de main* on 11 March, captured a bridge at Remagen, 90 miles upstream from Wesel. And on 22 March, Patton's 3rd Army managed to improvise a serviceable crossing at Oppenheim, 80 miles upstream from Remagen (note these distances, especially the 170 miles that separated Wesel and Oppenheim). The American armies quickly began to stream across the Rhine, and Bradley believed that the British could easily have followed them.

This argument did not wash with Montgomery, who never believed it important merely to capture enemy territory by moving in all directions over German real estate. His aim throughout was to vanquish the German army and capture important objectives. He had his eye on the big German ports on the Baltic and the North Sea. To get to these before the Russians, the British army had to continue its single-minded thrust north-east, so that Montgomery's meticulously prepared Rhine crossing was a vital part of the strategic plan. (See Map 13.) Shortly after the Rhine was crossed, Churchill and Brooke came from England to visit the bridgehead east of the river and join Montgomery for a picnic lunch. Afterwards Churchill urinated in the Rhine, a symbolic gesture.

With the Rhine behind them, the British now moved north-east through Germany. But this progression was not as speedy or as uninterrupted as the advance to Brussels in 1944. The German opposition was rapidly subdued, although the 55st Field Regiment suffered casualties, some fatal. Casualties so close to the end of hostilities were especially poignant. However, the end of the war was near and there were regular celebrations: a good deal of liquor flowed without damaging operational efficiency. The Regiment was almost daily on the move, travelling in a tactical formation, always prepared to be ordered into action at short notice. These regular changes of location provide a repetitive story. For the month of April 1945 I have therefore concentrated the diary extracts on days in which something out of the ordinary was taking place. These included the happy occasions when the Regiment liberated prisoners-of-war and foreign slave workers.

PP's diary contains typically English descriptions of the countryside in spring: he talks about the buds on the different trees and the various species of birds that were beginning to build their nests. On its travels, the Regiment was often billeted in German farms. The population everywhere was subdued but surprisingly cooperative. They were certainly not ill-fed, in contrast to the Dutch whom PP had encountered during the winter months. In March, Montgomery had published an order to all troops to prohibit fraternization with the German population; contact was to be on a 'business only' basis. However, this order was not taken too seriously by the troops in their search for what Montgomery himself had described, when he had commanded a division in France in 1940, as 'horizontal refreshment'.

25 March 1945
Buffaloes and DUKWs [*these were another type of vehicle that could drive across water*] crossing merrily and a tank raft going strong. Called on various artillery units. Two strong gins and back to lunch to find we move this PM – a paltry 2,000 yards. Moved straight away. We are now just inside the dyke beyond which is the Rhine. Burning buildings all over the far side. CRA came to tea and champagne cocktails.

26 March 1945
Thunder and lightning and heavy rain PM after overcast day. Laid the dust.

27 March 1945
Walked to HQRA 11th Armoured Division PM and back to tea at our HQRA. About three miles each way across country. Bit of a drinks party before dinner, champagne cocktails, CRA and staff in very good form. Hit bed before midnight.

28 March 1945
Our morning tour with CRA to 11th Armoured Division and 13th (HAC) Regiment, RHA, spoilt by finding them gone to their next positions during the night. Much better day for RAF. Hear XXX Corps armoured cars well out to south-east: as a right hook perhaps. General Adair visited us after lunch, walked round and had tea in the Mess. Very nice chap indeed and easy to talk to. Excellent cake and tarts by the cook. May move tomorrow. Dined at HQRA. CRA carved goose for about twelve. Long streams of traffic moving up road all day and all night to cross the large bridge that has been built [*by Royal Engineers*].

29 March 1945

CO called Conference 12:00. No move of Division before 04:00 [*30 March*]. General air of preparation and excitement. Our divisional objective is Hamburg. Overcast, cold, inclined to drizzle. 1,350-odd vehicles to cross the river before us and it is a very slow business over the bridge, particularly with armour. Hell of a row going on to north, probably the Canadians around Emmerich.

30 March 1945

Wakened 05:30. Doubt if we'll go before 08:00. Rain early and cold biting wind. We didn't go till about 11:30. Waited a long time on brink of river while solid jam ahead cleared itself. Crossed the Rhine at last, bridge about 350 yards long. We halted outside Rees. Half way to Isselburg we were ordered off road to let three battalions through. Tea ready and very low-grade salmon. Unlikely that we would move before 07:30 [*31 March*]. Hot meal 19:30, CO joined us. News is good. Four bridges at Rees now. Bed in tent let down from back of Humber [*staff car*].

31 March 1945

All up and ready about 07:00. No move before 09:30 and then had to pull out on road at 10:15. Regiment pulled up in rear of armoured battalions. Finally they did move off and eventually we followed. Heard that Johnson in 217 Battery killed a day or two ago [*he was the young officer who had a premonition on 10 February*]. Just after dusk got orders to harbour in tight group. Recced fields and barns for cookhouses and got in very slowly. Arranged left flank protection. Food trailer broke down on road and had to be ditched. RHQ fed very late. Bed 00:30 [*1 April*]. And slept very well.

1 April 1945

Easter Day. [*The Regiment as a whole was in Holland, in the Dutch territory north of the Reichswald*] Move off north and north-west towards Borenlo. Terrific welcome, all otherwise peaceful and no damage. Lovely birches along road just coming out. Everything is hedges, gardens, trees. The newspapers often write about armour racing here and there and I never believe it, but this is a bit of a race. We bat along well over twenty miles per hour for long stretches. One 75mm and one 88mm shell arrived in the area while I was lunching. Some dozen German soldiers we had captured went back on a Cromwell tank. It's lovely to see an unspoilt countryside although the tanks plough up some fields. I am tingling with the wind and very dirty.

2 April 1945
Fired guns about 15:00 on plan to support capture of airfield at Enschede. Runways just a heap of ruin and quite useless. All buildings camouflaged in trees for some distance from the actual field. Orders to get into action PDQ [*pretty damn quick*] south-east of Denchamp, to support attack on Nordhorn. Whole town of Denchamp turned out, we were greeted with roars of cheers. Five or six old people delighted to give me a bed and a glass of home-made cherry wine. 'We have waited five long years. The Germans took everything.'

4 April 1945
[*The Regiment was now in Germany*] Visited Brigade after lunch; heard about action of Ian Liddell's company and squadron at bridge over the Ems. 5 Coldstream got three 88mm guns, two 20mm guns, sixty prisoners of war and killed forty enemy, for the loss of about ten men. Also got the bridge intact over the Ems [*for this deed, Liddell was awarded the Victoria Cross. He was killed a few days later*]. Yesterday I saw cherry blossom and almond tree or something similar. Two obvious soldiers walked up to me and said they were Italians – in the Boche army I bet – so I sent them off to the cage [*where prisoners-of-war were held*] with a chap and a Sten gun. Barrie captured a couple of Boches the day before and the Batteries keep on getting the odd half-a-dozen here and there.

6 April 1945
Recce parties went down to Ems bridge and I took CP Officers through town and we looked round eastern exit for battery areas. Area I was given was in 3rd Division's FDLs. It was very built up and full of trees. Saw a dead Hausfrau with cycle in a gateway to a field where she had been caught by shell fire.

7 April 1945
Fire plan in morning for Lengerich. Bed at 03:00 in house with eleven civilians in cellar. Sergeant Brunscot [*Dutch interpreter*] shut them in for the night but before doing so held a pee parade, with a Sten gun. Eight women and three men lined up and pee'd as hard as they could on his order! Brunscot is very good at getting the lock on these Boches.

8 April 1945
Apparently an Italian officer gave himself up and said there were more waiting to be collected in the woods. Party went out from 374 Battery and Bombardier Taylor was shot up. Meanwhile a sergeant and one man

went round in trees and never heard of again. After that, Bill Taylor [*Major, OC 374 Battery*] got a couple of tanks and a party and went at it more cautiously. BSM Gregory of 373 Battery took a party round corner and in all they killed two or three and captured about eight.

PP letter to his father, 9 April 1945
The civilians we have met so far have been pretty docile and obey all orders. Some wave and smile and look mighty relieved, others look simply astounded at the columns of Allied might, others weep. I have noticed that they all look well-fed, a big contrast to the spotty under-nourished Dutch who show obviously the rigours of German domination for five years. The Dutch are delirious with joy and cannot do too much for us: working on roads in between the vehicles of a column, offering billets. The great majority in towns ask for cigarettes and chocolate and even biscuits. I have only known one Boche ask for anything and that was for a doctor as his wife had a cut forehead. We have met Italians, Russians and French as well; Yugoslavs and Poles; the highlight was the liberation of the number of British prisoners on one occasion.

PP diary, 10 April 1945
We all got into a regimental area I had recced yesterday. Saw red squirrel and a group of kingcups. Marshy ground but guns mostly kept near tracks. We hadn't quite enough range to cover Löningen, which Coldstream are moving towards. We therefore had to move forward again, to within 2,000 yards of new target. Despite enemy air bursts all around the place and a couple of swift ground bursts quite near my half-track, the traffic is still blocking the road. Guns arrived immediately and within half-an-hour two Batteries were firing to assist capture of Menslage at 2,900 yards' range. Many fires clearly visible and the church steeple was a fiery torch. Found a real bath in a large farm, and had water (full of small insects) boiled up outside and poured in. A couple of Polish girls, who had been taken from Poland five years ago, said they had been forced to come and work here. They wept with joy.

11 April 1945
Carew-Hunt [*Major, OC 373 Battery*], killed near bridge over River Hase [*70 miles north-east of the Rhine crossing at Wesel*]. He'd crawled forward to get a view, and was shot through shoulder and neck by Spandau. Very bad luck. This flat watery country certainly lends itself to defence and is no place for armour. There aren't enough infantry in an armoured division to capture bridgeheads over rivers and mop up woods and towns. [*See Map 13.*]

17 April 1945
Guards Armoured Division to follow 7th Armoured Division north-east and then turn off north-west towards Zeven and sit across communications between Bremen and Hamburg, while XXX Corps take Bremen. Terrific thunderstorm cleared the air and was very welcome at 19:00. Saw field of cowslips, very pretty but so dry, no smell.

18 April 1945
Hot and sunny. Small fire plan on Keltenburg, which was captured. Another fire plan on Visselhövede at 19:30. Hear that there are Werewolves about [*supposed German guerrilla fighters trained to harass Allied troops*]. A searchlight crew at Rethem found stabbed. I wonder.

20 April 1945
Deployed on road towards Westervesede. Regiment on road were halted and mortared and had a dozen casualties. One Troop of 373 Battery went into action to deal with mortars. Second Troop then came up. We had to turn the Battery round and fire on a different bearing, 170 degrees; we then laid them out again on 210 degrees to support the pursuing infantry. MO limping about, said he'd banged his leg bailing out of a truck, but later transpired he had got hit in the thigh. We found some German soldiers in civvies on the farms, including two officers who had resplendent uniforms, arms and ammo. hidden.

21 April 1945
Infantry Brigadier, CRA and CO of 5 Coldstream made plan to attack Rotenburg. Colonel Roddy [*Hill, Coldstream CO*] said that at this stage he begrudged every man hit. Fifteen Boches run into end of wood. Eventually Sergeant Ward produced four prisoners (three hit) and two *Panzerfausts*. Heaps of prisoners walking down road, with and without escorts.

22 April 1945
Attack on Rotenburg 09:30. CRA tells us to move to Weertzen to be better able to support infantry attack. Attack on Rotenburg went very well indeed. Two guns began shelling our area. I put RSM with a compass a mile away and eventually got cross-bearings. I fired on various Mike targets [*employing all the guns of the Regiment*]. Two men wounded.

24 April 1945
Cadged a run in 373 Battery's (captured) Mercedes and looked at

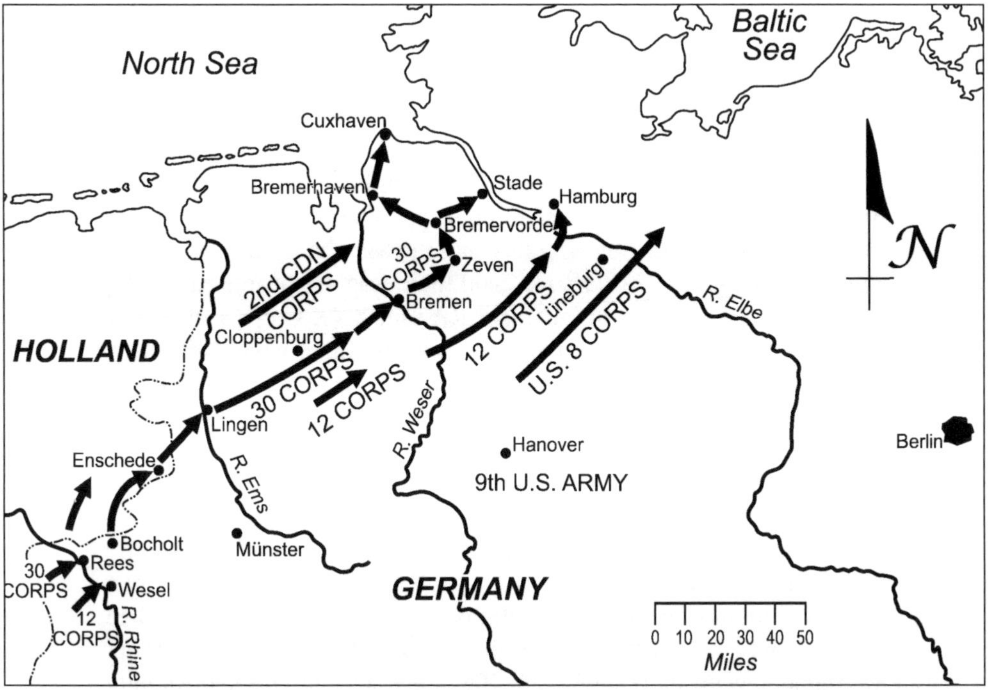

Map 13: The Rhine and the north German plain. From the time when the Anglo-Canadian forces had cut loose to make their sweeping advance to Belgium, Montgomery had been fixated on concentrating all Allied forces to make a major assault towards – and across – the north German plain. (There was a serious, almost disastrous, difference of opinion between Montgomery and Eisenhower on this subject.) The dramatic airborne crossing of the Rhine took place on 24 March 1945, although the Americans had already managed with great skill to cross the river upstream in two places. The Anglo-Canadian advance across Germany met a good deal of resistance, but it was unstoppable. The Guards Armoured Division, in which PP was serving, ended the fighting at the North Sea port of Cuxhaven. With a fine sense of drama, Montgomery received the unconditional surrender of all the German armies in the north, at his tactical headquarters on Lüneburg Heath.

Wiersdorf. Much gun fire to the south-west during the evening. Big party near Bremen I expect. There are a couple of RN officers at Divisional HQ. Bed for third night running in the same bed, a record since we crossed the Rhine.

26 April 1945

We liberated about 500 Russian and other female workers in an underground factory. They say there is a camp ahead of us with 9,000 British and Canadian prisoners-of-war in it. It's a terrific job for Military Government to sort them out and send them home, but it needs to be done quickly or someone has to feed them. I didn't realise until I saw it how far the Germans had been able to get with their scheme of relying on labour from every other country.

28 April 1945
Brigade static. But 8,000-odd prisoners-of-war liberated at Westertimke. Went to see their camp and raked up some cigarettes for them. There were 200 Guardsmen from Dunkirk and the Merchant Navy brother of our BSM Gregory [*373 Battery*]. Said there was reasonable treatment, except when there were SS guards. CRA said XXX Corps will shortly clear the peninsula between the Weser and the Elbe, which will mean virtually the end. No move before AM 30 April [*on that day, the Regiment was only 2 miles from Bremerhaven, the outlet to the sea from the city of Bremen*].

1 May 1945
Some cars brewed up in a village to north-west, and Spandau fire 1,000 yards away from the north. On to Weipen and found a good gun area. Had to push one of the females out of the house we wanted. Said they had only one shotgun and some cartridges (but they did not fit) but we found several more and a .22 rifle plus a wicked knife, apparently issued to the son in the Hitler Youth. Masses of food, eggs, bacon, bottled fruit as usual. Five wardrobes in passage crammed with stuff.

'The Führer Has Fallen in Action'
On 1 May 1945, PP heard the announcement on the German radio that *Der Führer ist gefallen*. Hitler had not of course been killed in action. When the Allied troops got to the bunker in Berlin that was the Führer's final headquarters, they soon discovered that he had shot himself. And his body was taken outside and burned, although not completely because there was not enough gasoline to do the job properly. Nevertheless, Hitler's end was an event of decisive importance. It meant that the war would be over within very few days. Admiral Dönitz ascended to the tottering throne, and from his headquarters at Flensburg started making preparations to surrender.

And on 6 May PP came to the Sandbostel concentration camp, the horrors of which are graphically described. On 7 May the Guards Armoured Division reached the naval base of Cuxhaven on the Baltic, on the promontory to the west of the estuary of the Elbe. The war was over. VE Day was announced for the next day. Another satisfying duty was to round up the still well-disciplined German troops. This surrender of the *élite* 7th Parachute Division makes a vivid story.

5 May 1945

Divisional artillery and 64th Medium Regiment fired into an uninhabited (?) area chosen from the map. A *feu de joie* of gunfire for one minute at 07:50. Hostilities ceased at 08:00. Civilians walking in the field in front of the guns; they lay down quickly and were absolutely petrified. Regimental Commemoration Service in an orchard full of blossom, and combined it with a burial service for Richard [*Major Carew-Hunt*] and four chaps killed with him.

6 May 1945

After lunch we went to Sandbostel, prisoner-of-war and concentration camps next-to-next. We were dusted with disinfectant, with squirts up sleeves and down blouse and trousers. Typhus in concentration camp. Corpses in huts so that you didn't know which were living and which were dead. Worst cases already moved to hospital. We didn't see anything of that except mass graves, and they were covering up the forty-seventh body in one as we watched. Staff said you could see their backbones through their stomachs. The whole place stank. Inmates defecated everywhere, even in huts and around them. Prisoners lived on turnips and water and little of that. Even the sort of porridge food we issue to them they can't even digest. Prisoners-of-war looked pretty fit in the other camp.

8 May 1945

[*The elite German 7th Parachute Division insisted that they would only surrender to the Guards Armoured Division, their enemy of many battles. They did this in disciplined order. Each unit came to attention, and salutes were exchanged*] CO and I looked at guns, which we arranged to neutralize. Very tidy heaps of ammunition and equipment. Got a holster for my Luger pistol and had to sign for it! How they were able to carry on with the broken-down collection of vehicles they have, I can't imagine: horses, carts, bicycles, motorcycles, half-tracks, army and civilian trucks and lorries, cars, captured British, Canadian, and American trucks. Some good Mercedes which we might be able to pick up later on. No aircraft left.

For PP, 7 May marked an important occasion for two reasons. First, the end of the war; and second, he was given command of the 55th Field Regiment, which was to be the high-water mark of his military career. He also received a Mention in Dispatches for his extremely efficient – but often frustrating – work in reconnoitring battery positions in a war of movement. His period of command was to be very busy.

He took full command at the beginning of June, with the rôle of transforming the regiment into an occupying force among an underfed and ill-organized German population. The guns departed on 10 June (following a very grand parade the previous day, described at the end of this chapter). A week later the Regiment was in Aachen, which had been captured by the Americans. PP and his men were to be engaged in controlling the Aachen sector of Germany's western frontier. This period, so soon after the end of hostilities, was to see vast numbers of displaced persons (DPs) trudging on foot to where they could find a home; 'denazification' trials of German citizens with a suspicious past; frustration on the part of the troops at the slow pace of their release, combined with unwelcome thoughts of service in the Far East; and a rampant black market, in which cigarettes became the most ubiquitous form of currency.

PP was particularly concerned with maintaining the morale and military efficiency of 55th Field Regiment. This meant looking after the welfare of the troops, with well-planned programmes to keep them happily occupied. These included establishing a club and leave centre, educational schemes, and amateur theatricals run by surprisingly talented members of the Regiment. The war in the Far East came to an end in mid-August 1945. The officers and men in Europe were being demobilized quickly, and the Regiment itself went into 'suspended animation' until the Territorial Army was re-formed in 1947. The Guards Armoured Division was disbanded in October. The Regular battalions remained, but the others marched off into history. PP was himself released before the end of September and returned to his legal practice in London. (*See Plate 24.*)

This book is a war diary, and details of 55th Field Regiment's days as an occupying force are likely to be anti-climatic. But the book needs a strong *finis*. This is provided by descriptions of two ceremonial occasions: one on 9 June and the other on 28 July. The earlier one was the more militarily significant, but the one at the end of July had an international flavour since it was the occasion when the City of Brussels thanked its liberators.

The Division had captured Brussels in early September 1944. As a tribute, the City Fathers of Brussels hosted a celebration on 28 July for large numbers of officers and men. Special standards were embroidered by the Belgians and presented to the Division. There was a great party atmosphere. Alongside a number of senior officers, PP was presented to the Burgomaster (Lord Mayor), who was dressed in a splendid uniform (Plate 22). The Division gave a ball in the *Hôtel de Ville*, and the British Ambassador, Sir Hughe Knatchbull-Hugessen, was much involved in the activities. His wife was dressed for the ball in a very patriotic fashion, with a red dress and blue shoulder straps (the colours of the Brigade of Guards).

On 9 June, the Guards Armoured Division staged a dramatic and moving

'Farewell to Armour' on the broad open area of the Rotenburg military airfield. Montgomery arrived with a large retinue; he was less informally dressed than he had been on the earlier occasions when PP had seen him. The thousands of guardsmen paraded in khaki rather than scarlet and gold, and music was provided by the regimental bands. The Brigade of Guards is celebrated for the splendour of its pageantry, but there has never been anything as powerful as this exhibition of discipline and efficiency at the end of a victorious campaign. The parade had a dramatic climax. After the tanks had passed by the saluting stand, they disappeared from view, to the strains of *Auld Lang Syne*. Some distance behind them the guardsmen on foot, in files six-deep, marched in Column of Route to salute Montgomery and the other generals. The Brigade had demonstrably become infantry again. Montgomery gave a speech, paying a warm tribute to the sacrifices and military skills of the Division. He also said that the unique excellence of guardsmen is to go to battle on foot, and no matter how proficient they had become as armoured warriors, it was appropriate that they should return to their traditional rôle. During the parade, all the gleaming guns in the Division were assembled and marched past en masse, and appropriately enough those in the Regiment that PP now commanded were on the right of the line.

Afterword

The Territorial Army: Past, Present and (Problematical) Future

The Territorial Army (TA) has existed in Britain for more than a century. In a bold reorganization by Lord Haldane, the Liberal Party's reforming Secretary of State for War, the TA was put together from a fragmented group of old-established Yeomanry cavalry and Volunteer infantry units, all manned by citizen soldiers. The TA played a major role in reinforcing the British army during the two large wars in the twentieth century. However, it was in the doldrums between 1945 and 1996, when new legislation called for some members of the TA to serve – some voluntarily and some not – on active service when there was no general mobilization. This was the beginning of the process of addressing the problem of reconstructing the force to provide direct support to the Regular army as it tackles the challenges it confronts in the twenty-first century.

'Men as shall voluntarily enrol themselves for the General defence of the Kingdom'

Peter Pettit served for almost twenty years on the active list of the Territorial Army: a period that included six years of full-time service, with almost two years at the battlefront. He had followed his father into the Honourable Artillery Company, and was followed in turn by his brother and two sons. Chapter 1 describes briefly the history of the HAC. But in view of the contribution made by the TA during the two world wars, it is important to examine the Territorial Army itself, since its rôle in the twenty-first century has not been robustly established and is being discussed in political and military circles and sometimes heatedly in the media.

The quotation that prefaces the last paragraph comes from the Parliamentary Bill, dated 27 March 1794, that established a force recruited to counter the threat of the militant French Republic that came into being after the Revolution. This force was the earliest precursor of the Territorial Army. It was mounted on well-bred horses with staying power, and received the splendid title of Yeomanry, which was a reflection of the independent yeoman farmers who filled its ranks. It is clear from the quotation that its purpose was the defence of the Realm, and that recruitment would be voluntary and not compulsory. After more than a century of service and with the outbreak of the Second Anglo-Boer War, the rôle of the Yeomanry was expanded to include service overseas, if members volunteered. Voluntary enlistment was always a cardinal principle of the TA, although during the two world wars the Territorials were subsumed into the Regular army and conscripts were sometimes sent to TA units. They served splendidly, but they did not consider themselves to be Territorials and virtually all of them finished their service when the war came to an end.

Membership of the Yeomanry was a source of pride. The local units were supervised by the Lord Lieutenant and High Sheriff, who were the most important grandees in each county and were empowered by the Crown to grant commissions. Arms and equipment were provided mainly by the government; and the often flamboyant uniforms were paid for by local subscriptions. The officers were invariably country landowners, and the men in the ranks were well-established and independent farmers who provided their own horses. The Yeomanry became a colourful part of British country life. Regular army officers were attached to the regiments for two or three years to supervise training, and a Yeomanry attachment was a popular posting with officers who enjoyed field sports. Captain John French, who eventually became a Field Marshal and Commander-in-Chief of the British Expeditionary Force in France in 1914, was a young officer in the 19th Hussars when he was appointed Adjutant of the Northumberland Hussars and performed this duty between 1881 and 1884.

At the beginning of the First World War, there were fifty-eight Yeomanry regiments: forty-four English, seven Scottish, five Welsh, and two Irish. By that time they had become part of the Territorial Force (as described below, in the section 'A Reserve Army for the Twentieth Century'). As in the Second Boer War, the First World War saw many members volunteering for service overseas, and they went to war with their horses. Many units did very well. The Westminster Dragoons were the first troops to enter Jerusalem as part of General Allenby's army in 1918.

Before the Yeomanry was established, the only type of citizen soldiering was in the Militia, which was established in the sixteenth century as an army reserve of foot-soldiers (with an origin that went even further back). Men were recruited by ballot from the very lowest ranks of society and were often embodied for long periods. Service was extremely unpopular. Not much could be said for its military efficiency and the system eventually expired. But during the middle of the nineteenth century, the government now saw a pressing need to provide a reserve for the Regular army. In 1852, the Militia was revived as a force recruited by voluntary enlistment and the members had to serve overseas if necessary. Cardwell's linked battalion system, introduced in 1881, organized each infantry regiment into two Regular battalions, with one overseas at full strength, and the other at home feeding men as needed to its overseas opposite number. The Militia now provided a third battalion composed of citizen soldiers who were committed to a month's training every year. Its rôle was to supply drafts to reinforce the Regular battalions, not to go on active service as complete Militia units.

It was hoped that the Militia would provide a supply of Regular recruits, and this happened to a limited degree. It was also a source of officers. Young men who failed to pass the entrance examination to Sandhurst or Woolwich were given a chance of receiving a Regular commission if they first became Subalterns in the Militia. They then sat a relatively simple examination and if they passed, they got into the Regular army through what was known as the 'Militia back door'. In 1893, a batch of 169 Militia Subalterns who got in through this 'back door,' included a tall young man called Trenchard. He was to have an extraordinary career. He became the 'Father of the Royal Air Force' and eventually earned five-star rank and a peerage.

During the 1880s, the terms of enlistment for soldiers in the Regular army were changed to what became known as short-service, which meant seven years with the colours and five years in the reserve. In this way, a substantial Regular army reserve was soon built up. This, and not the Militia, became the army's first-line reserve and would bring each battalion up to strength immediately after general mobilization. The full mobilization of the British Expeditionary Force in 1914 was only possible because the individual battalions had enough reserves to fill the ranks. The Militia reserve was as a consequence relegated to second-line status. There were even more pools of men: the miscellaneous collection of Yeomanry and Volunteers who were recruited exclusively for home service.

The Volunteers, mainly infantry, were formed a few years after the Militia had been set up. At about the same time, the Crimean War exposed the shortages and inadequacies of the Regular army. During the late 1850s, a threat was also seen from across the Channel, where the Emperor Napoleon III (in the words of the poet Victor Hugo, *Napoléon le petit*) was attempting to present to the world the image of his uncle, the first Emperor. There was great public enthusiasm in Britain for the Volunteer movement, and under the Cardwell system Volunteers began to form the fourth, fifth and even more battalions of each county regiment. The Volunteer battalions did not demonstrate much military uniformity and presented a picturesque patchwork of units. But musketry was strongly emphasized, which was something that gave the Volunteers considerable military value. Towards the end of the nineteenth century, the total number of Volunteer battalions was 238: 171 were based in England, 57 in Scotland and 10 in Wales. There were no Volunteers in Ireland at that time.

The Yeomanry and Volunteers were blooded during the Second Anglo-Boer War (1899–1902). This conflict was eventually to draw 500,000 men from Britain and the Empire into the field: the largest deployment of military manpower in British history. The call for reinforcements for the Regular army was met by an enthusiastic response from the Yeomanry and Volunteers. New mounted units were formed into battalions of Imperial Yeomanry, with individual companies coming from separate British Yeomanry regiments. The infantry terminology of battalions and companies was a reflection of the rôle of these units, as mounted infantry. This was a new and important military concept. The men were trained to be good shots and were mounted on sturdy ponies so they could move rapidly around the battlefield. Mounted infantry were the British army's response to the dangerous and elusive Boer Commandos. The British citizen soldiers saw much action and built a remarkable reputation.

The Volunteer infantry were also soon committed. They in fact had a forerunner, when two small detachments of Volunteers had served in the Egyptian campaigns of 1882 and 1885, carrying out specialist work on posts and telegraphs. The Second Anglo-Boer War was on a much larger scale. The first Volunteer force sent to South Africa was the extra-large battalion of City Imperial Volunteers (CIV) which was raised and equipped by businesses and other organizations in the City of London. (As explained in Chapter 1), the HAC Infantry supplied a company, and the HAC Artillery provided the officers and NCOs for a Field battery. These first drafts were followed by substantial reinforcements of Militia and Volunteer companies from county regiments. These citizen soldiers all experienced rough campaigning and heard shots fired in anger. Their prowess was remembered.

The experience of these men in South Africa changed the way in which the Yeomanry and Volunteers were regarded by politicians, generals, and the public. They had shown themselves to be serious soldiers and deserved a place in the British army's Order of Battle (ORBAT). But while the Yeomanry and Volunteers had returned from South Africa with an enhanced reputation, the war had revealed serious problems with the army as a whole. In brief, many people thought it outrageous that the British army had taken three years, and needed a ten-to-one superiority in numbers, to suppress a relatively small number of Boer farmers who were defending their homes. The Boer riflemen were not all crack shots but were on a par with the British, and tactically they were much better because they were more agile and had a better 'feel' for ground. The Boer superiority led to attempts to change British cavalry tactics: to steer them away from shock action with sabre and lance and learn to operate like mounted infantry. Nevertheless, the profound conservatism of British cavalry officers ensured that such a change did not take place, although – an important point – the British cavalry who went to war in 1914 were armed with the infantry rifle, the Short Magazine Lee–Enfield (SMLE), not the carbine they had used in South Africa. During the First Battle of Ypres (October–November 1914) the cavalry in their trenches used their SMLEs to great effect.

Before the Second Anglo-Boer War the British army – unlike the German and French – had no General Staff to control grand strategy, the deployment of armies, personnel matters and logistics. In Britain there was only a Commander-in-Chief, which was an archaic appointment that had been held for decades by Queen Victoria's cousin, the Duke of Cambridge. He was the personification of conservatism, whose attitudes had not changed since he had fought in the Crimea.

The 1899 plan for dispatching the army to South Africa and giving it realistic instructions about its rôle there was no fuller or more helpful than the plan that an earlier British army had received when it was sent in 1854 to fight the disastrous Crimean War. Immediately after the end of the South African war, the British government set up a Commission to report on what had happened. This was, to say the least, a sad story. After the Commission had made a very unfavourable report, a heavyweight three-man committee was set up under Lord Esher, to recommend action. It proposed the abolition of the post of Commander-in-Chief, and the formation of an Army Council of seven men: three civilians and four senior officers (who would be a General Staff in embryo). A Chief of the General Staff, later Chief of the Imperial General Staff (CIGS), was appointed to act as the military adviser to the Government and as the conduit for instructions from the Government to the army. It took some time for the system to operate efficiently, and it was 1915 before there was a fully effective CIGS. He was the formidable Lieutenant General Robertson, who had risen from the ranks and was eventually to become a Field Marshal.

Despite all the teething troubles, the General Staff made an important contribution during the years leading up to the First World War. Britain was able to develop plans to cooperate with the French army in the event of a war against Germany. The British Expeditionary Force (BEF) that was sent to France in 1914 was the best organized expedition of its type in British military history. However, whether the force was large enough for its task was a different matter altogether.

In addition to forming a General Staff to get a firm 'grip' on the army, there was a considerable need for a reorganization of the Yeomanry and Volunteers. This was planned and executed by a brainy and businesslike Secretary of State for War, Sir Richard Haldane, with the help of a number of talented military advisers.

A Reserve Army for the Twentieth Century

After being out of office for a decade, the Liberal Party in 1905 was elected to power with a rousing majority. The new premier Sir Henry Campbell-Bannerman put together a Ministry composed of men who were to leave a legacy of impressive achievement. They included three future Prime Ministers, Asquith, Lloyd George and Churchill. During its early days, the government pioneered the first major legislation devoted to what is now known as social welfare: old-age pensions, unemployment insurance, schemes to find work for the unemployed and other things. The army was also dramatically reorganized by Haldane: improvements that were in place when Britain found itself at war with Germany in 1914. The Liberal government was still then in office.

Haldane had no experience of military affairs, but he was a lawyer of high intellectual attainment, clear-thinking and energetic. He was later considered to have been the best Secretary of State for War ever to have held the post. He was wise enough at the beginning to select a number of experienced military assistants, including two seasoned staff officers, Lieutenant General Ian Hamilton and Major General Douglas Haig. These two generals were to hold high command during the First World War. Despite their earlier very effective administrative work on the staff, their performance as commanders was to be disappointing. Hamilton became Commander-in-Chief of the Gallipoli expedition, but was sacked after its failure. Haig commanded the BEF in France and Flanders during the last three years of the war, and his leadership was widely debated. Many views were favourable or at least sympathetic to Haig because of the great difficulties he faced, but many were highly critical of his performance during the years in which there were massive losses and little progress on the ground. Haig's diaries were first published during the 1950s, and Lord Beaverbrook observed that he had committed suicide thirty years after his death!

The post of Secretary of State for War was to be political head of the army. The navy, whose political head was the First Lord of the Admiralty, operated quite separately. An overall Ministry of Defence, running all branches of the armed forces, had to wait until the Second World War when Churchill took this job alongside his Prime Ministership. Haldane kept close touch with the navy because the rôles of the two armed services were complementary, and they were of course equally important. The possibility of a war with Germany was always present, and the Royal Navy remained the largest and best in the world, which was a matter of great importance because the Germans were building a powerful High Seas fleet. The German economy was extremely strong, the ambition of the Kaiser was unstoppable, and his political power was greater than that of the British monarch. In contrast, the army and navy in Britain were constrained by tight budgets. In 1913, the British defence budget was £75 million: 62 per cent for the navy and 38 per cent for the army. The tax needed to pay the £75 million called for a levy of less than £2 per capita: a small sum even in an age when wages were very low. Converting the 1913 budget to the value of money in 2013 brings the sum up to about £4 billion today. The armed forces in 2013 have fewer personnel than in 1913, but they have far greater offensive power. The vastly greater sophistication and cost of weapons accounts for the actual 2013 defence budget of £40 billion.

Regrettably, political realities in Britain meant that it was impossible to consider peacetime conscription to help prepare the country for a war on the European Continent, which was certain to be conducted by large armies. The Liberal government was resolutely unwilling to fund any form of conscription, although Field Marshal Lord Roberts, the most distinguished and revered soldier in the country, was at the time vigorously promoting a scheme to conscript all physically fit young men to undergo a few months' military service. This would have provided a massive reserve of partially trained men. A lively controversy on the subject of compulsory service was conducted in print. Hamilton, who was sponsored by Haldane, published a short book containing an elegant argument opposing conscription, and Roberts gave his name to a rejoinder. Roberts had the assistance of some skilled and persuasive advocates, and he got the better of the argument. But this did not bring the government any nearer to accepting compulsory service, which would have prepared the country for the war that came in 1914. The beginning of hostilities revealed that the general shortage of trained men was proving a grave handicap, and this was made worse by the heavy casualties that were soon being suffered.

Haldane's main task at the beginning was to articulate and execute the highest level of strategy: what is often called politico-military or grand strategy. This was defined in the following way by Basil Liddell Hart, the analyst who brought more expertise to this study than any other military thinker: 'The rôle of grand strategy is to coordinate and direct all the resources of a nation towards the attainment of the political object of the war – the goal defined by national policy.' In executing this strategy, Haldane confronted three demands that the British army had to meet. First, it had to continue policing a large and widespread British Empire. Second, it had to make long-range plans for conducting a possible war against Germany, in which Britain would be allied to France. With this in mind, the British General Staff was soon in regular although unofficial consultations with the French General Staff to develop a plan to dispatch a British Expeditionary Force to support the French army in the field. This was a matter that was to have huge ramifications. The third demand that Haldane faced was for the army to make realistic preparations for the defence of the country.

The first demand could be carried out through a continuation of the status quo, which was reasonably effective. At that time 113,000 men were deployed overseas in units kept at full strength, mainly in India but also in a number of other stations. In addition, 129,000 men were in Britain: recruits under training and men waiting to be shipped to overseas battalions. There was also in Britain a slightly larger number of Regular army reserves and Militia, who were available to boost the number of Regulars in the field if Britain went to war.

The second demand – providing an army to go to the aid of the French – called for 150,000 men. This force, which had been carefully planned by the General Staff following their discussions with the French, comprised six infantry divisions and one cavalry division, all at full strength and with a complete complement of equipment. This became eventually the British Expeditionary Force that went to France in 1914. It was the most perfectly organized and best trained military force that had ever left British shores. But the problem with the BEF was its size, which was soon shown to be totally inadequate. The scale of this force – and bearing in mind the likelihood that it would suffer heavy casualties in the first contact with the enemy – would soon put pressure on the overall numbers of the British army. In particular the strength of the Regular army stationed in Britain might be seriously reduced.

This situation exacerbated the third demand on the British army: to defend Britain from outside invasion. This had been the job of the Yeomanry and Volunteers. Haldane took them head-on, together with all their prejudices and vested interests, and constructed from the individual units an army he entitled the Territorial Force (TF). This comprised fourteen infantry and six cavalry divisions, with a total nominal size of 302,000 men. The officers and men were clothed in khaki, like the Regular army, and the individual units had their own badges and buttons; in the case of the infantry, these were the badges and buttons of the Regular regiments to which they were affiliated. For its time the TF was a very substantial force, with a major rôle when there was general mobilization: when Britain became for the first time since 1815 a 'nation at arms'.

Haldane virtually created the shape of the modern division, which was described succinctly by Hamilton: 'Off his own bat he did it; lopping off excrescences, adding guns, sappers, signallers, field hospitals, and all Army Service Corps administrative services.' An equally important point was that the TF divisions could be replicated because the mechanism was in place to do so. This was also described by Hamilton: 'The County Associations, who knew all about making, clothing, feeding and keeping troops, would have stamped out duplicates, triplicates and quadruplicates of their original quotas of Territorial troops, without too much friction or effort.' The administration of the TF was based on six military districts, formed after the end of the Second Boer War. Each district was intended to form a corps of three Regular divisions when war was declared. In peacetime, the Regular army hierarchy in the districts also supervised the Territorial units and sub-units which were spread over the territory of each district.

Nevertheless, the Territorial Force faced a number of problems. It was largely untrained and seriously under-strength with 250,000 men, a shortfall of 17 per cent. On the other hand, it was apparent soon after war was declared that the Royal Navy would defeat any enemy attempting to land on British shores, which made much of the TF superfluous. Could numbers of them be released for other duties, probably in France? There was the immediate difficulty that the TF was recruited for home defence, but this was soon overcome because large numbers soon agreed to serve overseas. The Militia (a force Haldane renamed Special Reserve) was also in being. Its members were obliged to serve abroad if called on, and Haldane took strong steps to amalgamate the Special Reserve and the Territorials, a move that was not totally successful because of the resistance of vested interests in the Militia. Many members of the Special Reserve served in the First World War. Even in the Second World War, one Royal Engineer regiment remained a Special Reserve unit; and some non-Regular officers continued to come from the Special Reserve.

A further, and perhaps more serious, problem shortly emerged. This was a subtle matter concerned with perceptions, and could not be assessed empirically. When numbers of Territorials were eventually fighting in France in the same uniform and under the same discipline as the Regulars, there is anecdotal evidence that the Regulars felt resentment and antipathy: perhaps a revival of similar attitudes before the war. Could this have been triggered by differences in social class between the two forces? Class was in those days a more prominent factor than it is now.

The officers and other ranks in the Regular army were rigidly divided by social class, and movement upward from the ranks to the officers' mess was extremely difficult, although not totally impossible. Officers came from the top 5 per cent of British society: about ½ million out of a total of 10 million families. There were five sources from which virtually all officers were recruited: the landed aristocracy (a very small group); the rather large numbers of gentry who had enough private money to live on, generally from the estates that they owned; sons of serving and retired service officers; sons of members of the learned professions, the Church, law and medicine; and (to a limited degree) those from prosperous industrial and commercial families. Education at a British public school (which means, in British English, a fee-paying private school) was desirable, and in many regiments, obligatory. But it was very rare indeed for a British army officer to have gone to a university, although most had graduated from Sandhurst or Woolwich, which did not provide an education of a university standard. In addition, the majority of officers received some financial subsidy from their families because their army pay was too small to cover their expenses.

In contrast, the other ranks in the Regular army came from the working class, and they included large numbers of unskilled labourers, many unemployed. (Army recruitment normally went up in step with increases in unemployment.)

The social backgrounds of the officers and men in the Yeomanry and Volunteers were not much different from those in the Regular army, although the officers included young men in advanced education, and others who were building careers in the professions and in fast-track jobs in business. The Territorial other ranks were mostly skilled members of the working class, and the Yeomanry were mainly farmers. Any resentment of the Territorial Force on the part of the Regulars was therefore due to factors other than social differences, and the obvious ones were a lack of military skill and inadequate experience of military discipline. During the course of the First World War, the Territorials were resented less and less by the Regulars for the simple reason that they were sharing the hardships and performing well in battle. However, antipathy simmered below the surface, and was to re-emerge during the Second World War. The next section, 'Lessons Learned', contains a dramatic example of a critical attitude on the part of a seasoned Regular officer who was later to command an HAC regiment on active service.

To reprise Haldane's specific contributions as Secretary of State for War:

i.   He made plans to maintain the army's rôle in policing the British Empire;
ii. He raised a superbly organized expeditionary force to go to France when war was declared;
iii. He constructed a large and well-balanced Territorial Force for home defence, and this was put together in such a way that it could be expanded when its members could be persuaded to serve overseas.

But, as I shall demonstrate, these three contributions were nullified decisively soon after war was declared.

Lessons Learned

Within very few weeks of the outbreak of hostilities in 1914, it became obvious that the deadly power of defensive fire had caught all the combatants by surprise. The size of the casualty lists came as a massive shock to armies in all countries. By the end of the year the BEF, which had appeared such a magnificent force in August, had lost more than half its strength in casualties. One of the tragedies was that the British army was eating its seed-corn, because it was losing experienced men whose greatest value would have been to train the vast influx of recruits. The loss of men in France and Flanders and the urgent need to provide leadership and instruction to what became known as the New Army put great pressure on the War Office to find reinforcements from overseas stations. Many units were shipped to the Western Front and later Gallipoli. In many cases they were replaced by the Territorial Force. In this way it was the Territorials who enabled the army to carry out its important task of garrisoning the Empire. Haldane's first achievement was therefore only made possible by means of last-minute improvisation.

Haldane's second achievement – raising and organizing the 150,000-strong BEF – was soon shown to be a disappointment because of the inadequate size of the force. The problem was made worse because of the casualties it suffered in 1914, and also because the French constantly stepped up their requests for reinforcements from across the Channel. These demands were met again by improvisation by the War Office in London, but the process was slow.

Finally, Haldane's contribution in raising the Territorial Force as the largest army reserve was forgotten very quickly. The TF was effectively strangled at birth by the new Secretary of State for War, appointed in August 1914, Field Marshal Lord Kitchener of Khartoum: the awesome K of K. His surprising unwillingness to build his New Army on the basis of the Territorial Force is unquestionably connected with the scepticism in Regular army circles about its effectiveness. K of K decided to build his force under the nominal control of the Regulars. It was an immense undertaking, and only a man of his capacity – military leader, proconsul and autocrat with an indomitable will – could have brought it off.

The fact that Haldane's three widely acclaimed achievements had before long been seriously modified with the coming of war provides a lesson of permanent value. It is a lesson that should be borne in mind when the shape of the twenty-first-century British army – including both Regulars and Territorials – is being studied and mapped out, as it is at the moment. *No matter how persuasive military plans may appear when they are developed in peacetime, the circumstances of war will inevitably cause these plans to collapse.* There was no one to blame for the British miscalculations before the First World War; every country made mistakes that were just as serious. The fact is that the forces released by war are too complex to be predicted, and the only policy advice that should be adopted is negative, that it is unwise to make substantial investments in plans for war when they are made in time of peace. Wars are won after the guns have started firing, the victors having greater intellectual depth and powers of recuperation – and generally much greater resources – than their opponents.

The solid shape of the BEF – a compact all-Regular force – did not survive after the end of 1914, as a result of the losses. During the following years, there was an enormous increase in the number of battalions and this, together with the massive and continuous drain of casualties, had two effects.

First, the social barrier between officers and men became porous; and second, battalions became more mixed. Over the course of the war, large numbers of men were commissioned who would not have been accepted before 1914, and the newcomers fought as steadfastly as the old, despite the appalling phrase that was often used to describe them, 'temporary gentlemen'. It is worth remembering that the only soldier during the war who earned the Victoria Cross on two occasions was a Territorial officer, Captain Chavasse, Medical Officer of the Liverpool Scottish.

As the war progressed, units received so many reinforcements from different sources that even a prestigious Regular battalion like 2 Royal Welsh Fusiliers had before the end of the war become a mixture of Regulars (not many of them left), New Army men, Territorials and conscripts. To the surprise of many, its fighting prowess was not weakened. In the British army, discipline and pride are the keys to military efficiency, and pride comes from regimental *esprit de corps*, which remained as strong as ever in a regiment with as long and bloody a history as the Royal Welsh Fusiliers.

In the war, twenty-eight Territorial infantry divisions were raised, the majority of which served overseas. Most received large numbers of reinforcements of New Army men and conscripts. The war provided little scope for cavalry on the Western Front, and many Yeomanry regiments served in the Middle East and saw considerable mounted action. The writing was nevertheless on the wall for the Yeomanry in its traditional rôle.

With the coming of peace and the departure of many war-service officers, and with the Regular army now reduced to its traditional size, the rigid social distinction between officers and men was reestablished. And the army resumed its normal rôle of garrisoning the British Empire, and also for a few years the Rhineland in west Germany. The Royal Flying Corps had by now given birth to an independent air arm, the Royal Air Force. But the Machine Gun Corps, an important innovation during the war, was disbanded and its Vickers machine guns passed on to the infantry battalions. The infantry regiments from what was now the Irish Free State also marched into history. The Tank Corps remained in being, although the future of the cavalry was widely questioned. The number of cavalry regiments was reduced by amalgamations, and gradually they began the process of exchanging their horses for tanks and armoured cars. This process had only finished a short while before the outbreak of war in 1939.

The infantry battalions of the Territorial Army, or TA (as it was soon to be called), returned in 1920 to part-time soldiering, and recruits slowly arrived to supplement the ranks of the war-time veterans who had survived and were happy to soldier on. The battalions now had the satisfaction of having participated with distinction in what became known as the Great War. The original fourteen infantry divisions remained, but some units were amalgamated; and in 1928 a complete Territorial Anti-Aircraft Artillery Division was formed. This development was to prove important in the war that broke out eleven years later.

However, many Yeomanry regiments began quickly to change. Of these, sixteen regiments kept their traditional cavalry rôle, although when war came they converted to armour and invariably performed well in the Western Desert and other theatres. A total of eight regiments were reduced in size and became armoured car companies in the Tank Corps. A further twenty-five became Field artillery regiments, a change that was welcomed because the soldiers kept their horses. In 1945, Peter Pettit was Second-in-Command and later Commanding Officer of the 55th Field Artillery Regiment (West Somerset Yeomanry), a unit that dated from 1794. During the 1920s there was no shortage of 18-pounder guns and ammunition for them, so the newly converted gunner regiments were able to have plentiful practice on Salisbury Plain.

The rising strength and aggressiveness of Nazi Germany during the 1930s caused British people in increasing numbers to fear that another war was on its way. British politicians were slow to respond to the danger, but rearmament was well under way by the end of 1937. The danger of war boosted the patriotic enthusiasm of young men, and recruitment into the Territorials picked up. The size of the TA was doubled in 1938 and the total of men enrolled increased to 300,000, a higher effective strength than the Territorial Force in 1914. As in the early years of the Territorial Force, the TA was still intended to make a major contribution if Britain became again a 'nation at arms'. By 1939 the HAC Infantry Battalion had become an officer-producing unit, and the HAC Artillery had given birth to three (later four) complete gunner regiments. Educated young men flocked to join the HAC, in the expectation that service in it would lead the way to a commission when war broke out. This happened to a substantial extent.

As in 1914, the enemy was going to be Germany, and Britain would be allied to France. But the British political and military leaders got things wrong and committed three cardinal errors. First, they assumed that the coming war would be a repeat of 1914. However, important differences had occurred undetected. The French army had by 1939 become disenchanted by war and was totally orientated to defence. The British Expeditionary Force that was sent to France in 1939 soon occupied permanent trench lines and started building concrete pill boxes. These were signs that the British army was also focussed on defence, although pill boxes lacked the technical sophistication of the Maginot Line. No one in Britain sensed the French army's reluctance to fight, nor the degree by which the German General Staff had developed revolutionary new battlefield tactics.

British political leaders in the 1930s were fixated on air power, and a disproportionate slice of the rising defence budget was devoted to fighter and bomber aircraft. This policy led to the second error that was made in 1939: reliance on the effectiveness of aerial bombardment. Soon after war was declared, bombers were sent to Germany in daylight raids and were rapidly destroyed by the German defences. (This was a lesson that had to be painfully relearned by the United States Army Air Force in 1942 and 1943, although its B-17s and B-24s that were sent out at that time bristled with heavy machine guns that unfortunately offered too little protection.) British bombing attacks began by night in 1940, but it was *two years* after the beginning of the war before the air marshals learned that the RAF's night navigation was hopelessly inadequate and most bombs were dropped miles from their targets. Then, with the help of radar, vast quantities of explosives began to be dumped on German cities. Despite the horrendous casualties and damage caused, these did not destroy the morale of the German population nor did they slow the production of German armaments, since the Germans quickly learned how to change the location of their factories.

The third British error – one that was to have appalling long-term consequences – was to underestimate the fighting power of the Japanese army, navy and air force. The loss of Hong Kong in late 1941 and Singapore in early 1942, together with the destruction of the battleships *Prince of Wales* and *Repulse*, were clear auguries for the end of the British Empire. Learning the early lessons of the war was a painful process for the British, but they demonstrated the truth of the maxim that the British lose every battle – except the last one.

The Territorial Army was mobilized when war was declared and many – perhaps too many – units joined the British Expeditionary Force, which within a few months was twice the size of its predecessor that left for France in 1914. There were seven Territorial divisions (about a quarter of the total strength of the TA) in France when the campaign came to its ignominious end in early June 1940. One serious loss to the TA was the encirclement and capture of the celebrated 51st (Highland) Division by a German division commanded by a general whose name would shortly become a household word, Erwin Rommel. The 51st was re-formed in Britain from Highland recruits eager to strike back at the enemy, and they fought with distinction in North Africa, Sicily and North-West Europe.

During the summer of 1940 after the fall of France and with the majority of the original Territorial Army in Britain, the troops were fully occupied in defence of the country, and also in receiving and learning to use new guns and heavy equipment. These were replacements for what had to be abandoned in France. Before the autumn, rigorous training began. In view of the defeat in France, the troops trained with intensity and most passed through the newly established Battle Schools. Many TA units received young Regular Commanding Officers, whose experience and belief in discipline increased the troops' fitness for war. Most of the divisions that eventually fought in North Africa had at least a year of training in Britain; those intended for the Far East had two years; and those who would participate in the invasion of Europe in 1944 had more than three years.

An instructive example of Regular attitudes to the Territorial Army came from 107th (South Notts Hussars) Regiment, Royal Horse Artillery, which (like 55th Field Regiment) dated from 1794. 107th Regiment was sent, with its horses, to Palestine (now Israel) in January 1940. This meant that it did not benefit from months of intensive training in Britain, although it undertook some training in Palestine before it was mechanized and sent in June 1940 to the Western Desert of North Africa. In the desert it fought for almost two years in battles in which, from early 1941, Rommel's Afrika Korps held the upper hand. Finally, in the bitter battle of Knightsbridge in May 1942, the Regiment was trapped and virtually wiped out. The casualties included the Commanding Officer and most of the other officers. Among these was Captain Graham Slinn, a remarkably tall young man who had already won two MCs, and who had been commissioned into the regiment from A Battery, HAC.

107th Regiment had a Regular Second-in-Command, Major Robert Daniell, RHA, an extremely experienced officer. He managed to escape the final battle by driving a truck flat-out through the German lines, moving so fast that the Germans were unable to train their gun sights on him. He was a forceful and direct man and he did not spare his criticisms of the 107th Regiment:

> There were two or three officers I liked, but the officers as a whole did not like me. I was a Regular officer, brought up in a Royal Horse Artillery Regiment and I was accustomed to carrying out anything I was told to do immediately to the best of my ability. I did not find that the majority of these officers copied me in any way whatsoever. They found difficulty in obeying orders in carrying out any operation that they themselves did not care for. I found that the Warrant Officers, NCOs, and men were of a very high standard. Their discipline was excellent, they themselves were strong and intelligent, and they took advantage of every order that was given them.

Before long Daniell was sent back to Britain, and was given command of the third of the HAC horse gunner regiments, 13th (HAC) Regiment, Royal Horse Artillery. This unit had been trained for more than three years under experienced Regular Commanding Officers before it was launched into battle in Normandy in June 1944. Daniell's opinion of the regiment was equally candid, but he found a unit different in important respects from the one with which he had fought in the desert:

> I could not speak more highly of this fine regiment, very well trained, staunch, brave and keen. My three battery commanders were of exceptionally high quality, especially Peter Gaunt, a man of great courage, always calm in moments of crisis, and an excellent gunner. He should have had a regiment of his own and he well deserved the DSO awarded to him at the end of the campaign. Sadly our casualties were to be very high, especially among the young FOOs, hand-picked and highly efficient after interminable months of training in England.

13th Regiment was unusually distinguished. However, fighting efficiency was more typical than not of the regiments and battalions in the Territorial Army that fought in the Second World War, especially those that had received long years of training and military discipline to prepare them for battle. After the end of the war, and following the complicated process of demobilization, the TA was re-formed in 1947, mainly from members who had fought in the war. The old enthusiasm was maintained, but the majority of members were officers and NCOs (some of whom agreed to step down in rank) and there was naturally a need for young recruits to make up the numbers. There was however an immediate impediment.

Because of continuing international tensions, the British government continued to conscript young men, in a process known as National Service. They served full-time for a finite period of eighteen months (later two years) followed by some years of reserve service, administered by the TA. The last National Serviceman was discharged from full-term service in May 1963. However, the reserve commitment was never fully implemented, and in most cases it meant only a single two-week summer camp, and even that stopped in 1957. By 1966, the whole scheme had come to an end, *de jure* as well as *de facto*. Some Territorials at the time felt that the end of National Service removed from the rolls many men with military experience, and this weakened the fabric of the TA.

After 1945, since potential recruits into the TA had to carry out National Service, there was a long hiatus in the life of the traditional all-volunteer force. But by the late 1960s, the TA – now again composed of volunteers – was seriously under-strength and still contained many men of the wartime generation. Young National Servicemen were unwilling to join because Britain was not under any serious international threat, and full-time service in peacetime had anyway reduced their enthusiasm for soldiering. The post-war years were a period of unparalleled prosperity in the country, and unemployment was low. Young men did not need to rely on a fortnight's summer camp for their annual vacation; two weeks on the Costa Brava were preferable, and they could afford the cost of a packaged holiday.

A further problem was that the main purpose of the army – and consequently the main purpose of the TA – was by no means clear. The situation was quite different from that before the two world wars. After 1945, a large proportion of the British army was serving in Germany as the British Army of the Rhine (BAOR), which eventually formed part of the North Atlantic Treaty Organization (NATO). But the threat of war with the Soviet Union gradually receded because of the danger, described in American military circles, of 'mutually assured destruction'. For a few years, the TA trained for civil defence, and at other times as a modern version of the wartime Home Guard. There was also the relatively short-lived Territorial Army Emergency Reserve (TAER or 'Ever-Readies'), who were given a financial bounty and better training facilities than the rest of the TA. Some members were called to active duty and acquitted themselves well.

However, inevitably many individual units amalgamated, and others were disbanded. In 1967, even the legendary 51st (Highland) Division ceased to exist. Decades passed with the TA maintaining a tenuous existence, sustained by the enthusiasm of its members. The name was changed more than once, but the traditional title of Territorial Army came back into use. The War Office kept the Territorial Army in being – not because of lobbying in influential circles, nor for reasons of sentiment – but because the volunteer spirit was felt to be important and the TA was anyway relatively inexpensive to run. And although Britain is unlikely ever again to be mobilized into a 'nation at arms', the TA was kept in being to fulfil a real purpose: although a purpose that was as yet undefined, at least until 1996.

Following the 1996 Reserve Forces Act, substantial numbers of Territorials have served – in some cases compulsorily – for a year attached to the Regular army on active service. Half the year has been needed for training, leaving six months for deployment in the field. The men and women are being fed into Regular units as individuals or in small groups. They have included some specialists: linguists, intelligence officers, medical officers, computer experts, police etc. Employers have been obliged to keep the volunteers' jobs open until they return, but regrettably some volunteers have lost their lives. This scheme is being expanded to embrace larger numbers (as discussed in the next section).

Facing an Uncertain Future

This book is a historical study: or at least it has been up to this concluding section. I am now going to embark on some speculation. Since the Territorial Army was re-formed in 1947 after the end of the Second World War, it has had a chequered existence, mainly because of the constant shortage of recruits. Attempts have been made to rationalize the TA, and this process is still continuing. Since the future is in the melting pot, I wish to give a strictly personal view. In stating this, I have not been privy to any information, statistical projections or plans for the future that have originated in any official source. The only data I discuss here are in the public domain.

There is a particular problem in visualizing the future of the Territorial Army. What must be done first is to define the future of the army as a whole, since the TA is only a part of it. Lessons can however be drawn from how Britain began the two world wars of the twentieth century.

In these, Britain faced initially a single enemy, Germany, a country that was compact, monolithic, powerful and aggressive. Britain at the beginning had a single ally, France, whose armed strength was comparable to Britain's. The inevitable theatre of war was north-west Europe. Most important of all, both wars were planned as conventional conflicts fought by traditional military forces (although during their course attacks on civilians became increasingly important).

In both world wars, Britain started with a Territorial Force/Army of about the same size as the Regulars, although in both wars newly enlisted volunteers and conscripts increased the total size of the army enough to reduce significantly the percentage accounted for by the Territorials. The Territorial Army was throughout closely integrated into the Regular army because of the affiliation of TA units with Regular regiments; and also because at the higher levels, Territorial formations were commanded by Regulars. There were no Territorial (two-star) divisional commanders, and very few (one-star) brigade commanders. (These included Brigadier 'Ginger' McKechnie, of the HAC Infantry, who commanded successfully an infantry brigade in the Italian campaign during the last two years of the Second World War.) There were many Territorial officers commanding regiments and battalions, although older men were often replaced by younger Regular Lieutenant Colonels. Field Marshal Montgomery insisted that battalion and regimental commanders should be no older than 35. Despite this, Peter Pettit was promoted to command 55th Field Regiment when he was 37, but he was an officer with unusually wide battle experience, and had received a DSO. A very important point that emerged from both world wars was that the TA units only became fully effective after they had received many months – and sometimes years – of uninterrupted training and military discipline.

Conflicts of the future will almost certainly not follow the predictable patterns of the First and Second World Wars. This is the major problem that is confronting military planners today. They are indeed moving into *terra incognita*. The military analyst Emile Simpson has characterized traditional warfare as 'bipolar', fought between nation states of roughly comparable strength. Conflicts today and in the future will be the opposite of 'bipolar'. They will be asymmetrical and diverse, with potential antagonists spread throughout the world in pockets rather than formed into compact armies. These antagonists are only rarely identified.

The hard experience of Iraq and Afghanistan has also provided lessons. General Petraeus, one of the few military leaders to have demonstrated 'grip' in his active command in this new type of warfare, is a scholar-soldier who wrote his PhD thesis at Princeton University on army morale, with special relevance to Vietnam. Petraeus believes that a successful strategy to combat insurgency must be 80 per cent political and only 20 per cent military: the opposite of the earlier American army doctrine of 'all or nothing – go in big, do the job, and get out quick'. Petraeus's type of war demands patience, skills and resources. It needs close army-air cooperation, and 'state-of-the-art' weapons, including Drones. The engagements themselves are likely to be widely spread over the whole battlefield, and conducted at a small unit level: by infantry companies and platoons, and Special Forces. It is a type of war for which the British are both experienced and well prepared.

Terrorism is the never-ending leitmotif of twenty-first century war. Iraq and Afghanistan have been serious conflicts, embarked on substantially in pursuit of powerful and menacing terrorists in the deep shadows – an assessment that was exaggerated in Iraq but was totally correct in Afghanistan. However, there is a widespread feeling that these two invasions turned out to be counter-productive because their outcome was to make terrorists more aggressive than before. Conventional warfare does not work. One unexpected reason why terrorists are so difficult to locate and neutralize comes from social science research. The people who speak loudest about their hatred of Western values are not the most likely ones to take action. The dangerous players in this hidden game communicate with one another and recruit new conspirators in different places, and they do this on the Internet which is a type of communication that can be penetrated by outsiders only with difficulty. In response, the American National Security Agency (NSA) has searched for and found a way of tapping into Internet messages 'of interest' in countries around the world. This has caused much controversy about breach of privacy.

Terrorists are elusive but often well-organized groups of fanatics who have no respect for human life – other people's or their own – and who are motivated by hatred of Western values. Their bitter antagonism embraces Christianity and Judaism; democracy and equality before the law, not least gender equality; Western sexual mores and addiction to alcohol; the presence of foreigners who cause wars and exploit mineral resources in lands where they are unwelcome; and the power of the dollar, and what fanatics consider to be Western economic imperialism. Rational argument has no meaning to terrorists. And 'winning hearts and minds' is not a realistic strategy. Force must be met by force, but force must be deployed with surgical finesse. The notion of 'blasting them back to the Stone Age' is an anachronism that was long ago discredited in Vietnam.

The danger area is the enormous expanse of territory with its huge population that stretches from western Africa across the middle of the globe. Some of the countries in this large region are antagonistic to each other, for nationalistic and/or sectarian antipathy based on religion. With the single exception of Israel, none of these countries can be called a firm friend of the United States and her allies, to whom they have attitudes ranging from watchfulness to ill-concealed hostility. In these countries terrorism is never a state policy, although some states are more tolerant than others of their fanatical minorities. In the middle of this enormous territory is the state of Israel, ally of the United States (as mentioned) and recipient of enormous subventions from her. Israel is a democracy surrounded by hostile and generally autocratic Islamic countries. Israel receives moral as well as material support from the United States, but the Israelis are mired in what seems to be an endless conflict with their neighbours – who ought to be fellow-citizens – the Palestinians. The American government, because of its alliance with Israel, continues its efforts to resolve this dispute although all its previous attempts to end it have been in vain. An additional complication is the confrontation between Israel and Iran, in which Israel has threatened a first strike against Iran's nuclear plant. If Israel's stand-off with the Palestinians demands a resolution on the grounds of equity, that with Iran is even more urgent because it has the potential of causing a disaster in the region.

Where in this vast tract of land will conflict arise? Western forces are already there, although within a short period most American and Allied troops will depart from Iraq and Afghanistan, leaving only a token force of military instructors in Afghanistan. These departures appear to be steps in a general process of American withdrawal from the complete region. The whole huge territory is open to unexpected explosions of trouble, and no one is able to guess where. American attention is being increasingly focussed on the Pacific, apparently because of the increase in Chinese naval power.

But anywhere in the world could be a locus of conflict. At a recent strategy conference at the United States Army War College, a group of senior officers was asked to suggest possible places where future war might break out. They produced an array of possibilities, every one of them carefully considered and rationally supported. In the 1990s, there was talk of future world-wide conflicts between continental blocs, something like the perpetual state of war visualized by George Orwell in *Nineteen Eighty-Four*. There is also the perennial problem of North Korea, a state that has nuclear weapons. These are dangerous, but less dangerous than the secretiveness and irrationality of the North Korean government. It is remotely possible that this country could ignite a spark that triggers a nuclear war. And there are the hostile neighbours India and Pakistan, which both made large investments in nuclear weapons mainly because they were suspicious of one another.

This is not the end of the possibilities, since conflict within the American hemisphere is not inconceivable, with the United States perhaps finding itself in some type of confrontation with Cuba, Venezuela, Colombia or Mexico. In this case there is no way in which British national interests would be involved, and in any event British participation would presumably be forbidden by the Monroe Doctrine. There will inevitably be occasions when Britain must retain her independence and stay out of a conflict. Harold Wilson's refusal during the 1960s to follow the Americans into Vietnam was a decision of decisive importance.

All speculations about future wars are valueless for serious strategic planning in which flesh must be put on the bones. There are simply too many possibilities – varying from the realistic, to the remotely possible, to the fanciful – for it to be realistic to set priorities. The only proposition that we are left with is the following: never make specific plans in advance for a possible war; devote all resources to responding to unanticipated contingencies. Resources should be nurtured and kept in good condition, but they should be deployed opportunistically.

How is this now likely to influence American, and then British, plans for the size, structure and deployment of military forces?

The first matter to look at is the relationship between the United States and Britain. Although Britain is unquestionably America's number one military ally, its horsepower is vastly less. When France and Britain were allied in 1914, they possessed military resources in the approximate ratio of 50:50. The present ratio between the United States and Britain is nearer 93:7 (calculated from the two countries' defence budgets). The American armed services are stronger although not larger than those of any other country – even China and Russia – a fact that the United States uses to justify its self-imposed task of acting as 'the peace keeper of the world'. America is a generous and idealistic country with no imperialist ambitions. But it wishes to preserve human rights and spread democracy: ambitions that have led the country into military adventures against opponents who are profoundly antagonistic to the values for which the Americans are prepared to fight.

In addition to her Regular army, the United States also has a very large auxiliary force. But in contrast to the Territorial Army, the American National Guard is run on a State and not a Federal basis. It is therefore to some extent 'an army within an army', with all ranks up to (two-star) Major General being filled from within. By law complete units and formations can be drafted overseas if needed, and the American army has fought in Iraq and Afghanistan with large numbers of units of the National Guard serving alongside the Regulars. The pay and benefits of the National Guard are attractive by British standards, e.g. National Guard service is pensionable. Nevertheless, there have been the expected problems for the men and women drafted overseas, because of the strain on their families and worries about their civilian jobs. Many members have lost their lives.

But although it is clear that America is going to call the shots, there are good reasons for suggesting that Britain is able 'to punch above its weight'. These are that the British army has had continual experience of low-level warfare since the end of the Second World War. It is far more experienced than any European army, even the French despite the French involvement in quelling insurgencies during the last days of the French Empire. In addition, the British have excellent Special Forces; high-quality military intelligence; and an admirable record in developing sophisticated weapons, e.g. Vertical Take-Off and Landing (VTOL) fighter aircraft.

Traditionally, the British have a strong understanding of military strategy, as was demonstrated during the Second World War. And I am willing to give an opinion based on 'gut feel'. If Britain had been in a position to make the sole independent decision about whether or not to invade Iraq and Afghanistan, the answer would have been 'no' in both cases. In Iraq, the intelligence was not strong enough that the Iraqis possessed Weapons of Mass Destruction, the *casus belli.* And Britain had suffered nothing but bruising and sometimes disastrous experiences in Afghanistan since the 1840s, with the inevitable danger that there would be an unacceptable risk of repetition.

The British are America's main ally. Because of this, it is logical that both armies should plan to use the same weapons and ammunition to simplify logistics. There is also a need for continuous joint training, at a battalion level and below, between the American and British units. The long and complex story of Anglo-American cooperation in North Africa and Europe has been told in earlier chapters of this book. During the two-and-a-half years between America's entry into the war and the middle of 1944, the British had taken the greater overall share in determining strategy and providing operational leadership. During the invasion of France, the land, sea and air commanders were all British. But in September 1944 a decisive line was crossed when the American army in Europe became larger than the British, and from then on the gap widened continuously until the end of the war. In the autumn of 1944, the Americans provided two army groups, and the British and Canadians one. General Eisenhower therefore took over operational command of all three. This set the pattern for the future.

In 1945, the Royal Navy's Pacific Fleet became Task Force 57, a much respected command attached to the United States Navy. (The armoured decks of the British carriers were envied by the Americans, whose carriers had wooden decks.) More recently, the British provided an armoured brigade that played an important part in the victorious re-conquest of Kuwait in 1992. In Iraq and Afghanistan, the British army was responsible for conducting operations in specific regions, under the overall direction of the American Commander-in-Chief. Following these precedents, it makes most sense to plan the British army as an independent formation working hand-in-glove with the Americans in peace and war, but Britain must be an ally who will occasionally say 'no'.

This proposal excludes the possibility of Britain 'going it alone', as she did during the Falklands War of 1982. The political decision made during the twenty-first century to scale back the size of the British armed forces – like the decision made during the 1960s to abandon British commitments east of Suez – is a calculated risk. Today it would be highly problematical for the army to engage in a Falklands-type operation. There would be great difficulty in providing strong enough naval support, and logistics would be an enormous challenge in a war conducted over such large distances. The fact that the British Ministry of Defence and military chiefs have accepted the limitation in the size of the armed forces demonstrates their belief that Britain is unlikely to fight a serious war alone, and they therefore believe that it is an acceptable risk that Britain should not prepare for one.

Lord Salisbury, British Prime Minister for three separate periods between 1885 and 1902 – a time when the British Empire was approaching its zenith –

believed that the British Regular army should operate like a fire brigade. The army at the time was surprisingly small (certainly in comparison with the major European powers), and Salisbury believed that it should be an organization of seasoned and continuously trained professionals who are accustomed to active service. After the army had been re-organized after the Second Anglo-Boer War, Salisbury's vision became a reality, and the BEF that went to France in 1914 demonstrated its quality. A century later, the fire brigade concept has a surprisingly contemporary relevance.

It is virtually certain that Britain will never again find herself a 'nation at arms', engaged in any conflict like the two world wars of the twentieth century. It is also probable that the United States, from whom Britain will take a lead, will not engage in any major operation with political overtones on the scale of Iraq and Afghanistan. In contrast to these two incursions, America has been remarkably circumspect about involvement in insurrections that have no closing date, such as Libya and Syria.

If there are to be wars in the future – a fair certainty – these are most likely to be unexpected 'brushfire' affairs, with terrorists as their driving force. The Western powers should therefore respond to these like a fire brigade. But the world has become a much more complicated place during the more than a century since Salisbury coined his graphic description. A contemporary military fire brigade will have an overall strength determined by the seriousness of the threat; and it must contain a balance of four elements:

i.   A conventional military component of all arms, including Drones;
ii. A force of special troops for tasks of particular difficulty and secrecy;
iii. A partly civilian group composed of experts with politico-military experience;
iv. Intelligence tentacles that are sensitive to the smallest signals.

These four components are of equal importance, but are likely to vary a good deal in size.

Command and control will be a new art-form, because of the need to prepare for unpredictable, complex and politically delicate emergencies. Composing, organizing and training such a force will be the major job of the peacetime army in both the United States and Britain. This will of course include both Regulars and Reserves.

This brings me to what is known of the present official deliberations about the armed services in general and the TA in particular. Much was known about the government plans even before the publication of the Ministry of Defence White Paper in June 2013. This whole matter has been subject to vigorous comment in the 'serious' newspapers, including many letters of protest from retired officers.

The first major problem facing British military planners is the future total size of the army. This has been determined by the best professional forecasts of its future tasks, as well as the relatively small size of the military budget. This is planned to be 112,000 men and women: prima facie a remarkably small number, indeed a smaller force than the British have fielded since before the French Revolutionary War. Before the 1960s, Britain had to defend and police a worldwide empire; and during the years of the Communist threat to Western Europe, it had to find substantial numbers of troops for service in Germany. NATO is no longer making heavy demands on British manpower and British forces are already being withdrawn from the European Continent. The total strength of 112,000 has been judged sufficient for the type of small-scale, high-intensity warfare that has been conducted during the twenty-first century.

The most serious loss from the shrinkage of the army has been to the regiments that have been amalgamated and disbanded: something that has unquestionably damaged *esprit de corps*. The army is nevertheless tough, well-trained and well-armed, and the majority of soldiers wear medals for active service overseas. There is strong comradeship – loyalty to their mates – in the fighting units that compensates to some extent for the disappearance of long-established regiments. The most controversial part of the government's plan is the proposal to cut back the Regulars by 20,000, although the budget for military hardware will be kept intact. Dispensing with the services of so many experienced Regular soldiers is already causing hardship.

The second major problem facing the army is that the gap caused by the reduction in the numbers of Regulars will be filled by 30,000 Territorials: an increase in the strength of the TA by more than 50 per cent. The ratio of Regulars to Territorials according to the present plan will be 73:27, which means that the TA will inevitably pick up more of the strain. Its members at the moment go on active service in the way described as 'trickling' into established military units. But their now greater absolute and relative strength will almost certainly mean that members will be dispatched to the seat of conflict in larger groups: in rifle platoons or even companies. This has already happened to a limited degree in Cyprus, where the British army has supported the United Nations. In addition, the TA has provided training teams to help the Ugandan army, and this is the sort of activity that might be repeated in the future.

The TA has mobilized 1,200 men and women each year since 2003: a total of 15,000 to date. They have served in the Balkans, Iraq, Afghanistan and Cyprus; and 2,100 Territorials helped with the organization of the London Olympic Games in 2012. Territorial officers are also, for the first time, receiving one-star appointments and even two-stars in a couple of cases.

These developments demonstrate how the 1996 Act has produced much positive action: and of course a complete change in the TA's terms of service since it was founded in 1908. However, the new configuration of the Territorial

Army has not eliminated three fundamental problems, although steps are being taken to tackle them: *general recruitment*; *recruiting officers*; *preparing the Reserves for action.*

General recruitment: there will be improved terms of service, and these should provide a boost in recruitment. As an example, the number of paid training days was in 2012 increased to forty, which meant a greater financial incentive to join and a means of improving training. Also, for the first time, Reserve service will be pensionable. With a look to the future, a serious effort is being made to encourage teenage members of the Army Cadets to join the TA. They bring much enthusiasm and a surprisingly high standard of military education.

But most importantly, the Ministry of Defence is tackling the recruitment problem aggressively, by using television advertising to trigger interest. The advertising is planned to prompt potential recruits to find out more by attending recruitment events and reading pamphlets, which are produced in large numbers. These cover many specific topics that describe and explain how reserve service is personally rewarding and offers reasonable pay and benefits.

The television advertising is planned and executed by a prominent advertising agency, JWT (acronym for J. Walter Thompson). The campaign was based on market research that revealed that the Territorial Army is seen as an essentially amateur organization, 'weekend warriors'. One change that was quickly made was to introduce a new name, Army Reserve. The television commercials feature Reservists in Helmand Province, Afghanistan, talking about the serious jobs they are carrying out on active service. The advertisements are targeted at men and women in their late teens and early twenties who have a sense of adventure. A difficult problem is that these young people do not spend much time watching mass-market television programmes, although they are constant users of the Internet. JWT therefore runs the commercials online, and they are shot live and piped out in real time. This technique represents a genuine innovation in how television messages are distributed.

At the same time, the Ministry of Defence is in touch with employers. Financial 'sweeteners' – sums of money that are not enormous but certainly not trivial – are offered to encourage the cooperation of employers to release their young staff for military service and keep their jobs open on their return (as is actually required by law).

The effects of the advertising are being carefully monitored, by behavioral measures – direct enquiries from potential recruits that are logged – and also by a tracking of psychological attitudes to the Army Reserve. It is expected that there will be small, progressive improvements in public perceptions. The first signals from the campaign are positive. However, the emphasis of the recruitment effort is on the rank and file.

Recruiting officers: a force of 30,000 Territorials will require perhaps 1,500 officers, 5 per cent of the total. This is a reasonable ratio because any war that is being prepared for will be a conflict of companies and platoons. Sandhurst is commissioning batches of TA officers from short courses, but there is no indication that this rate of training will increase the total to 1,500 in the near future. Officers are young men and women who are likely to have progressive careers in civilian life, so that it is especially difficult for them to take time off to join the army for a year.

Preparing the Reservists for war: the most intractable difficulty of all is the need to prepare the members of the Army Reserve for war by improving their physical fitness and intensifying their training to make them equal in effectiveness to the Regular army. The First and Second World Wars demonstrated clearly that Territorial soldiers do not become fully efficient without many months and even years of full-time training and discipline.

The fact that Territorials have served and performed well on active service since 1996, confirms the wisdom of the system of 'trickling' them in relatively small numbers into Regular units. In recent discussions with two young Reservists, a lance corporal and a Subaltern, I heard at first hand how well the process has worked.

The experience of both soldiers confirmed two specific things: first, that the six-month training before deployment had been intense and realistic, and an admirable way of bringing them 'up to speed'. The second point was that success was largely because the two men had been fed into rifle platoons already serving in the front line: sub-units of about twenty-five men of whom three were Reservists. After some suspicion on the part of the Regulars, the Reservists soon learned to 'pull their weight'. The Subaltern, as a Platoon Commander in a battalion of Foot Guards, came under fire on a dozen occasions; also, when accompanied by an interpreter, he engaged many times in dialogues with wary Afghans. Interestingly, his views on the soldierly qualities of the Regular and Reserve soldiers he was commanding were accepted without hesitation by his Company Commander and Commanding Officer: proof that he was being treated as one of the family.

These experiences nevertheless leave open the considerable potential problems of mobilizing complete platoons and companies of Reservists and sending them on active service. This policy is being viewed with considerable circumspection by the Ministry of Defence, but the fact that 27 per cent of the army will, it is hoped, be composed of Reservists means that this difficulty cannot be ducked forever. The experience will certainly not be the same as 'trickling' small numbers into sub-units on the ground. The army will be moving into unknown territory although, if one takes a historical perspective, the British army can be seen to have crossed into similar territory almost a century ago.

Soon after war was declared in 1914, the London Scottish, the first contingent of the Territorial Force to go to war, sailed to France and was soon in action north of Messines, in the Ypres sector. After less than three months of battle, the BEF was in serious straits, and the London Scottish – which was full of brave, highly motivated but basically untrained young men, many with defective rifles – was pushed into the line to 'plug a gap'. The battalion had received no more training than its peacetime commitment, and had no Regulars in the ranks, but it fought heroically. It suffered 394 casualties: more than 50 per cent of its total strength.

In the twenty-first century, the Territorials who are sent into action to support the Regulars are being fed into existing units as individual reinforcements or small groups, and they can learn a good deal from their comrades in the ranks. But, as I have argued, the TA sub-units who will be deployed are soon likely to be larger. In the First World War, the London Scottish quickly soon filled up with reinforcements and it became part of a large and growing British force. More battles followed, then more reinforcements so that the ranks were filled again. This is most unlikely to happen in the twenty-first century, when there is a top limit to total numbers.

Stories of military heroism can do more than boost the morale of new generations of warriors. They can also reveal lessons of contemporary operational value. It is not very likely that the circumstances of the battalion action at Messines will ever be repeated, but it cannot be absolutely guaranteed that this will never happen. The danger of inadequate preparation for war is a point that I have tried to underscore in this chapter. I have also emphasized the all-too-common danger that carefully developed plans will go awry. In war the only thing that can be reliably expected is, paradoxically, the unexpected.

Glossary

'A' ECHELON: The transport in a regiment that followed behind the Fighting or 'F' Echelon (the troops in contact with the enemy). 'A' Echelon travelled a 'tactical bound' in rear, and provided the immediate re-supply of ammunition, food, water etc.

AIMING POST: Metal post painted black and white that was stuck in the ground in front of each gun. The line of the gun to the target (the Zero Line) was set by map and prismatic compass and marked by the position of the aiming post. The gun was then sighted on the aiming post.

AIR OBSERVATION POST (AOP): Light aircraft (usually Austers) piloted by Royal Artillery officers who observed the fall of shot, sending corrections to the guns by radio. Widely used in the Italian campaign but employed less in North-West Europe, because of the greater amount of hostile air activity.

ANTI-AIRCRAFT (AA) WEAPONS: Important throughout the Second World War, in which there were more such regiments than in any other branch of the Royal Artillery. Light AA regiments used 40mm (2-pounder) Bofors guns. Heavy AA regiments used 3.7in and 4.5in. The majority of Heavy AA regiments remained in Britain as protection against German bombing, although Heavy AA regiments also accompanied the larger British formations overseas. The German army had the extremely effective 88mm and 105mm flak guns.

ANTI-TANK (AT) WEAPONS: Of growing importance during the Second World War, in an effort to keep pace with the rapidly increasing armour and size of German tanks. British AT weapons employed armour-piercing (AP) ammunition, and grew in hitting power from .55in anti-tank rifles (of very little use), to guns of various calibres: first the 2-pounder; then the 57mm 6-pounder (the weapon used for the longest period); and finally the 76mm 17-pounder, with a 3,000m range and a muzzle velocity of 950m per second. None of these was a match for the most formidable German tanks.

German anti-tank weapons were better than those used by the Allied armies. The main German AT guns were 50mm and the incomparable 88mm, which was employed with deadly effect during the last four years of the war. It had a 4,000m range, with a high rate of fire, and muzzle velocity of 1,130m per second. The 88mm was an anti-aircraft weapon engineered to point horizontally. The British 3.7in anti-aircraft gun had a similar calibre, but the carriage could not be adapted for horizontal firing. It was astonishing that the British army showed no interest in following the German example in improvising new carriages. But there is some evidence that the power of the 88mm gun was not brought to the attention of the authorities in Britain until the end of the African campaign. The Germans also possessed formidable self-propelled anti-tank guns, notably the *Jagdpanzer*, which was low on the ground and mounted the 88mm gun.

ARMOURED CAR: An armoured car, carrying a 20mm gun, ran on wheels and not on tracks. This made for speed when the going was good, but for difficulties when the going was rough. The best known Armoured Car regiment in the Second World War was the 11th Hussars (the 'Cherry Pickers') who built a formidable reputation during the whole of the campaign in north Africa. Armoured car regiments had an establishment of 635 all ranks, plus 67 vehicles. Reconnaissance regiments had an establishment of 796 all ranks, plus 52 armoured cars and 63 Universal Carriers.

ARMOUR ORGANIZATION: The number of troops and tanks varied according to casualties and replacements. The figures below are those for the full establishment. (The same qualification is also true for 'Infantry Organization'.) The following structure of armoured formations dates from 1944. By that time, the lesson had penetrated that a division had to be a balanced force, containing substantial strength in armour and infantry

• Troop of tanks, commanded by a subaltern;
• Squadron of three troops plus headquarters, commanded by a major;
• Regiment of three squadrons plus headquarters, commanded by a lieutenant colonel. Establishment of 663 all ranks and 78 tanks;
• Armoured brigade of three regiments and a motor battalion, commanded by a brigadier;
• Armoured division composed of one armoured brigade; one reconnaissance regiment; one infantry brigade; four artillery regiments; engineers, signals and various services. Commanded by a major general.

A single armoured division was usually one of the divisions in a corps, the others being infantry. The Russian and German armies included complete armoured corps; and the Russians even had tank armies.

ARMY: Large formation, usually comprising three corps. Commanded by a full general (four-star).

ARMY GROUP: The largest formation employed during the Second World War, and usually comprising three separate armies. The Russian and German armies, being the largest that fought in the Second World War, pioneered the formation of army groups. The Allies followed in North-West Europe. The British had one army group, commanded by Montgomery who was a (five-star) field marshal; the Americans had two army groups, each commanded by a (four-star) general.

ARMY GROUP ROYAL ARTILLERY (AGRA): *See* 'Artillery Organization'.

ARTILLERY ORGANIZATION: During the Second World War, the organization of Field artillery supporting infantry is described below. There was a similar organization for the Royal Horse Artillery supporting armour.

• Troop (four guns) commanded by a captain, supporting a company.
• Battery of two troops (eight guns) commanded by a major, supporting a battalion and working in close cooperation with it. When Peter Pettit took 481 Battery to Normandy, its strength was 184 all ranks.
• Regiment of 3 batteries (average of 700 all ranks plus 24 guns) commanded by a lieutenant colonel, supporting a brigade and working intimately with it.
• Three Field regiments, one Anti-Aircraft regiment, and one Anti-Tank regiment, commanded by a brigadier (Commander Royal Artillery or CRA), supporting a division.
• Army Group Royal Artillery (AGRA) usually composed of one Heavy, three Medium and one Field regiments. An AGRA was commanded by a brigadier (CAGRA) and was available to support higher formations where needed.
• Variable number of divisional artillery formations, supporting a corps.
• Variable number of corps artillery formations, commanded by a Major General Royal Artillery (MGRA), supporting an army.

The last of these concentrations enabled the British army to employ the huge artillery fire power – from more than a thousand guns – that made such a contribution to victory during the battles of El Alamein, Tunisia, the invasion of Italy and the crossing of the Rhine. In Normandy, the Allied armies were supported on a number of occasions by large numbers of heavy bombing aircraft based in Britain. This bombardment was of questionable value because the devastation on the ground made it difficult for attacking armour and infantry to advance. *See* 'Collateral Damage'.

ASSAULT COURSE: System developed in Britain after the army had been evacuated from France at Dunkirk. It was aimed at schooling soldiers in close-quarter battle. An Assault Course called for soldiers to crawl through ditches, swing from ropes, cross streams on rope bridges, traverse barbed wire entanglements: all under live rounds fired over their heads. Many men thought that Assault Courses made a refreshing change from the deadening routine of conventional military training.

BARRAGE, MOVING/CREEPING: Belt of fire moving forward, usually 100yd in front of advancing troops, and creeping forward at their rate of advance.

BARRAGE, STATIONARY/STANDING: Belt of fire aimed at a specific target.

BATTALION: Basic infantry unit, with an establishment in 1944 of 845 all ranks. *See* 'Infantry Organization'.

BATTLEDRESS (BD): Serviceable khaki serge uniform with many pockets. Short waist-length jacket, a cause of complaint that BD was not warm enough around the middle. Closed up to the neck, except for officers who had open necks, showing a khaki shirt and tie. Over the battledress, soldiers fitted robust and well-designed webbing equipment, including short gaiters. Black 'ammunition' boots issued to the troops were not waterproof. American boots, with composition soles, were very much stronger. Soldiers who were campaigning in northern Europe and during the winter in southern Europe and north Africa all fought in battledress. In cold weather, it was supplemented by greatcoats, leather jerkins and (for tank crews) insulated one-piece tank suits.

BATTLE DRILL and BATTLE SCHOOLS: Established after the British army had been evacuated from France. Schools were set up all over Britain, partly to compensate for the lack of experienced men who could teach tactics. The schools taught Battle Drill as an automatic routine, with the intention of inculcating an immediate response to tactical problems. Over time the system attracted criticism because it was thought to discourage junior officers and NCOs of all ranks from using their own initiative. In contrast, the German army always laid great stress on the individual initiative that should be displayed by all junior ranks.

BAZOOKA: Weapon of American origin. Anti-tank rocket launcher fired at short range by soldiers in rifle platoons.

BEACHES: There were five beaches assaulted in Normandy on D-Day. From west to east, they were: *Utah* (American), *Omaha* (American), *Gold* (British), *Juno* (Canadian) and *Sword* (British).

BEARING: Compass bearing from gun to target, measured in degrees (or mils for American guns which had differently calibrated sights).

BEATEN ZONE: When a weapon is sighted on a specific target the Beaten Zone describes the area in which the missile will land. It is a measure of the accuracy and offensive characteristics of the weapon. (Different weapons produce Beaten Zones that are unique to them.)

'B' ECHELON: Third line of transport behind 'F' and 'A' Echelons. 'B' Echelon moved a 'tactical bound' behind 'A' Echelon. The task of 'B' Echelon was to receive supplies from the rear and feed them forward. 'B' Echelon was commanded by the unit quartermaster, and the unit clerks travelled with it.

BISHOP SELF-PROPELLED GUN: *See* 'Field Guns'.

BIVOUAC/ 'BIVVY': Small tent accommodating two men sleeping on ground sheets.

BOBBIN: A tank that laid mats for crossing sand and shingles. *See* 'Funnies'.

BRACKET: Gunfire straddling a target.

BREN GUN: *See* 'Machine Guns'.

BREN GUN CARRIER: *See* 'Universal Carrier'.

BRIDGE-LAYER: A tank mounted with bridging equipment. *See* 'Funnies'.

BRIGADE: *See* 'Armour Organization', 'Artillery Organization' and 'Infantry Organization'.

BUFFALO: Tracked amphibious armoured vehicle, best known for ferrying British troops across the Rhine in late March 1945. *See* 'Funnies'.

CARTRIDGE: Container (for 25-pounder guns) armed with one, two, three or four (supercharge) bags of propellant, depending on the range of the target. The cartridge was loaded behind the shell to speed it on its way.

CASUALTY CLEARING STATION (CCS): Location to which casualties were moved after receiving first aid at a Regimental Aid Post. They received further treatment at the CCS, and most would then be shipped to hospitals in the rear.

CHARGE, PROPELLANT: *See* 'Cartridge'.

CHURCHILL TANK: 40-ton, relatively slow but well-armoured tank designed to provide close support to the infantry. Widely used by the British army in Tunisia, Sicily and North-West Europe. Earlier variants had unsatisfactorily small guns, but later ones were equipped with 6-pounder and then 75mm guns. However, even these were outmatched by the German Tiger tank and especially by the 88mm anti-tank gun.

COLLATERAL DAMAGE: Gunfire and (especially) air bombardment that often landed on locations outside the target area. There were two causes. The first was less-than-accurate targeting; the second was that troops and equipment sometimes got too close to the beaten zone of the guns or bombs. One of the most serious types of collateral damage during the Second World War was casualties to troops as a result of 'friendly fire'. This caused serious losses at the beginning of the *Cobra* American offensive in Normandy. Another type of collateral damage was to buildings, the result of which might impede advancing infantry and armour. This became a serious problem during the Anglo-Canadian assaults through Caen in July 1944.

COMMANDING OFFICER (CO): Lieutenant colonel commanding an armoured regiment, artillery regiment or infantry battalion.

COMMAND POST (CP): Fixed location of artillery commander. Generally run by an officer of junior rank, because COs and BCs were usually with the formations or units that they were supporting.

COMPANY: *See* 'Infantry Organization'.

COMPO RATION: Boxed ration issued to British troops in North-West Europe, holding a day's supply of food. It provided two balanced meals in cans and dehydrated form plus a snack, and contained enough calories for an active life. The Compo was popular with troops, particularly because the boxes came in a number of varieties. *See* Plate 12.

CONCENTRATION AREA: Attacking troops were assembled in a concentration area, a 'tactical bound' behind the Forming-Up Place (FUP), to which they moved when ordered.

CORPS (a group of divisions): *See* 'Armour Organization', 'Artillery Organization' and 'Infantry Organization'.

COUNTER-BATTERY FIRE: Batteries were always vulnerable to counter-battery fire from the enemy, and this caused them to move location at frequent, irregular intervals. Opposing batteries could be located visually, and sometimes by sound and by Radar. In the British army, Medium regiments were often used for counter-battery fire, because the guns had a longer range than Field guns and were therefore protected from enemy response.

CRAB/FLAIL: A Sherman tank equipped with rotating chains in front that could effectively blow up mines. An earlier version had been called the 'Scorpion'. *See* 'Funnies'.

CROCODILE: A Churchill tank equipped with a powerful napalm flame thrower. *See* 'Funnies'.

CROMWELL TANK: Robust British tank designed as a fast 'cruiser'. ('Cruisers' tended to sacrifice armour for speed.) 19 tons, with a 6-pounder or 75mm gun. The Cromwell replaced the Sherman in some British armoured divisions towards the end of the Second World War.

D-DAY: American nomenclature for the day of a major military operation. However, after it had been used for the invasion of Normandy on 6 June 1944, it was not employed again in the original way.

DEFENSIVE FIRE (DF) TASK; and DF/SOS TASK: An important target because it was the likely location of an enemy attack. If there was one location that was especially dangerous, it was described as DF/SOS. When guns were out of action, their sights were set on the SOS target (or the DF/SOS if one had been located).

DENIMS: Light khaki working dress, resembling overalls. In North-West Europe, the troops often went into battle in denims in warm weather.

DIVISION (group of brigades): *See* 'Armour Organization', 'Artillery Organization' and 'Infantry Organization'.

DUKW (pronounced 'Duck'): A floating 2½-ton wheeled truck. Its body contained sealed empty tanks that gave it buoyancy. Two small propellers drove it through moderate sea at 5 knots. It could travel 50mph on land, and was large enough to carry artillery, cargo and men.

DUPLEX-DRIVE (DD) TANK: A Sherman tank with a heavy canvas screen around the body that enabled the tank to swim ashore from the sea, driven by propellers. Despite the ingenuity of this design, DD tanks were very vulnerable in rough water and frequently foundered, with disastrous consequences. *See* 'Funnies'.

EASTINGS: Parallel lines of longitude, ranging from west to east. The intersection of Eastings and Northings provided a map grid. *See* 'Grid Reference'.

FASCINE TANK: Vehicle carrying large bundles of stout sticks – fascines – for filling trenches. *See* 'Funnies'.

'F' ECHELON: The small number of vehicles at the headquarters of units and sub-units when they are actually in battle. These vehicles were restricted to Jeeps, Universal Carriers and half-tracks.

FIELD GUN: The best of all Field guns during the Second World War was the British 25-pounder which came into use in 1939–1940, replacing the 18-pounder used in the First World War. The 25-pounder was robust; it had a 40 degree angle of fire so that it could serve as a howitzer as well as a Field gun; and it had the exceptional range of 13,400yd (on supercharge). Later models were fitted with a muzzle brake. The British army also used a number of self-propelled guns (SP) mounted on tank chassis. The best were the Priest (using a 105mm American gun plus a cupola in the front holding a .5in machine gun) and the Sexton (with a 25-pounder on a Sherman tank chassis). The Bishop (also mounting a 25-pounder) was a failure. The German army had the excellent 76mm field gun; also the *Wespe* (Wasp), a self-propelled 105mm howitzer. Similarly, the main American field gun was a 105mm howitzer.

FIREFLY: Sherman tank equipped with a 76mm long-barrel 17-pounder gun. In the last months of the Second World War a quarter of all Sherman tanks had these heavier guns, although they were outperformed by the German 88mm.

FIRE FOR EFFECT: *See* 'Gunfire'.

FIRE ORDER: Executive order to call on fire. It specifies range and bearing of the target; type of ammunition; and number of rounds to be fired.

FIRE PLAN: Artillery order setting out all the details of fire support for units and formations planning military operations. A fire plan is sometimes very complex because it is normally confined to brigades, divisions, and larger formations. It specifies, for each artillery unit, timings, targets, types of fire (e.g. harassing) and ammunition (e.g. HE, smoke etc.) Fire plans became important during the First World War as a result of the large scale set-piece attacks made between 1914 and 1918.

FLAIL: *See* 'Crab'.

FLYING DUSTBIN: *See* 'Petard'.

FORMATION: Brigades and above were described as formations. Regiments and battalions and below were described as units.

FORMING-UP PLACE (FUP): Location where attacking troops assembled before crossing the Start Line (SL) to make an attack.

FORWARD DEFENDED LOCALITIES (FDLs): In the Second World War the front was rarely a continuous line of trenches. It was made up of individual positions, often on high ground, defended by infantry with their own support weapons and artillery on call. The gaps between the FDLs were controlled by fire and infantry patrols. The modern name for FDLs is Forward Edge of the Battle Area (FEBA).

FORWARD OBSERVATION OFFICER (FOO): An officer accompanying the supported unit or sub-unit and engaging opportunity targets. British army binoculars had degrees etched into the lens of one of the eye pieces. This device helped an FOO to order reasonably accurate switches, left and right of a target. He was normally accompanied by a signaller, who transmitted orders to the gun position. An FOO was usually the commander of one of the gun troops in a battery. In engagements involving a whole battalion, the battery commander accompanied the infantry CO and had his own radio in his 'F' Echelon vehicle. Within a battalion, the 3in mortar platoon employed a Mobile Fire Controller, a senior NCO carrying his own radio.

'FUNNIES': One of the most remarkable senior officers in the British army during the Second World War was Major General Hobart, who was Field Marshal Montgomery's brother-in-law.

Hobart was brilliant although abrasive. At Churchill's urging, he was asked to form and lead 79th Armoured Division, a formation that made a striking contribution to the victory in North-West Europe. It contained the vehicles that became known as the 'Funnies'. These were the Bobbin, Bridge-layer, Buffalo, Crab/Flail, Crocodile, Duplex-Drive (DD) Tank, Fascine and Petard. The 'Funnies' were under the direct command of 21st Army Group, and various units were 'farmed out' to separate army formations to carry out specific tasks. The American army only used the DD Tanks but many foundered on the journey to Omaha Beach. Most of the other 'Funnies' were built from British tank chassis, and the Americans were unwilling to use them for logistical reasons.

GENERAL OFFICER COMMANDING (GOC): An officer commanding a division and above. Ranks ranged from major general to field marshal.

GRID REFERENCE (GR): Map grids are based on the intersection of numbered Eastings (advancing from west to east) and Northings (advancing from south to north). The squares on a 1in to 1-mile map measure 150mm (or ⅝in) both vertically and horizontally. Here is an example from a real map. The grid based on the 41 Easting and the 20 Northing is square 4120.

This is not precise enough for targeting. The Eastings are therefore divided into ten sub-units, and so are the Northings: thus producing 100 small cells. The bearing of a target half way (five-tenths) between the Eastings, and a similar distance between the Northings becomes 415205. This is a six-figure grid reference.

It is possible to make an even more exact bearing with large-scale maps. The Eastings can be divided by 100, and so can the Northings, to produce 10,000 tiny cells. This makes it possible to produce an eight-figure grid reference, e.g. 41552055.

GUNFIRE: Firing live rounds at the enemy. Now known as 'Fire for Effect'.

GUN PIT: Field guns were dug into shallow gun pits wherever possible. Although these pits gave a good deal of protection, the wall could not be too high because it would impede the firing of the gun.

GUN POSITION: Guns were normally deployed as a battery, although sometimes as a troop. These were concealed from enemy view (except from the air), since nearly all gun fire was indirect. Firing over open sights directly at the enemy was extremely rare, and probably meant that the gun position was being overrun. Static OPs and mobile FOOs were in touch with the gun position by radio. If time allowed, static OPs were also connected with the gun position by telephone line.

HALF-TRACK: Clumsy, partially armoured truck with wheels in front and tracks in the rear. This arrangement enabled it to move over difficult ground. Big enough to carry an officer, signallers and a good deal of kit.

HARASSING FIRE: Gunfire intended to hamper enemy movements, impede their operations, and damage their morale.

HEADQUARTERS (HQ): Central location of a unit or sub-unit. The former contained the Commanding Officer and his immediate aides: Second-in-Command, Adjutant, Intelligence Officer (IO), Signals Officer (SO), Transport Officer (MTO), Medical Officer (MO), plus numbers of NCOs and other ranks. In a battalion, the supporting Battery Commander would be present when action was imminent or underway.

HEAVY GUN: British Heavy regiments contained sixteen guns, and were normally under the command of an army. The main weapons were 7.2in howitzer, 9.2in howitzer, 9.2in gun and the American-made 155mm gun. The German army had the 'Hummel' 150mm self-propelled howitzer; also a 170mm gun.

H-HOUR: American nomenclature for the hour and minute of an attack.

HIGH-EXPLOSIVE SQUASH HEAD (HESH): *See* 'Shells'.

HUMMEL: *See* 'Heavy Gun'.

INFANTRY ORGANIZATION: Infantry, the 'Queen of the Battlefield', was organized in 1944 and in subsequent years in the following way (with some variations).

• Three sections (each of a corporal and ten men) formed a rifle platoon, commanded by a subaltern;

• Three platoons and a small headquarters formed a rifle company, commanded by a major;

• Four rifle companies, one support company, one headquarters company and a battalion headquarters formed a battalion, commanded by a lieutenant colonel. Establishment of 845 all ranks;

• Three battalions and a brigade headquarters formed a brigade, commanded by a brigadier;

• Three brigades, one support (machine-gun) battalion, one reconnaissance regiment, three Field artillery regiments, one Light AA artillery regiment, one Anti-Tank artillery regiment, plus engineers, signals, and a range of services made up a division, commanded by a major general. An infantry division represents a complete 'orchestra of war'. Establishment of 18,347 all ranks;

• Usually three divisions in a corps (it was quite common for divisions to transfer between corps).

INTERDICTION: Gunfire or air bombardment aimed at targets that had an indirect influence on the battlefield, e.g. road and rail communications used by the enemy to transport troops to the front. This was an important strategy before the invasion of France in June 1944.

JAGDPANZER: *See* 'Anti-Tank (AT) Weapons'.

JEEP: American ¼-ton vehicle named from the acronym General Purpose (GP). Four-wheel drive; agile over rough ground; draughty because there were no sides and only a thin canvas top. One of the most important innovations of the Second World War, produced in enormous numbers. Extremely popular, and employed in all parts of the world for many years during and after the war.

KING TIGER: *See* 'Tiger, Panzer Mark VI Tank'.

LAND LINE: Telephone line laid (and dug in if possible) between a static OP and a gun position. It protected conversation from being intercepted by the enemy: always a danger with radio communication.

LIGHT AID DETACHMENT (LAD): Each armoured and artillery regiment had a group of skilled technicians, with appropriate cranes, winches and other equipment. Many of these men were in the Royal Electrical and Mechanical Engineers (REME). The job of the LAD was to salvage damaged tanks and guns, and tow away those in difficulties. The LAD made repairs where possible; otherwise they removed the vehicle or gun to workshops in the rear.

LIMBER: Heavy case on two wheels containing shells and cartridges. It was towed immediately behind its gun. It fell out of use when 3-ton trucks took over from QUADs as towing vehicles.

MACHINE GUN: Extremely important weapon in both world wars. In the Second World War, the main machine guns used by the British army were:

• *Sub-machine guns*: The American Thompson (Tommy gun) and the British STEN. The Tommy gun was far more reliable than the STEN, which was mass-produced in enormous quantities. They both used 9mm ammunition;

• *Light machine guns (LMG)*: The British-built Bren gun, based on a Czech design. This was a highly effective platoon weapon, fed by a magazine of twenty-nine rounds of .303in ammunition. It could be carried by one soldier, although it was operated by two men, one aiming and the other feeding the gun with full magazines. The British soldier's webbing equipment had two pouches on the belt that could hold Bren gun magazines. The gun could fire single shots or bursts;

• *Medium machine guns*: The celebrated British Vickers guns that had been used since before the First World War. Used .303in ammunition, belt-fed for continuous firing; water-cooled jacket around the barrel; maximum range of over 2,000yd although mostly fired at ranges under 1,000yd. Could be used for indirect fire, using a special sight. The guns had a cigar-shaped Beaten Zone stretching away from the gun, and this made them particularly suitable for enfilading enemy troops from the flank. Most effective with a narrow arc of fire, and not sprayed from side-to-side (in the Hollywood style). The main problem with the Vickers gun was its weight. They had a large barrel, a bipod and a can containing water for cooling, plus the belts of ammunition, so that a gun crew normally comprised three men. During the First World War, a special regiment was formed, the Machine Gun Corps, which was disbanded in 1918. Before the Second World War, a new system was introduced. Vickers guns were concentrated within support (or machine-gun) regiments, which were distributed one to each division;

   • *Heavy machine guns*: American Browning guns using .5in ammunition, and packing a heavy punch. Used in a number of British and American tanks. Also widely used in American aircraft, both fighters and bombers.

The German army had generally better machine guns than the Allies. The German Schmeisser sub-machine gun (sometimes known as a machine pistol) was the envy of Allied troops. Many British subalterns tried to 'liberate' one for their own use. The best machine gun of the Second World War was the German Spandau, Model 42. Like the Vickers gun it was belt-fed (with fifty rounds), but was portable and could easily be carried by one soldier. It had an exceptionally high rate of fire, which gave it a characteristic sound, like tearing fabric.

MAP REFERENCE: *See* 'Grid Reference'.

MEAN POINT OF IMPACT (MPI): Arithmetical average of the grid references of the points of impact of a barrage; in simple terms, the impact point of a typical round.

MEAT AND VEGETABLES (M&V): Canned rations that were reasonably popular with troops before the introduction of Compo.

MECHANICAL/MOTOR TRANSPORT (MT): The main MT in an artillery regiment was 15cwt trucks; 3-ton trucks (necessary to carry ammunition); QUAD tractors (to tow guns); Jeeps; Universal Carriers; staff cars; and (more rarely) half-tracks.

MEDIUM GUNS: Artillery regiments (of sixteen Medium guns) were under the command of corps and mainly used for counter-battery fire (because of their long reach). The main Medium gun was the 5.5in gun howitzer, which replaced the earlier 6in model.

MOBILE FIRE CONTROLLER: *See* 'Forward Observation Officer'.

MORTAR: Mortar fire was first used extensively during the First World War. Mortars fire at an extremely high angle so that their bombs can be aimed at enemy trenches. They are terror weapons, and there is evidence that many if not most of the psychological casualties in the Second World War were caused by mortar fire. Mortars are smooth-bore, which makes them relatively inaccurate, with a large oblong Beaten Zone pointing away from the mortar tube. The main mortars used by the British army in the Second World War were:

   • 2in. A platoon weapon, used exclusively for firing smoke; range 500yd;

   • 3in. An infantry battalion weapon, organized in a platoon of eight mortars. They could fire 10-pound bombs, high explosive (fragmentation) and smoke. The normal rate of fire was five rounds per minute, but this could be doubled on occasions. Maximum range 2,800yd. Fire was controlled from a static OP or by a Mobile Fire Controller. A platoon of 3in mortars could bring down more fire in a minute than a troop of 25-pounders, because the high rate of mortar fire caused more destruction than the much heavier artillery shells;

   • 4.2in. This large mortar, firing a 20-pound bomb, had a maximum range of 4,100yd. It was originally used by the Royal Engineers; then by support (machine-gun) battalions; and finally after the Second World War by the Royal Artillery.

The German 81mm mortar was similar to the British 3in, but was generally better because of its superior range. By far the best mortar used during the Second World War was the German *Nebelwerfer*. This was a six-barrel multiple mortar with a calibre of 150mm, and was terrifyingly effective. The Royal Army Medical Corps estimated that 70 per cent of infantry casualties in Normandy were the result of enemy mortar fire.

MUZZLE BRAKE: Metal device attached to the end of a gun barrel to dampen the shock of firing. This reduced the recoil and increased the rate of fire. It came into use with 25-pounders during the last year of the war. (*See Plate 2.*)

NAVY, ARMY AND AIR FORCE INSTITUTES (NAAFI): A private corporation that was run on a non-profit basis. Set up after the First World War, it established canteens for junior NCOs and other ranks in most camps all over Britain and overseas. It also ran NAAFI shops to provide goods to military families (on the same lines as the American Post Exchanges, or PXs). NAAFI did an important job for service people on active service by providing a range of comforts for sale at low prices, e.g. packaged foods and confectionery, tobacco, toiletries like soap and razor blades, soft drinks and beer (in modest quantities). For officers, NAAFI also arranged limited supplies of hard liquor.

NEBELWERFER: *See* 'Mortar'.

NORTHINGS: Parallel lines of latitude, ranging from south to north. The intersections of Eastings and Northings provided a map grid. *See* 'Grid Reference'.

OBSERVATION POST (OP), STATIC: Position on the ground (occasionally in a building) from which fire was controlled. *See also* 'Forward Observation Officer (FOO)'. A static OP had to be concealed from enemy sight while offering good view of target. Good communications necessary with gun position, by radio and (if possible) by land line.

OFFICER CADET TRAINING UNIT (OCTU): An army unit providing an intensive course (varying from seventeen to thirty weeks, depending on the branch of service) for cadets: potential officers who had been carefully selected during the months they had to serve in the ranks. If they passed the rigorous OCTU course they were immediately commissioned. Training included the duties of a private soldier, so that young officers could do a private's job better than most men in that rank; but more importantly the cadets were trained in tactical leadership as well as being educated in military organization, military law and other subjects. The objective was to provide a compressed version of the much longer courses offered before the war at the Royal Military College and the Royal Military Academy.

OFFICER COMMANDING: Commander of a sub-unit, i.e. squadron and troop in armour; battery and troop in artillery; and company and platoon in infantry.

OPERATIONS: Major operations were given code names to disguise their identity. Examples were *Torch* (the invasion of North-West Africa); *Husky* (the invasion of Sicily); *Overlord* (the invasion of North-West Europe); *Epsom*, *Charnwood*, *Goodwood* and *Totalize* (operations designed to break into and through the defences of Caen); *Cobra* (the American break-out at St Lô); and *Market Garden* (the unsuccessful plan to seize the river crossings in southern Holland, the last of which was at Arnhem: an operation aimed at a major assault into Germany).

OPPORTUNITY TARGET: An enemy target that suddenly appeared on the battlefield, e.g. bodies of troops or concentrations of armour. As soon as such a target was spotted from a static OP or by an FOO or AOP, orders were dispatched to the gun position and fire could immediately be brought down.

ORDER OF BATTLE (ORBAT): Table detailing the organization of a formation or unit, including the strength in officers and men and the inventory of major items of equipment.

ORDERS ('O') GROUP: Before any operation, the commander assembled his subordinates to receive their orders. In a battalion, the 'O' Group would comprise the 'R' Group (*see* 'Reconnaissance ('R') Group'), plus the Second-in-Command, the company commanders, the support platoon commanders, IO, SO and MO. About twenty men in all, spread out over the ground as far as possible to reduce casualties if they were fired on.

PANTHER (PANZER, MARK V) TANK: The first gigantic German tank. 50 tons, 35mph, 75mm gun. For added reinforcement, these large vehicles added to their massive armour a thick mud-like protective paste, with layers of sandbags on top.

PANZER: German word for tank. It was given a broad meaning, to describe what in 1940 was a new type of warfare. This was also called *Blitzkrieg* (lightning war).

PANZERFAUST: Hand-held German rocket launcher that could severely damage a tank if fired at ranges up to 150m.

PANZER MARK III and PANZER MARK IV TANKS: Immediate predecessors of the Panther and Tiger. Panzer III: 22 tons, 28mph, 50mm gun. Panzer IV: 26 tons, 30mph, 75mm gun.

PETARD: Tank mounting a heavy mortar that could hurl a big projectile named the 'Flying Dustbin'. *See* 'Funnies'.

PETROL, OIL and LUBRICANTS (POL): All vehicles needed regular (often daily) replenishments; it was the driver's job to see that this was done and the appropriate paperwork completed.

PLATOON: *See* 'Infantry Organization'.

'POTATO MASHER': Long-handled German hand grenade, called a stick grenade. Because the handle acted like a lever, the 'Potato Masher' had a greater range than the British and American grenades that were thrown like a ball.

PREDICTED FIRE: Fire not checked by a ranging shot. It was aimed at a grid reference on a map and called a predicted target. (This was distinct from a registered target, which was the result of observation of the fall of shot.)

PREMATURE: An unfortunate accident when a shell explodes before reaching its target. If this happens shortly after the shell leaves the barrel, it could cause serious casualties in the gun position. Prematures are usually caused by guns being fired continuously, causing the barrel to be overheated.

PRIEST: *See* 'Field Gun'.

PROJECTILE INFANTRY, ANTI-TANK (PIAT): British infantry platoon weapon that hurled an anti-tank grenade from a tube. Like a *Panzerfaust*, it had to be fired from a very short range, although it did not have the punch of the German weapon.

QUAD: Tractor to tow field guns. Four-wheel drive and an enclosed cabin with a sloping top. Later in the Second World War, 3-ton trucks took over the task of gun towing, and also made limbers unnecessary.

RADIO: British radio sets used in the field employed Radio Telephony (RT), not Morse code. The main man-pack models used by the infantry were the 18, 21 and 38 sets, with a low power output which made them unreliable. Those used by the armour and artillery, notably the 19 and 22 sets, were carried in a vehicle and were much more powerful and reliable. All sets were battery-powered and were designed before the era of the transistor.

The phonetic alphabet universally used for clear communications was as follows: able, baker, charlie, dog, easy, fox, george, how, item, jig, king, love, mike, nan, oboe, peter, queen, roger, sugar, tare, uncle, victor, william, x-ray, yoke, zebra. In 1956 the phonetic alphabet was changed to make it uniform in all NATO forces.

Grid references had a special importance in radio procedure. Grid references of enemy positions were always transmitted in clear. Grid references of friendly locations were always coded. The reason that enemy grid references were not coded was because this would enable the enemy to break the code.

There was a range of code names for specific military appointments. Here are some typical examples: *Sheldrake* (artillery); *Sunray* (Commanding Officer or Officer Commanding); *Sunray Minor* (Second-in-Command); *Acorn* (Intelligence Officer); *Pronto* (Signals Officer).

RANGE: Distance in yards (metres since the mid-1950s) from gun position to target.

RANGING SHOT: Fire from one gun, which (after correction) was then called a registered target, to establish the bearing and range for a battery (or less commonly) a troop. This was different from a predicted target.

RANKS, ARTILLERY: The Royal Artillery has its own nomenclature. The ranks for soldiers and NCOs are: Gunner, Lance Bombardier, Bombardier, Lance Sergeant (abolished after 1946),

Sergeant, Battery Quartermaster Sergeant, Battery Sergeant Major, Regimental Quartermaster Sergeant, Regimental Sergeant Major. Among commissioned officers, a Second Lieutenant in the Royal Horse Artillery is called a Cornet (a term also used in the Household Cavalry).

RECONNAISSANCE (RECCE): Careful and thorough 'hands on' survey of the ground over which military action will take place. A military adage: 'time taken in reconnaissance is never wasted'.

RECONNAISSANCE CORPS: Established in 1941 and absorbed into the Royal Armoured Corps in 1944. Its rôle was to recce in armoured cars and Universal Carriers, but then to fight dismounted. One Reconnaissance regiment was allocated to each infantry division. *See* 'Armoured Cars'.

RECONNAISSANCE ('R') GROUP: Made up of the commander of a planned operation, accompanied by a small group of aides. A battalion CO would take his Intelligence Officer and supporting Battery Commander; also an RAF representative if tactical air support was planned. The group also had one or two soldiers for protection.

REGIMENT: *See* 'Armour Organization' and 'Artillery Organization'.

REGIMENTAL AID POST (RAP): Location of Medical Officer and his orderlies during military operations. The RAP was usually in a forward location, but one protected from enemy fire. Wounded troops were given first aid and most were sent back as quickly as possible to a Casualty Clearing Station.

RENDEZVOUS (RV): Precise location where a meeting in the field will take place. Normally a grid reference (coded if broadcast by radio).

'REPEAT': A gunnery fire order to bring down fire again in accordance with the immediately preceding fire order. The word 'repeat' was never used in radio procedure as a request to repeat a message. The correct phrase was 'say again'.

'ROGER' and 'WILCO': Abbreviations widely used in radio procedure. 'ROGER': message received and understood; 'WILCO': will comply. 'WILCO' was abandoned during the 1960s, and 'ROGER' was used for both meanings.

ROYAL MILITARY ACADEMY (RMA) and ROYAL MILITARY COLLEGE: Institutions set up in the early nineteenth century to prepare officer cadets for commissions in the Regular army. The RMA (known as 'the Shop') was in Woolwich, and trained cadets intended for the more technical branches: artillery, engineers, signals etc. The course lasted two years. The RMC was for cadets going to the infantry and cavalry, and was concentrated into eighteen months. Before the Second World War, entrance to the RMA and RMC was by written examinations and interviews. Fees were charged although scholarships were available, on merit and for the sons of ex-officers.

After the Second World War, both institutions were amalgamated and established as the Royal Military Academy, Sandhurst (RMAS). Fees were abolished. Since the end of the Second World War the course length has varied. During recent years, cadets (now including women) take a six-month course and enter army service with a short-service commission. Suitable young officers can be granted Regular commissions and return to Sandhurst for additional training. An important change since the Second World War is that 80 per cent of officers now have three-year university degrees and go to Sandhurst after they have graduated.

In contrast to officer training in the United States, Sandhurst does not offer a university level education. In America, West Point (for the army), Annapolis (for the navy and marines) and Colorado (for the air force) provide a rigorous four-year degree, with an engineering orientation. Many young officers are also commissioned from the Reserve Officer Training Corps (ROTC) established at major universities. (General Colin Powell entered the army in this way.) A surprising number of American officers return to university for graduate studies. It is sometimes jokingly said that young officers in the American army are better educated but not as well trained as their British counterparts.

SCHMEISSER: *See* 'Machine Gun'.
SCORPION: *See* 'Crab/Flail'.
SECTION: *See* 'Infantry Organization'.
SELF-PROPELLED GUN: *See* 'Field Gun'.
SEXTON: *See* 'Field Gun'.
SHELLS: The types of shell fired by 25-pounders were as follows:
  • *High explosive (HE)*: producing shock and fragmentation and aimed at enemy materiel and troops. Used on a huge scale in the First World War to destroy enemy trenches and barbed wire entanglements;
  • Fragmentation/anti-personnel: air-burst to drench a large area with shrapnel and shell fragments;
  • *Smoke*: to blanket enemy positions and impede their visibility. There were two types of smoke shell. The first exploded on impact. The second, called base-ejection, exploded in the air above a target and caused a downward stream of smoke;
  • *Anti-tank*: two types: solid shot and High-Explosive Squash Head (HESH). A HESH shell had a plastic head and when it hit a tank with great force it squashed against the armour. This dislodged a hot scab of metal inside the turret that caused great damage inside, particularly to the crew.
  • *Star shell*: this was fired into the air and exploded with a bright light that descended to the earth on a parachute, which provided powerful illumination of the battlefield.
SHERMAN TANK: Cruiser tank manufactured in the United States and used in larger quantities than any other tank by the Allied armies during the Second World War. The Sherman arrived in the desert just before the Battle of El Alamein. It was high off the ground, was reliable and fast, but it had two serious weaknesses. First, the armour was thin although this was improved in 1944. The tank was gasoline-driven, powered by two Pratt &Whitney aircraft engines which belched flame when they were started. The fuel tank and the ammunition racks were just under the vehicle's skin, which made it horrifyingly easy to catch fire if hit. Second, the Sherman was under-gunned. By the autumn of 1944 a quarter of all Shermans had received 76mm long-barrel 17-pounder guns, which were a great improvement although this weapon was no match for the German 88mm. *See* 'Firefly'. Towards the end of the war many British armoured divisions replaced their Shermans with Cromwells.
SIGNALS INTELLIGENCE (*SIGINT*): Highly secret intelligence from the British code-breaking unit at Bletchley Park, north of London. It was sometimes known as Ultra (for Ultra-Secret), and was shared by only a tiny handful of top people. Some of the intelligence findings were passed to divisional commanders, but the source was not revealed.
SITREP: Situation report.
SLIT TRENCH: Shallow oblong trench big enough to hold two men. Sometimes called a Doover. When a new position was occupied, troops were put immediately to work digging slit trenches.
SPANDAU, MODEL 42: *See* 'Machine Gun'.
SPECIAL FORCES: The two main British Special Forces established during the Second World War were the Commandos and the Special Air Service (SAS). The Commandos, who wore green berets, were raised in 1940 at the instigation of Winston Churchill, and were hard-hitting units less than a battalion in size. Their job was to raid targets on the coast of occupied Europe, but later in the war they were used for small-scale shock actions demanding surprise and speed, supported by heavy fire from automatic weapons. The SAS was an infiltration force made up of small groups of men, a platoon or smaller in size. They sprang from adventurous independent organizations raised during the campaign in North Africa: the Long-Range Desert Group (LRDG), the Special Boat Service (SBS) and Popski's Private Army (PPA). After the Second World War, a handful of Commando units remained in the Royal Marines. The SAS has flourished and is today an important (and highly secret) part of the British army. Field Marshal Montgomery did not approve of Special

Forces, because in his opinion they skimmed off the best men, thus weakening the overall quality of the infantry.

SQUADRON: *See* 'Armour Organization'.

START LINE (SL): Line crossed at the beginning of an operation from troops moving forward from the FUP. Another military adage: 'the Start Line must be secure'.

STEEL HELMET ('TIN HAT'): Rimmed helmet of manganese steel introduced into the British army in 1916. Effective against metal splinters, but could not protect against a rifle bullet. The steel helmet was not often worn by FOOs. PP mentions two young officers in Tunisia who were killed by head wounds because they preferred to wear in action their blue and red Royal Artillery side caps. (These caps were widely worn in all branches of the army during the Second World War; the soldiers gave them a very impolite nickname.)

STONK: Code word first used in the Western Desert during the Second World War, standing for 'Standard Concentration', meaning a 575yd linear target engaged by any number of regiments. (After the Second World War, the length was reduced to 525yd, as a linear target for a single regiment.) Soon after it came in use, Stonk began to be employed as a common description of a heavy artillery or mortar bombardment, and was used as both a noun and a verb.

SUB-UNIT: Groups of men smaller than regiments and battalions, e.g. squadrons and troops in armoured regiments; batteries and troops in artillery regiments; and companies and platoons in infantry battalions.

SUPPORT WEAPONS: Within a battalion, the support weapons were 3in mortars; anti-tank guns (6-pounders, later replaced by 17-pounders); and the explosives used by assault pioneers. Within a support (machine-gun) battalion, there were Vickers medium machine guns; and (later in the war) 4.2in mortars.

SURVEYING-IN: The process of bringing groups of guns onto a common map grid. Once a grid was established for a battery, it was shortly afterwards integrated into a regimental grid, and then into grids for more guns, culminating in a theatre grid. The more quickly this was done, the larger amounts of fire power an OP could bring down on a target.

SWITCH: Change of bearing for a gun or group of guns. Measured in degrees left or right (mils for American guns).

'TACTICAL BOUND': Distance between groups of troops and/or vehicles. The distance should be short enough to make movement between the groups easy, but this was determined by the shape of the ground and also the activity of the enemy. There were occasions when 'B' Echelon would be 5 miles behind 'A' Echelon, and 'A' Echelon would be 2 miles behind 'F' Echelon. However, these examples are not generalizable.

TACTICAL EXERCISE WITHOUT TROOPS (TEWT): A method of training young officers in battlefield tactics. They walk over a piece of ground armed with tactical maps. Under the guidance of a more senior officer, syndicates of juniors work out answers to specific tactical problems. At the end there is Directing Staff (DS) Solution, representing the best answer to each problem.

TANK: *See* 'Churchill', 'Cromwell', 'Firefly', 'Sherman', 'Panzer III', 'Panzer IV', 'Panther', 'Tiger', 'King Tiger'.

TANK TRANSPORTER: Long, wheeled road vehicle that could transport tanks from place to place. Transporters were often used to move tanks even when action was imminent. Their value was that they minimized wear on tank tracks, and they saved gasoline. (A tank on its tracks normally needed 1 gallon per mile.)

TARGETS: Code names for artillery targets were identified by the following code words, using the phonetic alphabet of the Second World War:

Mike: guns of a regiment;
Uncle: guns of a division;
Yoke: guns of an AGRA;

Victor: guns of a corps;

William: guns of an army.

TIGER (PANZER MARK VI) TANK: Formidable German vehicle: 62 tons, 25mph, 88mm gun. The King Tiger was the ultimate tank: 70 tons, 15–24mph, 88mm gun. The armour plating on these tanks could not be penetrated by any Allied guns, particularly after the tanks had been fortified with protective paste and sandbags.

TROOP: *See* 'Armour Organization', 'Artillery Organization'.

ULTRA: See 'Signals Intelligence'.

UNIT: Armoured regiment, artillery regiment, or infantry battalion.

UNIVERSAL CARRIER: Formerly known as the Bren Gun Carrier, the Universal Carrier did long service during the Second World War. It was a 3-ton tracked vehicle, armoured on the front and sides but with an open top. It had a crew of three, but a dozen soldiers could find a place on board as it moved around the battlefield. It was often used in the 'F' Echelon of artillery and infantry units. The Universal Carrier was a precursor of the Armoured Personnel Carrier (APC) for infantry, introduced during the 1960s.

VE DAY: American terminology for the conclusion of the Second World War in Europe, 8 May 1945. This did not represent the complete end of the war. VJ Day marked the end of the war in the Far East on 14 August 1945.

V1 AND V2: German *Vergeltungswaffen* (Vengeance Weapons). The V1 was a pilotless flying bomb that fell in large numbers on south-east England between June and September 1944: 2,419 on London alone. The V1 caused over 8,000 casualties and had a serious effect on British morale, since the bomb could be seen and heard in flight, but when the engine stopped everyone below knew that 1 ton of explosive would shortly land. V1s were called Doodlebugs by the long-suffering British population, and Buzz Bombs by the Americans. They were dispatched from specially built sites on the western coast of France and Belgium, and these became the targets of continuous Allied bombing. Clearing the launch sites was a major objective of the advancing British and Canadian troops after the Battle of Normandy had been won.

Unlike the V1s, the V2s were rockets that were launched from sites in the Low Countries. They shot high into the stratosphere, and 1,300 of them landed on area targets in southern England, causing 2,500 fatal casualties. There was no precision in the targeting. They approached silently and caused a large explosion. (Since they travelled faster than the speed of sound, there was no warning.) There were no counter-measures, short of capturing the launch sites themselves. The V2s operated between October 1944 and March 1945, and many V2s landed on targets in Belgium, notably Antwerp; these were noted by PP. The V1s and V2s caused serious loss of life and damage, but they were in no way war-winning weapons.

VICKERS MACHINE GUN: *See* 'Machine Guns'.

WAGON LINE (WL): The location of the vehicles used to tow the guns, in a relatively protected place within reach of the gun position.

WESPE: *See* 'Field Guns'.

'WILCO': *See* 'Roger' and 'Wilco'.

ZERO HOUR: Out-of-date terminology for H-Hour.

ZERO LINE: The compass bearing between a gun and its target. Switches to left or right were based on the Zero Line.

Bibliography

Much to my wife's irritation, I am an inveterate and incorrigible collector of books. I not only read them for enjoyment and enlightenment, but I dig into them for facts to underpin my own writing.

This book is based on the diary that Peter Pettit wrote day-by-day during his two years of active service, but this is not the book's only empirical source. The work is structured to be part general history and part diary, with the diary adding the immediacy and vividness that bring the history to life. History and diary are interleaved throughout the book and are roughly equal in length. More than a hundred titles from my library are listed below, all of which I have consulted in writing the history component of the book. They include British army war diaries and some personal diaries. These all represent primary sources because they are first-hand and were written at the time. There are also a number of memoirs, which are first-hand but were not written when the events described took place. The other books on the list are secondary works, based on their authors' generally rigorous use of existing facts, documents, statements by authoritative figures, and the testimony of participants. Some of this material is in the public domain and some is unpublished. These works are the best of their type that have emerged from the enormously rich literature of the Second World War.

Alanbrooke, Field Marshal Lord, *War Diaries, 1939–1945*, London: Weidenfeld & Nicolson, 2001

Alexander of Tunis, Field Marshal Earl and John North, *The Alexander Memoirs, 1940–1945*, London: Cassell, 1962

Ambrose, Stephen E., *D-Day, June 6 1944. The Climactic Battle of World War II*, Norwalk, CT: Easton Press, 1995

Armstrong, Geoffrey, *The Sparks Fly Upward*, East Wittering, West Sussex: Gooday Publishers, 1991

Atkinson, Rick, *An Army at Dawn. The War in North Africa, 1942–1943*, New York: Henry Holt, 2002

Bamford, James, 'They Know Much More Than You Think', *New York Review of Books*, 15 August 2013

Belchem, Major General David, *Victory in Normandy*, London: Chatto & Windus, 1981

Bennett, Ralph, *Ultra and Mediterranean Strategy. The Never-Before-Told Story of How Ultra First Proved Itself in Battle, Turning Defeat Into Victory*, New York: William Morrow, 1989

Bishop, Chris, *The Military Atlas of World War II*, London: Amber Books – Igloo, 2005

Blumenson, Martin, *The Patton Papers, 1940–1945*, New York: Da Capo Press, 1996

Borneman, Walter R., *The Admirals, Nimitz, Halsey, Leahy, and King – The Five-Star Admirals Who Won the War at Sea* New York: Little, Brown and Company, 2012

Bradley, Omar N., *A Soldier's Story*, Chicago, IL: Rand McNally, 1951

Bradley, Omar N. and Clay Blair, *A General's Life, an Autobiography*, New York: Simon & Schuster, 1983

British Army War Diaries (Kew, Surrey: National Archives):
> Second World War, 59th Division, WO171/571
> Second World War, 78th Division, WO171/168
> Second World War, 11th (HAC) Regiment, Royal Horse Artillery, WO166/1461; WO169/1430; WO169/4560

British Ministry of Defence, *Ministry of Defence Paper on Future Reserves, 2002 (FR20)*; media editorials: *Economist*, 7 July 2012, 19 January 2013; *Telegraph* (Weekly Overseas Edition), 11 January 2012, 11 July 2012, 27 February 2013, 10 July 2013, 18 September 2013, 23 October 2013

British Ministry of Defence, *Reserves in the Future Force 2020: Valuable and Valued*, June 2013

Budiansky, Stephen, *Battle of Wits. The Complete Story of Codebreaking in World War II*, New York: The Free Press, 2000

Butcher, Captain Harry C., *My Three Years with Eisenhower*, New York: Simon & Schuster, 1946

Carafano, James Jay, *After D-Day. Operation Cobra and the Normandy Breakout*, Boulder, CO: Lynne Rienner, 2000

Citino, Robert M., *The Path to Blitzkrieg. Doctrine and Training in the German Army, 1920–1939*, Mechanicsburg, PA: Stackpole Books, 2008

Clarke, Sir Rupert, *With Alex at War from the Irrawaddy to the Po, 1941–1945*, Barnsley, South Yorkshire: Pen & Sword – Leo Cooper, 2000

Colquhoun, James, *Action Front. A History of 'C' Battery, HAC, in War and Peace*, London: Leo Cooper, 1992

Corrigan, Gordon, *The Second World War. A Military History*, New York: St Martin's Press, 2011

Crosswell, D.K.R., *The Chief of Staff. The Military Career of General Walter Bedell Smith*, New York: Greenwood Press, 1991

Cunningham of Hyndhope, Admiral of the Fleet Viscount, *A Sailor's Odyssey*, London: Hutchinson, 1951

Daglish, Ian, *Goodwood. The British Offensive in Normandy, July 1944*, Mechanicsburg, PA: Stackpole Books, 2009

Daniell, Brigadier R.B.T., *Journal of a Horse Gunner. India to the Baltic, via El Alamein*, Sevenoaks, Kent: Buckland Publications, 1998

Davies, W.J.K., *German Army Handbook, 1939–1945*, New York: Arco Publishing, 1984

de Guingand, Major General Sir Francis, *Operation Victory*, London: Hodder & Stoughton, 1947

Delaforce, Patrick, *The Fighting Wessex Wyverns. From Normandy to Bremerhaven with the 43rd Wessex Division*, Stroud, Glos: Sutton, 1994

de Lannoy, François, *21st Army Group, Normandie 1944*, Bayeux, France: Heimdal, 2003

d'Este, Carlo, *Bitter Victory. The Battle for Sicily, 1943*, New York: E.P. Dutton, 1988

d'Este, Carlo, *Decision in Normandy*, New York: E.P. Dutton, 1983

d'Este, Carlo, *Patton. A Genius for War*, New York: HarperCollins, 1995

Doherty, Richard, *In the Ranks of Death. The Irish in the Second World War*, Barnsley, South Yorkshire: Pen & Sword, 2010

Doherty, Richard, *Ubique. The Royal Artillery in the Second World War*, Stroud, Glos: The History Press, 2008

Doherty, Richard, *Normandy 1944. The Road to Victory*, Staplehurst, Kent: Spellmount, 2004

Dueck, Colin, 'Geography and World Politics', *Claremont Review of Books*, Spring 2013

Dunn, Bill Newton, *Big Wing. The Biography of Air Chief Marshal Sir Trafford Lee-Mallory*, Shrewsbury, Salop: Airlife, 1992

Edwards, Roger, *Panzer. A Revolution in Warfare, 1939–1945*, London: Arms & Armour Press, 1989

Eisenhower, Dwight D., *Crusade in Europe*, Norwalk, CT: Easton Press, 1997

Eisenhower, Dwight D. with Robert H. Ferrell (ed.), *The Eisenhower Diaries*, New York: W.W. Norton, 1981

Ensor, R.C.K., *England, 1870–1914*, Oxford: Oxford University Press, 1960

Fletcher, David, *Tanks in Camera, 1940–1943. Archive Photographs from the Tank Museum*, Stroud, Glos: Sutton Publishing – Budding Books, 2000

Ford, Ken, *Assault on Germany. The Battle for Geilenkirchen*, Barnsley, South Yorkshire: Pen & Sword, 2009

Ford, Ken, *Battleaxe Division. From Africa to Italy with the 78th Division, 1942–1945*, Stroud, Glos: Sutton Publishing, 1999

Forty, George, *British Army Handbook, 1939–1945*, Stroud, Glos: Sutton Publishing, 1998

Fraser, David, *Knight's Cross. A Life of Field Marshal Erwin Rommel*, New York, HarperCollins, 1993

Fraser, David, *Alanbrooke*, New York: Atheneum, 1982

French, David, *Military Identities. The Regimental System, the British Army, and the British People, c.1870–2000*, Oxford: Oxford University Press, 2005

French, David, *Raising Churchill's Army. The British Army and the War Against Germany*, Oxford: Oxford University Press, 2000

Frost, Major General John, *A Drop Too Many*, London: Sphere Books, 1988

Funk, Arthur Layton, *The Politics of Torch. The Allied Landings and the Algiers Putsch, 1942*, Lawrence, KS: University Press of Kansas, 1974

Funk & Wagnalls, *New Encyclopedia Year Book*, Willard, OH: World Books, 2013

Gavin, General James M., *On to Berlin. The Battles of an Airborne Commander*, New York: Bantam Books, 1985

Gilbert, Martin, *Churchill, a Life, Volume II*, London: Folio Society, 2004

Gill, Ronald and John Groves, *Club Route in Europe. The Story of XXX Corps in the European Campaign*, Hannover, Germany: Werner Degener, 1946

Gordon-Duff, Lieutenant Colonel Lachlan, *With the Gordon Highlanders to the Boer War and Beyond. The Story of Captain Lachlan Gordon-Duff*, Staplehurst, Kent: Spellmount, 2000

Graham, Dominick, *The Price of Command. A Biography of General Guy Simonds*, Toronto, Canada: Stoddart Publishing, 1993

Haig, Douglas, with Gary Sheffield and John Bourne (eds), *War Diaries and Letters, 1914–1918*, London: Weidenfeld & Nicolson, 2005

Hamilton, Nigel, *Monty*, London: Hamish Hamilton: Vol I: *The Making of the General, 1887–1942*, 1981; Vol II: *Master of the Battlefield. Monty's War Years, 1942–1944*, 1983; Vol III: *The Field Marshal, 1944–1976*, 1986

Harris, Marshal of the RAF Sir Arthur, *Bomber Offensive*, London: Collins, 1947

Hart, B.H. Liddell, *History of the Second World War*, London: Collins, 1970

Hart, Peter, *To the Last Round. South Notts Hussars, 1939–1942*, Barnsley, South Yorkshire: Pen & Sword – Leo Cooper, 1996

Haskew, Michael H., *Artillery. From the Civil War to the Present Day*, New York: Metro Books, 2008

Horrocks, Lieutenant General Sir Brian, *A Full Life*, London: Collins, 1960

Imperial War Museum, *The British Army. The Definitive History of the Twentieth Century*, London: Cassell, 2007

Jobson, Philip, *Royal Artillery. Glossary of Terms and Abbreviations, Historical and Modern*, Stroud, Glos: The History Press, 2008

Johnson, David, *V1, V2. Hitler's Vengeance on London*, New York: Stein & Day, 1982

Johnson, Brigadier R.F., *Regimental Fire! The Honourable Artillery Company in World War II*, London: HAC, and Williams, Lea, 1958

Jones, John Philip, *Johnny. The Legend and Tragedy of General Sir Ian Hamilton*, Barnsley, South Yorkshire: Pen & Sword, 2012

Keegan, John, *The Second World War*, Norwalk, CT: Easton Press, 1989

Keegan, John, *Six Armies in Normandy. From D-Day to the Liberation of Paris, June 6 – August 25 1944*, New York: Viking Press, 1982

Kelly, Orr, *Meeting the Fox. The Allied Invasion of Africa, from Operation Torch to Kasserine Pass to Victory in Tunisia*, New York: John Wiley, 2002

Makepeace-Warne, Anthony, *Brassey's Companion to the British Army*, London: Brassey's, 1995

Merewood, Jack, *To War with the Bays. A Tank Gunner Remembers, 1939–1945*, Cardiff: 1st The Queen's Dragoon Guards, 1996

Mileham, Patrick, *The Yeomanry Regiments. Over 200 Years of Tradition*, Staplehurst, Kent: Spellmount, 2003

Montgomery of Alamein, Field Marshal the Viscount, *Memoirs*, London: Collins, 1958

Morgan, Lieutenant General Sir Frederick, *Overture to Overlord*, Garden City, New York: Doubleday, 1950

Morgan, Ted, *FDR. A Biography*, New York: Simon & Schuster, 1985

Neillands, Robin, *The Battle of Normandy, 1944*, London: Cassell, 2002

Nicolson, Nigel, *Long Life. Memoirs*, New York: G.P. Putnam's Sons, 1998

Nicolson, Nigel, *Alex. The Life of Field Marshal Earl Alexander of Tunis*, London: Weidenfeld & Nicolson, 1973

Orange, Vincent, *Tedder. Quietly in Command*, London: Frank Cass, 2004

Orange, Vincent, *Coningham. A Biography of Air Marshal Sir Arthur Coningham*, Washington, DC: Center for Air Force History, 1990

Persico, Joseph E., *Roosevelt's Centurions. FDR and the Commanders He Led To Victory in World War II*, New York: Random House, 2013

Pettit, Paul E., 'The Shadow of War', n.d., unpublished

Pettit, Paul E., 'When We Were Horsed', n.d., unpublished

Place, Timothy Harrison, *Military Training in the British Army, 1940–1945*, London: Frank Cass, 2000

Pogue, Forrest C., *George C. Marshall. Organizer of Victory, 1943–1945,* New York: Viking Press, 1973

Porch, Douglas, *The Path to Victory. The Mediterranean Theater in World War II*, New York: Farrar, Strauss & Giroux, 2004

Powers, Thomas, 'Warrior Petraeus', *New York Review of Books*, 7 March 2013

Pownall, Lieutenant General Sir Henry, *Chief of Staff, Diaries, Volume I, 1933–1940*, London: Archon Books – Leo Cooper, 1973

Richardson, General Sir Charles, *Send for Freddie*, London: William Kimber, 1987

Ridgway, General Matthew B. with Harold H. Martin, *Soldier. Memoirs,* New York: Harper, 1956

Rolf, David, *The Bloody Road to Tunis. The Destruction of the Axis Forces in North Africa, November 1942 – May 1943*, London: Greenhill Books, 2001

Rommel, Erwin with B.H. Liddell Hart (ed.), *The Rommel Papers*, Norwalk, CT: Easton Press, 1988

Rosse, Captain the Earl of and Colonel E.R. Hill, *The Story of the Guards Armoured Division*, London: Geoffrey Bles, 1956

The Royal Artillery Commemoration Book, 1939–1945, London: RA Benevolent Fund, and G. Bell, 1950

Roynon, Gavin, *Massacre of the Innocents. The Crofton Diaries, Ypres, 1914–1915*, Stroud, Glos: Sutton, 2004

Simpson, Emile, *War from the Ground Up: Twenty-First Century Combat as Politics*, London: Hurst Publishers, 2013

Stewart, Adrian, *The Campaigns of Alexander of Tunis, 1940–1945*, Barnsley, South Yorkshire: Pen & Sword, 2008

Taylor, A.J.P., *England, 1914–1945*, London: Folio Society, 2000

Taylor, A.J.P., *The Second World War. An Illustrated History*, London: Purnell, 1975

Taylor, General Maxwell D., *Swords and Plowshares,* New York: W.W. Norton, 1972

Tedder, Marshal of the Royal Air Force Lord, *With Prejudice. The War Memoirs,* London: Cassell, 1966

Terraine, John, *A Time of Courage. The Royal Air Force in the European War, 1939–1945*, New York: Macmillan, 1985

United States Strategic Bombing Survey, *The Effects of Strategic Bombing on the German War Economy*, Washington, DC: Overall Economic Effects Division, J. Kenneth Galbraith, Director, 1945

Walker, G. Goold, *The Honourable Artillery Company, 1537–1947*, Aldershot, Hampshire: Gale & Polden, 1954

Warner, Oliver, *Admiral of the Fleet Cunningham of Hyndhope. The Battle of the Mediterranean*, Athens, OH: Ohio University Press, 1967

Warner, Philip, Horrocks. *The General Who Led from the Front*, London: Hamish Hamilton, 1984

Wavell, General Sir Archibald, *Generals and Generalship. The Lees Knowles Lectures Delivered at Trinity College, Cambridge, in 1939*, Harmondsworth, Middlesex: Penguin Books, 1941

Weigley, Russell F., *Eisenhower's Lieutenants. The Campaigns in France and Germany, 1944–1945*, Bloomington, IN: Indiana University Press, 1981

Westlake, Ray, *The Territorial Battalions. A Pictorial History, 1859–1985*, Staplehurst, Kent: Spellmount, 1986

Whitaker, W. Denis and Shelagh Whitaker, *Rhineland. The Battle to End the War*, New York: St Martin's Press, 1989

Whiting, Charles, *Kasserine. First Blood. The Battlefield Slaughter of American Troops by Rommel's Afrika Korps,* New York: Stein & Day, 1984

Wilmot, Chester, *The Struggle for Europe*, London: Collins, 1952

Winton, Harold R., *To Change an Army. General Sir John Burnett-Stuart and British Armoured Doctrine, 1927–1938,* Lawrence, KS: University Press of Kansas, 1988

Winton, John, *Cunningham. The Greatest Admiral Since Nelson*, London: John Murray, 1998

Wolseley, Lord with Adrian Preston (ed.), *In Relief of Gordon. Lord Wolseley's Campaign Journal of the Khartoum Relief Expedition, 1884–1885*, London: Hutchinson, 1967

Index

Main text only, excluding maps and plates (both of which have detailed captions), and Glossary and Bibliography (both arranged alphabetically). Titles (knighthoods etc.) are only shown for living generals.